# Praise

This book should be required reading for all technology and business leaders who are serious about digital transformation. It takes you on a provocative, fun, and comprehensive tour of the key areas that will promote and ignite agility, creativity, learning, community, and collaboration.

This book may be about taking a seat, but this is no time to be sitting still! IT leaders will be convinced that their job is now about incentivizing and inspiring courage, passion, and technical excellence in service of business objectives rather than blindly servicing requirements. You will find practical advice on how to deal with projects, scope creep, IT assets, governance, security, risk management, quality, and shadow IT.

—**Jason Cox, Director**, Systems Engineering,
The Walt Disney Company

In his first book, *The Art of Business Value*, Mark brought together a unique understanding of modern techniques—Agile, DevOps, and Continuous Delivery. In *A Seat at the Table* he grabs hold of these concepts and disrupts the conventional dynamics around the role of the CIO in any organization. His progressive thinking is unmatched and a must read for leadership and practitioners of all kinds.

—**Luke McCormack**, former CIO of the
Department of Homeland Security

Mark has found the IT leadership cheese after Agile moved it. Finally, an idea of how to structure IT, including leadership and the teams, and joining the business and IT together!

—**Joshua Seckel**, Chief Engineer at WhiteHawk CEC, Inc.

High-performing organizations see technology as a strategic capability of their business. The walls, inertia, and confusion of seats, sides, and responsibilities does not exist for them. Yet many organizations still retain legacy mind-sets and behaviors that limit their opportunities to improve, innovate, and inspire their people. Mark shows the steps needed to break free of these challenges and unlock potential, speed, and growth. His advice is pragmatic, practical, and to the point.

—**Barry O'Reilly**, co-author of *The Lean Enterprise*

"Agile" is more than a new software development practice; it is a new way to think, engage, and lead. As Mark Schwartz points out in his compelling new book, *A Seat at the Table*, when CIOs re-conceptualize their role based on Agile principles, they will stop worrying about having a seat at the table and start realizing all of the full potential of IT.

—**Martha Heller**, CEO of Heller Search Associates and author of *Be the Business: CIOs in the New Era of IT*

I use to feel guilty when someone would ask me how do I get my leadership to understand DevOps if they refuse to accept it. My answer was, basically, you can't. Now I can give them a copy of *A Seat at the Table*.

—**John Willis**, Co-Author *The DevOps Handbook*

Fresh thinking and useful advice fill the pages of Mark Schwartz's *A Seat at the Table*, which strikes an encouraging, instructive tone about the future of IT leadership and the CIO's expanding business role. "If we cannot know the future, then we have to think a bit differently," he writes. And he does just that. Mark's argument that IT executives must change their behaviors—dropping the "command and control" mindset in favor of community building and Agile leadership practices—resonates throughout this well-organized, thoughtful book. While attaining that "seat at the table" often refers to CIO career goals, the ideas and approaches explored in this book are essential reading for anyone hoping to advance in the IT profession today.

—**Maryfran Johnson**, Executive Director of CIO Programs,
IDG (International Data Group)

Mark Schwartz is a rare combination: a deep thinker who has also applied lean, Agile, and DevOps principles at the highest level, leading an extraordinary Agile transformation in the US Federal Government at USCIS. In this book, he shows how modern IT leaders succeed by driving business outcomes rather than operating an order-taking function. This shift in organizational mindset is critical to any successful technology transformation but requires substantial changes in behavior at every level, and Mark's thorough analysis will prove invaluable to leaders who must execute it.

—**Jez Humble**, CTO, DevOps Research & Assessment LLC

If you're a CIO, read this book. If you're not a CIO but work closely with one, read this book. Mark Schwartz is the best of iconoclasts. He brings deep insights from his unique erudition and real-world experience—ranging from a startup to government agency—in untangling the dilemma of the CIO in the second decade of Agile. There aren't many people who can swing from Horace to Daniel Pink without losing a breath. And there aren't many who can critique Agile and Waterfall with equal insight. This is a surprising book—well worth your (20%) time.

—**Sam Guckenheimer**, Product Owner,
Visual Studio Team Services, Microsoft

As with his book *The Art of Business Value*, Mark Schwartz directly confronts the tensions that exist across the corporate IT landscape, showing us how we got here and what to do about it. Almost every page contains a situation I've seen in my day-to-day work, but that have not been articulated before. [*A Seat at the Table* is] required reading for anyone seeking to understand how IT should work with an organization to achieve success in an Agile age.

—**Ian Miell**, Lead Software Architect, Financial Services

# *a* **Seat** *at the* **Table**

25 NW 23rd Pl, Suite 6314
Portland, OR 97210

First Edition
Printed in the United States of America
10 9 8 7 6 5 4 3

Cover and book design by Devon Smith
Author photograph by Gary Landsman

Library of Congress Catalog-in-Publication Data
2017948982
ISBN: 978-194278-8119
ePub: 978-194278-8126
Kindle: 978-194278-8133
PDF: 978-194278-8140

Publisher's note to readers: Many of the ideas, quotations, and paraphrases attributed to different
thinkers and industry leaders herein are excerpted from informal conversations, correspondence,
interviews, conference round-tables, and other forms of oral communication that took place
over the development and writing of this book. Although the author(s) and publisher have made
every effort to ensure that the information in this book was correct at press time, the author
and publisher do not assume and hereby disclaim any liability to any party for any loss, damage,
or disruption caused by errors or omissions, whether such errors or omissions result from
negligence, accident, or any other cause.

For information about special discounts for bulk purchases or for information
on booking authors for an event, please visit our website at ITRevolution.com.

# *a* Seat *at the* Table

## MARK SCHWARTZ

IT Revolution
Portland, Oregon

To the talented and hard-working government employees,
so resilient in the face of impediments, criticism, and abuse.
I have so much fun working alongside you.

# CONTENTS

**INTRODUCTION** xi

*PART I* **FINDING THE TABLE** 1

  1 SITTING ALONE 3

  2 KEPT FROM THE TABLE 25

  3 A NIMBLE APPROACH TO THE TABLE 45

*PART II* **EARNING THE SEAT** 67

  4 PLANNING 69

  5 REQUIREMENTS 89

  6 TRANSFORMATION 107

  7 ENTERPRISE ARCHITECTURE 125

  8 BUILD VERSUS BUY 143

  9 GOVERNANCE AND OVERSIGHT 161

  10 RISK 197

  11 QUALITY 219

  12 SHADOW IT 237

*PART III* **SITTING AT THE TABLE** 257

  13 THE CIO'S PLACE AT THE TABLE 259

  14 EXHORTATION AND TABLE MANNERS 283

**REFERENCES** 291

**NOTES** 299

**ACKNOWLEDGMENTS** 309

**ABOUT THE AUTHOR** 311

# INTRODUCTION

The demand that I make of my reader is that he should devote his whole life to reading my works.

—**James Joyce,** *interview*

Let these things be believed as resembling the truth.

—**Xenophanes,** *Fragments*

As I was writing my last book, *The Art of Business Value*, something at the back of my mind kept nagging me. It finally made its way onto the page in a chapter I wrote called "The CIO," where I looked at the role of the CIO in delivering and defining business value. The issue, as I saw it at the time, was that Agile approaches seem to remove the CIO—and the rest of IT leadership—from the value-delivery process.

For example, in Scrum, an Agile software development framework, the delivery team works directly with a product owner, who is generally drawn from the business. The product owner decides what will be valuable and works with the rest of the business to see that the value is harvested once the product is delivered. The delivery team—the autonomous delivery team—figures out the best way to deliver the solution. The team listens only to the product owner on questions of value.

Considering the above, what role does the CIO play in delivering value?

This question puzzled me, because I had previously thought that the CIO (me) had some responsibility for delivering IT value. This seemed to lead to a broader set of questions. Is the Agile team responsible for delivering business value, or is the product owner (or someone else drawn from the business) responsible for delivering business value, and the team responsible only for delivering product that will be used for delivering business value? Why do we need IT management? And if we do, how should they involve themselves in the delivery process?

> What is the relationship between IT and the business, and how does it change as we introduce Agile and Lean approaches?

The more I thought about these questions, the clearer it became that to answer them, I would first need to understand some more fundamental points: How does an IT department fit into its broader enterprise? What is the relationship between IT and the business. And, how does the relationship change as we introduce Agile and Lean approaches?

There are three main places to look for answers to these questions. The first is in the literature of the CIO—the many books, conferences, blogs, and podcasts on how to be an IT leader. What I found there was pretty much nothing at all; no discussion on what it meant to be an IT leader in the age of Agility, just a great deal of speculation on how to gain a "seat at the table," or a recognition of IT's strategic value.

The second place to look is in the literature of Agile, Lean, and DevOps practices. There, I read that IT leaders had a role to play in driving the adoption of Agile practices in their organizations...but then what? What was the role of the IT leader once Agile practices had been adopted?

The third place to look is in our own experiences, my personal experiences and those of my friends and associates. The best I could do was to reflect on my own mistakes as I bumbled around trying to figure out what I was supposed to be doing as an Agile CIO.

I think I can promise that every point I make in this book is an answer to some moment of dumbness in my career. I love the idea that I learned about in Chris Avery's article, that in making an organization Agile one should "provoke and observe."[1] I have provoked, and I have observed.

What I have observed, mostly, is confusion. Martha Heller, in her book *The CIO Paradox: Battling the Contradictions of IT Leadership*, sums it up beautifully: the CIO role, and by extension the role of all IT leadership, is filled with contradictions and impossibilities.[2] And when I reflected on the fact that Agilists don't talk much about CIOs and CIOs don't talk much about Agilists, the reason suddenly became clear to me. The reason—I think—is that the way the CIO role is defined, conceived, and executed today is incompatible with Agile thinking.

> The way the CIO role is defined, conceived, and executed today is incompatible with Agile thinking.

There is a fundamental disconnect between the two. Interestingly, I find that the way the CIO role is defined, conceived, and executed today is incompatible with pretty much everything, particularly the delivery of business value. That, perhaps, is the point of Heller's book.

That is why this book is filled with hope. I believe that if we reconceive the role of IT leadership based on Agile principles, we can make sense of all this confusion and turn IT into a value-creation engine. Agile, Lean, and DevOps approaches are radical game changers.

They are a different way to think about how IT fits into the enterprise, a different way to think about how IT leaders lead, and a different way to think about harnessing technology to accomplish the objectives of the enterprise.

The worst thing we can do is to try to squeeze Agile ideas about project execution into a business context that was created with Waterfall approaches in mind. Unfortunately, that is what we do. The Waterfall, I will show, is so deeply ingrained in the way we think about IT leadership that we barely notice it. On the other hand, by importing Agile ideas into the leadership context, we can align delivery with management, oversight, governance, risk management, and all the other things that IT leaders have always worried about.

It seems to me that honest and open conversations are not taking place at the interface between management and Agile delivery teams. The important questions are obscured by rhetoric that says, "We need immediate cultural change so that we can become Agile!" That attitude, as I pointed out in *The Art of Business Value*, is strangely non-Agile—what we really need to do is experiment and learn about how an Agile approach to IT works within the broader business context that is the enterprise.*

That context—given the history of business management over the last few decades—is of an IT organization that is separate from *the business* and stands in a fraught and tenuous relationship with it. Agile approaches hold out the promise of solving this problem-

---

* I should note that Kanban, as described by David Anderson in *Kanban: Successful Evolutionary Change for Your Technology Business*, does suggest incrementally moving toward the Lean approach.

atic relationship but have focused on the micro-context of individual teams and not yet effectively taken on the macro-context of enterprise dynamics. The problem of what Agile looks like at enterprise scale is treated as a problem of how to scale Agile.

This, I say, is because we are not having honest and direct conversations. Are Agile teams saying to the senior people in their companies, "Stay out of our way! Your job is to be servant-leaders and help us!"? Or are they saying, "We are going to do this initiative without any requirements—instead, we are going to have discussions about what will create value"? Instead, I hear mumbling about user stories—yes, of course you can give us requirements; just write them in this new format. Agile teams, fearing that management will resist their Agile practices, are trying hard to frame those practices in ways they think will be palatable to management, but they are hiding critical, disruptive ideas in the process.

> Honest and open conversations are not taking place at the interface between management and Agile delivery teams.

Are managers saying to their teams, "Yes, you are empowered and autonomous, but sometimes you produce sucky code, and not all of you are competent, and it's part of my responsibility to fix this"? Or are they saying, "Right, we shouldn't slavishly follow a plan, but no one in the senior executive team can figure out where we are on anything, and they're getting antsy"? Or, "Great job keeping the users happy—but the company's strategic goals aren't being met"? Or even just, "I feel excluded from your process"?

There are ways to deal with all of these issues, if they are raised openly. What I want to do in this book is to take these matters head-on, and show that they lead us to interesting places. Think of me as a tour guide pointing out highlights as we travel through the rough terrain of IT leadership today.

This book is a meditation, or series of meditations, on what IT leadership means in an Agile world. I plan to take each of the areas that we have thought of as IT leadership concerns and twist them around, look at them from odd angles, and arrive at an idea of how they appear from an Agile perspective. I will explain what I see as the fundamental incompatibility of the CIO role—as it has been defined—with Agile and Lean thinking, which represent the best ways we know for IT to deliver value. I will provide a primer on Agile and Lean thinking from an IT executive's perspective.

Ultimately, I will show that the only way to become an Agile IT leader is to be courageous—to throw off many of the attitudes and assumptions that have left the CIO meekly begging for a seat at the table, to proceed in bold strokes, and to lead the enterprise in seizing opportunities to create business value through technology.

> The idea that IT is an independent unit that must be brought under control is a great destroyer of business value.

Part I explains what I see as the fundamental problem of IT leadership in the Agile world: the old idea that the primary role of IT leaders in an enterprise is to demonstrate control over an independent-contractor-like gang of technical folks, thereby justifying a "seat at the table" for IT. The idea that IT is an independent unit that must be brought under control is not only incompatible with Agile thinking, but a great destroyer of business value.

Part II is organized like many typical books for CIOs, with a chapter touching on each of the classic concerns of IT Leadership—governance, oversight, Enterprise Architecture, building versus buying, security, and so on. But there is a twist. As I take up each of these concerns, I try to show how we should be thinking about them in an Agile context if we are to have a frank and open conversation. Let's not pretend that user stories are simply a way of expressing requirements, but instead admit that there is something fundamentally wrong with the idea of a requirement as it is traditionally understood. By the end of Part II, I hope you will see why I believe that leading IT is fundamentally different in an Agile world, and thoroughly inconsistent with the traditional paradigm of gaining a seat at the table by demonstrating control over the geeks.

In Part III, I pull the pieces together to show what IT leadership does look like in an Agile world, and how IT leaders need to change their behavior in order to make the transition from Waterfall IT to Agile IT. The good news is that, by leading in an Agile way, we can tear down the wall between IT and the business and claim that seat at the table that has so often remained elusive for CIOs working within the traditional paradigm.

This book builds upon some of the ideas I presented in *The Art of Business Value*, though it is not necessary for readers to have read that book to follow the arguments in this one. In *The Art of Business Value*, I made the case that business value cannot be a guide for IT unless it is first framed—translated into a concrete set of values—by the organization's leadership team. *The Art of Business Value* examined the enterprise as a Complex Adaptive System (CAS), with emergent needs and constantly changing interpretations of business value. In this book, we are looking at how IT leaders can deliver business value to their companies with this in mind.

You will find a few themes running through this book. First, that we have locked ourselves into a frame of reference that is getting in our way as we try to become Agile. This frame of reference includes the notions of project, system, application, investment, architecture, skill set, and accountability. We have, to be honest, made a jumble of these concepts. If we sort them out and think more clearly about them, then we can resolve some of our questions about how to reconcile IT leadership and Agile approaches.

Second, that the business value of IT is more like the value of an intangible asset, which I will call—despite some disconcerting connotations of the term—the Enterprise Architecture. The asset view of IT will substitute for the outdated project view in my vision for what IT leadership must become. IT delivery is about making incremental adjustments to that asset. The asset supports the business's operations and competitive strategy; it has latent value to the extent that it will support future needs with minimal additional investment.

Third, underlying all of these changes—all of the problems with plan-driven approaches, all of the advantages of Agile approaches— is a confusion about how to deal with uncertainty and risk. What I call the "contractor-control paradigm"— our old way of doing IT—is really about trying to make risk go away, when risk is really the essence of what we do. The job of the CIO is to bring a reasonable attitude toward uncertainty into the company's decision-making process.

> The job of the CIO is to bring a reasonable attitude toward uncertainty into the company's decision-making process.

Fourth and last, that the business should be thought of as a community, or perhaps as a Complex Adaptive System, which needs to be led and managed through an inspect-and-adapt, feedback-and-vision-oriented approach because of its complexity. As a result, "control" doesn't look like what it used to, and a CIO trying to gain a seat at the table through demonstrating the old kind of control is going to set his or her company back three or four decades in its ability to compete. Reductionist management theory has led us to believe that business strategy and tactics require making plans and then executing them. This in turn has led us to make important decisions based on point-in-time snapshots of what we call data but what are really assumptions about the future. But we have learned that the pliability of software lets us test those assumptions, which leads to better decision making.

Along the way, I will focus on two critical questions:

- How can we harness Agility to achieve the best value for the enterprise?
- How can IT redefine its relationship with the enterprise to maximize this value, and in the process, earn that seat at the table?

## Who This Book is For

In this book, I will be talking mainly about Enterprise IT—that is, the kind of IT that provides capabilities to users within companies, rather than digital products that are sold to customers. Digital product companies—unsurprisingly—are generally organized around products delivered to customers, a model where analogies to other types of product organizations arguably work well. When this model is applied to Enterprise IT, however, it leads to a problematic relationship in which IT as the provider of products and services is held at arm's length from its customers, who happen to be its fellow employees.

In much of the book I draw my examples from software development. I find that many of the book's themes are most vivid in the software world, and that happens to be the world where much of my experience lies. But I am really talking about all types of IT delivery capability. In chapter 8, I will specifically address capabilities acquired "off the shelf" and broaden the discussion, albeit briefly, to include hardware.

If you are a CIO, you need to not only understand this Agile revolution, but also to do something about it. This book will explain it all, and what it all means for you. I will show you why this is a deep and important change and why you need to adapt to it—and I will show you how.

If you are in another IT leadership position, your concerns are similar to those of the CIO. You play a role that links IT delivery to IT and business strategy, and you need to acknowledge the importance of the change that Agile approaches bring to both. The IT practitioners you lead have new expectations of you: you will need to manage in a Complex Adaptive System, function as a servant-leader, and remove impediments. There is a new language, and along with it, a new way of thinking. As you prepare for a CIO or more senior IT leadership role, you need to learn how Agility changes the way you create value for the enterprise.

If you are an Agile practitioner, then you have not yet figured out the role management and leadership play in your practice. I say that with confidence, as I have been part of the Agile community for more than a decade. I have not found one book that effectively connects our team-based Agile, Lean, and DevOps practices to the role that senior IT leadership plays. At best, we have told managers and leaders to keep their hands off. This book brings together the literature of Agile thinking and the literature of IT leadership.

If you are a consultant supporting an Agile transformation, I will try to give you insight into how CIOs think and a language for discussing this transformation with them. Without the ideas in this book, I am afraid you will find yourself reinforcing many of the old ideas about IT leadership—obstacles to your Agile transformation.

If you are a fan of Italian pastas, you might want to read this book because of its unique—perhaps unprecedented—use of pasta metaphors in an IT context.

Perhaps you are a senior executive in a non-IT discipline: maybe a CFO, CMO, CEO, or COO. This book will help you work with your IT organization to harness nimbleness, flexibility, speed, leanness, and responsiveness to create competitive advantages through IT.

As with all things Agile, this book is intended as a contribution, an increment, and a trial that is subject to feedback and improvement. I can't say it better than Xenophanes did 2,500 years ago: "Let these things be believed as resembling the truth."

# Part I

## *Finding the Table*

# 1

# SITTING ALONE

I don't know why we are here, but I'm pretty sure that it is not in order to enjoy ourselves.

**—Ludwig Wittgenstein**, *conversational remark*

Well chaps, first I'd like to say a few vile things more or less at random, not only because it is expected of me but also because I enjoy it.

**—Donald Barthelme**, *Snow White*

I've read a number of books on IT leadership and how to be a good CIO. None of them mention the major change of the last two decades: the rise of Agile and Lean practices for IT delivery. I've read plenty of books on Agile and Lean practices for IT delivery. None of them explain the role of IT leadership in an Agile world. The two domains are evolving separately: the field of IT leadership continues to frame its problems in its same old ways, oblivious to the deep changes brought on by the Agile revolution, while the Agile world, ever suspicious of management, proceeds as if it can manage without the involvement of IT leaders.

Surprisingly, this divergence continues despite the deep influence of Agile and Lean thinking on general—that is, non-IT—management. The disciplines continue to evolve separately even though corporate strategy is increasingly about both agility and IT strategy. The two worlds do not converge, even though IT leadership books advise CIOs to pull themselves closer to strategy formulation and claim a "seat at the table." But while the other C-level executives around the table are discussing the need for agility, senior IT leaders, eager to gain or retain a seat at the strategy table, are pursuing the path of demonstrating the value of IT . . . by locking in old-school practices that encourage rigidity.

Agile and Lean thinking represent, simply, the best way we know of practicing IT. The techniques of Continuous Delivery (CD) and DevOps might have originated with the so-called "unicorns"—the leading technology companies—but they have spread quickly through the "horses" to the "donkeys," dramatically increasing their deployment velocity and market responsiveness and in the process becoming table stakes for playing in competitive industries. The Puppet Labs and DORA *2016 State of DevOps Report* found that those high-performing horses and donkeys spent 22% less time on unplanned work (a proxy for quality) and 50% less time remediating security flaws, experienced 2,555 times shorter lead times, and had employees who were 2.2 times more likely to recommend their companies as a place to work.[1] The stock market bets happily on those horses, as they show a 50% higher growth in their market capitalization over three years.[2]

Admittedly, IT is *always* changing, and rapidly. Suddenly, we were delivering for desktops rather than mainframes; for client-server architectures rather than monolithic ones; for distributed abacuses, n-tier whatchamacallits, clouds, extra-large-size data, re-oriented objects, etc. Our services became microservices, apparently skipping right over milliservices on their way to becoming nanoservices. Our Businesses had Intelligences and our Internet filled with Things. We outsourced, we insourced. In this context, it is tempting to see the Agile/Lean movement as simply a buzz term that describes how we deliver IT product today.

In fact, these changes of the last 15 years are revolutionary: they are not about the mechanics of IT system delivery, but about what IT is, how it should be managed and led, and how it fits into the enterprise. Yet somehow, the literature on IT leadership and the techniques taught to current and future CIOs through books, seminars, conferences, and membership organizations continue to emphasize a decades-old, control-oriented paradigm that is inconsistent with the new Agile ways of thinking. This inconsistency, as I will show, runs deep—there are very good reasons why the CIO community is not taking advantage of the powerful changes brought on by the Agile revolution (revolution, yes—it even has a manifesto!).

Because of this divergence, senior IT leadership is pulled from one new marketing buzzword to the next, drawn to the trend of the day, while missing the deeper currents that could change the way technology is used to drive business value. Locked into an understanding of its role that involves protecting or striving for a seat at the table, practicing governance, finding cost efficiencies, executing projects against defined milestones, and delivering service with a smile, IT leadership is blindsided by IT-like initiatives it plays no part in—initiatives executed by shadow IT organizations, rogue developers, and the newly knighted Chief Digital Officers and Chief Data Officers.

> The prevailing wisdom about what makes for good CIO leadership would make an Agile thinker squirm.

Indeed, the prevailing wisdom about what makes for good CIO leadership would make an Agile thinker squirm.

As the project reaches each gate in a series, the project is reviewed with sponsors, the project team, and the project management office for progress against goals and key risks.

Each gate calls for a go/no-go decision for the next stage of activity and funding.[3]

So say Richard Hunter and George Westerman in *The Real Business of IT: How CIOs Create and Communicate Value*, perhaps missing the point that this is a faithful description of the old school Stage-Gate or Waterfall model that Agile approaches reject. One CIO, answering the question of how to maintain control over IT in Martha Heller's book *The CIO Paradox*, says, "You do that through very rigorous architectural thinking, planning, and review."[4] The Agile Manifesto, on the contrary, says that "the best architectures emerge from self-organizing teams"[5]; its focus is on experimentation and evolution rather than on trying to plan architecture "very rigorously" in advance.

While Agile organizations increase delivery velocity on the theory that rapid feedback cycles and early delivery of value are critical, Heller advises CIOs to "understand that one of the most evolved of all executive traits is the ability to be patient, the ability to balance the need for speed with the patience to set things up correctly."[6] Hunter and Westerman seem to agree: "Successful CIOs don't skip steps, and they don't run them out of sequence."[7]

> Risk is managed not through cautious planning but through bold experiments.

But Agile and Lean approaches recommend that teams put product in the hands of users quickly and then continuously refine both the product and the team's practices, rather than waiting for perfection before starting or "moving on to the next step." Risk is managed not through cautious planning but through bold experiments combined with frequent inspection, feedback, and adaptation.

When Hunter and Westerman say that IT must demonstrate value through "on-time project delivery, on-budget project delivery, and 'first time right' application delivery,"[8] are they aware that the Agile community speaks instead of maximizing business value delivered, creating minimal viable products which are later incrementally enhanced, and even of testing in production?

IT leadership experts have struggled to express the practical implications of the changes brought on by our increasingly Agile, digital-service-driven world. George Westerman, in his book *Leading Digital: Turning Technology into Business Transformation*, encourages us all to become digital masters. Digital masters, he says, "use technology better than their competitors do and gain huge benefits…[they] see technology as a way to change the way they do business."[9] Well, of course they do.

Peter Weill and Jeanne W. Ross think it's important that businesses become IT savvy. "IT-savvy firms distinguish themselves from others by building and using a platform of digitized processes…to disengage people from processes that are better performed by machines," they explain.[10] To me, that sounds more like the slogan of the Industrial Revolution, not advice for IT leaders adjusting to the digital age. I don't disagree with these thinkers, but how exactly (or even approximately) should IT leaders make their companies IT-savvy digital masters?

I don't mean to pick on these authors—and especially not Heller— who've written much that is helpful and to the point. But the implications of the last few decades—the changes brought on by the Agile, Lean, and DevOps movements and the increasing importance of digital services—are much more profound than these easy pronouncements would indicate.

Surprisingly—and ominously—Agile thinking has gone right around IT leadership to influence non-IT executives, with books like Eric Ries's *The Lean Startup*, which makes validated learning a critical goal for the enterprise and argues for moving quickly to implement minimal viable products and hasten corporate learning. In fact, Agile and Lean approaches—which, in truth, are management techniques rather than technical practices—have spawned literature that bears on general corporate leadership. Non-IT executives can learn how to apply intrinsic motivation techniques from Daniel Pink's *Drive*, and can learn to see the business as a Complex Adaptive System—an evolving organism that continuously adapts to environmental factors and incentives set by leadership—from *The Biology of Business: Decoding the Natural Laws of Enterprise*, edited by Henry Clippinger III.[11]

The literature on autonomous teams in the workplace is substantial—Harvard Business School Press, for example, publishes Richard Hackman's classic book on the subject, *Leading Teams: Setting the Stage for Great Performances*. General Stanley McChrystal's book *Team of Teams* draws lessons for businesses from the military's increasingly agile ways of organizing to fight global terrorism. And the Beyond Budgeting movement teaches executives that the artificial annual budgeting cycle is not agile enough for corporate planning. All of these ideas have been deeply influenced by Agile IT thinking. While the writers on IT leadership are talking about the "need to be digital," non-IT leadership is already absorbing the lessons of actually becoming digital.

To further complicate matters, senior executives, and indeed everyone in the enterprise, have become more sophisticated in their use and understanding of the technology. They have high-speed wireless networks at home, smart watches and fitness bands, media streaming out of their devices and into their sensory organs. They shop online and ask Google, Siri, or Alexa when they have a question. Their standards for usability and functionality are high and climbing. Many of IT's partners and users have learned to talk intelligently about the cloud; they know about big data and predictive analytics; their wearable devices have more computing power than IT's servers had a few years ago. I mean, ordinary folks in the company have already learned just to hit the restart button on devices that aren't working right—what more can we teach them?

Any C-level executive can see that Facebook is changing the features on its site every day, while IT projects in his or her own company are still spitting out dribs and drabs on quarterly or annual release cycles. Yes, there are very good reasons why IT is run the way it is, and yes, IT leaders increasingly understand why Agile and Lean techniques are important for *product delivery* and *project execution*. But that is just the point—they are framing the new ideas in Agile and Lean thinking in terms of an old paradigm and missing their deeper implications. As I will argue later, IT leaders should not even be talking about product delivery and project execution. The world has moved on, and we should be glad of that—the old model wasn't working all that well for IT leadership.

> Many IT leaders are framing the new ideas in Agile and Lean thinking in terms of an old paradigm and missing their deeper implications.

Perhaps the most far-reaching change to consider is in whom executive leaders look to as their corporate models—whose strategies, cultures, and competitive tactics they study in business school and try to emulate. Netflix, Google, Amazon; the "unicorn" leaders of the technology world, of course. These companies are not just business role models but familiar and important to the company's executives in their daily lives. Leaders want to run their companies more like these successful technology companies, and who is in the way? Generally, it is the IT department, which is still producing more Gantt charts than useful product.

Non-IT executives are now speaking the language and technique of IT. But many IT executives are not.

If not adapting to Agility, then what *are* CIOs concerned with?

The typical book or blog on IT leadership asserts—as it has for decades now—that the CIO needs to claim a seat at the table*— that is, a place among the strategic-thinking C-level executives who report to the CEO. In her book *The New IT: How Technology Leaders are Enabling Business Strategy in the Digital Age*, Jill Dyche devotes an entire chapter to "Getting and Keeping a Seat at the Table." In the *EY* study "The DNA of the CIO," the authors say that "securing a seat at the top management table is—and should be—a key priority for CIOs," but point out that less than one in five CIOs occupy such a seat.[11] A 2016 article in *InfoWorld* called "CIO's May Finally Get a Seat at the Grown-Ups' Table" starts out "for as long as I can remember, CIOs have obsessed about getting a seat at the executive table."[12]

Some of these obsessive CIOs already have one, of course, but those who don't, according to these sources, must learn to put technology aside and develop the skills of C-level executives: financial savvy, polished communication, strategic visioning, and customer intimacy. It is interesting that this is posed as some kind of a difficulty. These writers seem to assume that CIOs are naturally all

---

* Note that the phrase is used ambiguously, either to mean a seat at the board of directors table or at the CEO's table of executives, who weigh in on strategic decisions.

introverted, anti-social techno-nerds. Is the invitation to join the strategic table being withheld because the CEO doesn't believe that IT is strategic, or because he or she does not believe that someone with technological savvy is capable of playing a strategic role?

How, according to these books, should the CIO go about gaining the coveted seat at the table? There apparently are a number of preconditions, according to the literature. "Show value for money before you try to prove that IT is an investment in future business performance," Hunter and Westerman say.[13] Let's think carefully about that statement. IT leadership should *first* focus on things other than future business performance (to demonstrate trustworthiness) *before* doing the things that the business is trusting IT to do (influence future business performance). Does that sound right?

The CIO must, according to the literature, "sell" the accomplishments of IT. He or she must show the ability to think and act like an executive and demonstrate that he or she can be trusted to keep the business's interests in mind—most importantly, by *controlling* the costs and schedules of IT projects. Hunter and Westerman give examples of ways CIOs can prove IT's value through measurements, including uptime, application performance, on-time project completion, and "first time right application delivery."[14] The not-so-hidden assumption here is that IT is not businesslike; the CIO must prove something, show business value, demonstrate business savvy. The CIO must *earn* a seat at the table.

As a consequence, IT leadership has been obsessed with demonstrating value by establishing control over IT project execution. According to a 2015 survey by the CIO Executive Council, 53% of senior IT leaders believe that "proving the business value of IT's contributions" is "highly important" and a further 39% believe it is "important."[15] IT leaders set up project management offices

(PMOs)—not only to *ensure* on-time and on-budget delivery but also to *prove* that such delivery is occurring. Because proving on-time delivery is the price of a seat at the table, the CIO must fight against anything that would make it harder to demonstrate that control. PMOs, for example, are encouraged to be enemies of the dreaded "scope creep"—that is, changes that the business stakeholders request when they realize that a system won't actually meet their needs as specified...but which might make it difficult for IT to show that it is delivering on schedule.

There is a danger that the CIO's struggle to prove that he or she is delivering value will actually *destroy* business value for the company. Because not all IT-related spending is directly under his or her control, the CIO is often forced to exert influence through policies, standards, bureaucracy, and no-saying. IT "adds value" by *constraining* solution formulation and delivery through its Enterprise Architecture standards, by *slowing down* delivery to users through its governance processes and maturity models, and by *adding overhead* through risk-averse security policies. By saying "no" to any work that would make it difficult to show that IT is under control—scope changes, exceptions to standards, newly unveiled technologies—IT is swallowing up forkfuls of potential business value.

> Any IT leader who focuses on *demonstrating* value is simply wasting company resources.

I'll go further: any IT leader who focuses on *demonstrating* value is simply wasting company resources; IT leaders should direct all their focus to *delivering* value. Which of the other executives at the table puts that kind of effort into demonstrating that they are adding value? Is the CFO preparing slide shows on how drafting the annual financial statements is valuable?

The prevailing wisdom further requires that IT leadership—to justify a seat at the table, of course—demonstrate that IT is "aligned" with the business. "The root cause of most of the challenges confronting IT organizations today is the CIO's inability to lead and manage alignment, starting with IT/business alignment," according to George Lin in *CIO Wisdom*.[16] I am particularly struck by the framing in *IT Governance*: governance, the authors say, "ensures compliance with the enterprise's overall vision and values."[17] It is revealing that they think governance is about compliance: the vision and values come from somewhere else, and IT must comply with them.

> IT leaders should direct all their focus to delivering value.

Although aligning with strategies formulated outside of IT would seem to absolve the CIO of some responsibility for results, it actually doesn't work that way: the more senior a corporate executive is, the more likely he is to blame IT when things go wrong.[18] Or, as Martha Heller puts it, "there are only two types of projects: business successes and IT failures."[19] => *Defensiveness*

Nor is the whole idea of earning a seat by demonstrating value very effective. The same CIO Executive Council study asked what the prevailing perception of IT was by business stakeholders. Fifty-eight percent said that IT was perceived as a service provider or just a cost center; 28% as a separate but partnering group; 11% as a peer; and just a startling 3% as a business game changer.[20] I haven't seen a study on this, but what percentage of respondents would say that technology itself—as opposed to the IT department—is a business game changer? High, I'd think. What then does it tell us that only 3% think that the IT department is a business game changer?

Perhaps the reason business stakeholders perceive IT as a service provider is that—um, well—we have defined the role of IT to be a service provider. "The CIO is responsible for the smooth running of 24-7 IT operations, IT governance, and implementation of new projects," according to Weill and Ross.[21] Funny that the role doesn't

> The job of the CIO is to bring a reasonable attitude toward uncertainty into the company's decision-making process.

involve outcomes, isn't it? If we continue to define IT as a *function*, then we will never find a seat at the table.

That role is too passive—"implementation" not "formulation"; "governance" not "roadmap." Investments and projects somehow come to the CIO from somewhere else, and IT delivers on them. While pointing out that more than 70%[22] of IT spending typically goes to keeping the lights on, which is presumably non-strategic activity, the experts still advise that CIOs demand a seat at the strategic table. But if most of IT's effort is simply wiping up messes or filling the salt shakers, taking orders and delivering the dishes, and perhaps helping those at the table choose their wines, how can a seat at that table be appropriate?[†]

This passivity bleeds over into an attitude that IT's function is to serve the rest of the enterprise. Somehow, IT cannot shake the notion that its role is about providing "customer service" to the rest of the business. But why? Does finance provide customer service? Marketing? Mustn't we admit that IT leadership's obsequious attempt to charm its way to the strategy table by pleasing other executives further undermines its chance of gaining that seat? A business function

---

[†] No disrespect to janitorial or service-profession functions intended; my point is just that it is hard to argue that they are strategic to the company.

that merely serves the real strategy creators can never deserve a seat at the strategy creators' table.

So, the CIO is fighting for a seat at the strategy table by demonstrating basic competence, believing that the rest of the organization considers IT to be non-businesslike, potentially misaligned, and in danger of destroying business value. The CIO demonstrates basic competence by showing that IT is none of those things—that, in fact, it is delivering good service. Is it any wonder that the business perceives IT as a service provider and not as a game changer?

We can all agree that adding business value is a good thing, but a CIO trying to *prove* that he or she is doing so is in for a tough struggle. I've read—and written—CIO resumes. Sure, we say that we saved the company umpteen million dollars by automating the schmoo process or consolidating our whatsits. But, as we all know, that's assuming a particular baseline (really?) and assuming that the results were actually realized (were the former executors of the schmoo process let go, at no cost to the company?); it is ignoring the question of whether that cost-saving was more important to the company than other things IT could have been working on; it assumes that customer service and employee satisfaction didn't decline; and it especially avoids the question of whether a different CIO could have achieved even more benefit at less cost, or simply eliminated the schmoo process entirely rather than automating it. Perhaps a better CIO would have seen that the industry is changing in ways that will soon make the process irrelevant? The business value delivered is more the result of a well-written presentation than a business reality.

I agree with Douglas Hubbard's point in *How to Measure Anything*, that anything can be measured if it can be *defined*;[23] the problem here is that the definition of IT's value is simply wrong, or at best, confused. In *Leading Digital*, Westerman, Bonnet, and McAfee frame it as, I think, most people do: "It starts with competence in delivering services reliably, economically, and at very high quality."[24] But is this what we mean by IT adding value to the enterprise? Weren't we talking about a strategic function, about a digital world in which the company uses IT to compete?

> There is a deeper problem with this idea of demonstrating competence, and that is the intrusion of uncertainty into the realm of IT decision-making.

I have discussed the challenge of defining business value in *The Art of Business Value*; even more challenging in this case is defining what we mean by business value *delivered by IT*. Business value is delivered by the enterprise with support from IT—IT is part of a whole, a complex system in which its ability to deliver value depends on factors outside of IT. The only way that IT can *deliver* business value itself is through cost-cutting within the IT cost structure—in all other cases that I can think of, IT is delivering *product* that might or might not then be used by *someone else* to deliver business value.

Aside from the problems of measurement, there is a deeper problem with this idea of demonstrating competence, and that is the intrusion of uncertainty into the realm of IT decision-making. The CIO is asked to demonstrate that he or she is in control of IT investments by showing that he or she can deliver on business cases according to plan. Projects should be on time, within budget, and at a high level of "quality," whatever that word might mean.

Here's the problem: plans are about the future, and the future is uncertain. In the case of IT projects, the uncertainty is extremely high. In truth, an excellent CIO is one who makes good decisions about risk and adapts plans over time based on unexpected events and changes in the company's needs. But if the CIO is trying to justify a seat at the table based on his or her control of an uncertain future, he or she will be off eating in the corner of the room or banished to a side table in the kitchen.

Let's listen to Westerman, Bonnet, and McAfee:

> In the long-distant past, we were taught that IT was the keeper of technology and that IT leaders were service-providers to the rest of the business. Their job was to stay aligned with business strategy, taking orders from the business and delivering new systems. If they kept the systems running and delivered new projects on time, then all was good. That time is over, and has been for many years.[25]

It has been over for many years. But we have not shaken the idea.

In the twenty-first century, there are very few C-level executives out there who seriously doubt that IT adds value to the business. The rest of the enterprise does not want IT to treat them like customers, and does not want IT to "align" with them. What they want is for IT to deliver *outcomes*.[26] This screams out for an Agile and Lean solution: deliver value—outcomes—quickly and frequently, and trim away everything else, since everything else is simply waste.

Getting a seat at the table is not so much about learning to wear a suit and tie instead of a Nirvana T-shirt; it's about guiding the enterprise in its use of technology and information assets. Given the importance of digital technology, and given which companies now serve as role models for executive leadership, it might be that instead of CIOs learning to wear suits, the

> Instead of CIOs learning to wear suits, the rest of the executive team should be ready to start dressing down.

rest of the executive team should be ready to start dressing down. Or perhaps the business should be learning how to align with IT, rather than the other way around.

Stop laughing. This is just another way of saying that businesses need to become digital masters who are IT savvy.

So, there we have it: the CIO is being told—and told loudly—that he or she must earn a seat at the table by proving that he or she can control IT delivery—a discipline in which uncertainty is the norm—and deliver business value—difficult to define—while for the most part being restricted to delivering only product. If the CIO does these things, then he or she is probably destroying business value and doing non-strategic things, and therefore does not deserve a seat at the table. What will this CIO be doing with his or her time? Creating bureaucratic policies to try to establish "control," denying that IT is too expensive, pretending to have near-certainty in situations where uncertainty is the norm, and saying no to anything that might interfere with his or her ability to prove that he or she is adding value.

This all comes at a time when businesses want to become IT-savvy digital masters. In Westerman, Bonnet, and McAfee's research, "many executives told us that, given their IT units' poor performance, they were going to find a different way to conduct their digital transformations. The business executives were going to move forward despite their IT units, not with them."[27] Again, this bears some deeper thought. We know that IT organizations are often filled with motivated, intelligent, and experienced professionals. If particular skill sets are missing from the IT organization, they can be hired, just as they can be hired into any other part of the organization. There is no *a priori* reason that IT cannot lead the business's digital transformation. The fact that organizations widely don't believe this suggests that there is something wrong with the way we have been defining IT.

You would be disappointed if you thought to turn to the Agile community for ideas on how senior IT leadership should act. The nicest way to characterize the Agile community's treatment of senior IT leadership is, well, neglectful.

When the Agile literature does think to mention senior IT leadership, it does so in the context of driving cultural and organizational change to make room for Agile practices. It assigns two roles to IT management. The first is to empower teams to be autonomous. The second is to help drive the cultural change that will allow the adoption of Agile techniques. These both come down to the same thing: management's job is to force itself to stay out of the way.

In a way, the Agile community is suffering from the same insecurity as the CIO community. While CIOs feel that they need to justify their existence and claim a seat at the table, the Agile community is stuck on the idea that it has no place until dramatic cultural and organizational changes happen.[tt] The enterprise is assumed to be naturally resistant to Agile ideas, and Agility has to fight to claim a seat at the other table—the PMO table, that is. I have argued elsewhere that the fist-pounding demand for cultural change is misguided: there is a place right now for an agile approach to Agility, cultural change or no.[28]

But the real inconsistency—or paradox, if you prefer—is that Agile approaches seem to *remove* IT leaders from the value-creation

---

[tt] Thanks to Gojko Adzic for pointing out to me that Kanban is different in this regard—it advocates moving incrementally from the status quo. On the other hand, I hear very little of that attitude in discussions in the Agile community.

process. In an Agile process, visioning, refinement, and acceptance of system capabilities are in the hands of product experts and users— that is, the folks from the business side. Delivery teams work directly with users and product owners from the enterprise lines of business to decide what is valuable and to create solutions. Where does this leave IT leaders who have always believed themselves responsible for making sure that IT delivers business value?

According to Ken Schwaber and Jeff Sutherland, the creators of Scrum, "Self-organizing teams choose how best to accomplish their work, rather than being directed by others outside the team."[29] A product owner, generally drawn from the business, is responsible for maximizing the value of the product that the development team produces.[30] For the product owner to succeed, they say, "the entire organization must respect his or her decisions...the Development Team isn't allowed to act on what anyone else says."[31] It is hard to see how the team could be more autonomous: the product owner decides *what* they should do, they decide *how* they should do it, and no one else— presumably including IT leaders—is allowed to give them direction.

Now, this is considered a fairly extreme statement of Scrum's views, and other Agile frameworks describe the autonomy of the team differently. Extreme Programming (XP) is less prescriptive and speaks instead of the development team working with "onsite customers," but the general idea is still to empower the team to deal directly with non-IT "business" people to create valuable solutions. The autonomy of the team is further extended in the DevOps model, where a team has "full stack" responsibility for a product: not just development, but also testing, operations, security, and infrastructure engineering.

Let's face it, in this world, IT leadership can sometimes become a useless barnacle on the ship of value delivery, a parsley garnish on a bowl of chocolate pudding, an elephant-shaped stapler on the dinner table.

Imagine the ancient Greeks with their autonomous city-states. They found a way to govern locally through direct democracy. Of course, the city-states were autonomous—you might even say that they worked at cross-purposes. There was no real vision of a single Greek nation that brought those city-states together. Now imagine the Romans with an altogether different vision. Initially a republican vision, theirs was ultimately a vision of empire; their governance structures were set up to unify diverse city-states under a common vision. They had an enterprise view. The Greeks, with their loose collection of autonomous teams, could not compete and eventually were amalgamated into the Roman Empire. Or would you say that the Greeks were the ones who were successful, given that their culture was so vibrant and considering all of their achievements in philosophy, drama, science, and math? Not to mention the fact that, when the Roman Empire declined, what was left was a more-or-less Greek Byzantine Empire? Well, the battle between Greeks and Romans continues.

Our poor IT leaders are Roman emperors trying to find a job in a Greek civilization. It's not surprising that 91% of senior IT leaders think that their job is becoming harder.[32]

When IT leadership finds itself separated from the day-to-day creation of value but nevertheless has responsibilities—security, Enterprise Architecture, cost control, reporting on accomplishments, switching from Python to Ruby and back again, sounding good in front of its peers at conferences—it asserts its control through bureaucracy.

Mike Cohn's wording on this subject is telling. "A Scrum team's job," he says, "is to self-organize around the challenges, and within the boundaries and constraints put in place by management."[33]

Management's role is to *constrain*, to put *boundaries* on the team's ability to create solutions. Cohn is right, though I don't think this is quite what he means. How else can management have influence on a fully autonomous team that is not supposed to listen to them other than by setting up a bureaucracy of rules and constraints? IT security formulates controls and demands that teams produce documentation to show compliance. Enterprise Architecture develops standards that the project teams must follow. The PMO adds paperwork to project reporting and to quality assurance gates. IT leaders write their value delivery story in policy papers rather than in software code.

> IT leaders write their value delivery story in policy papers rather than in software code.

What Cohn meant, I think, is that management *defines the problem* by indicating its boundaries. The team, after all, needs to know what problem it is trying to solve, and what sorts of solutions will be considered effective in solving the problem. We might better say that management sets the *criteria* for success. I admit that is a good point, Mike, but I'd rather take your words out of context for a moment.

Even granting Mike Cohn the right to mean what he means, in Scrum it is actually the product owner, the person drawn from the business side rather than IT, who defines the boundaries of the problem. IT management is relegated to the role of policy-writing bureaucrats who still control that constraining, no-saying, wonkified gate to production. Tom Demarco et al. talk evocatively about template zombies.[34] I love that formulation. IT has been biting itself in the neck for decades, and can't seem to stop. Given the several generations of IT we've been through, our templates have had baby templates by now, and this population explosion has placed severe demands on the scarce resource of delivery team time.

The Agile movement is undermining itself by—in effect—encouraging senior IT leadership to fabricate bureaucracy and manufacture constraints. It does this by not admitting that there is a continuing role for IT management even after the Agile transformation is accomplished, by forcing the CIO to eat brains. It is interesting that both the CIO literature, with its obsession with earning a seat at the table, and the Agile literature, with its emphasis on autonomous teams, both wind up compelling IT leadership to destroy business value.

Yes, I am saying that Agile development adds bureaucracy and waste. #CheekySmile.

The thing is, Agile and Lean approaches work—they lead to good outcomes for the enterprise. They provide excellent ways for IT leaders to lead. They reduce risk, improve quality, and most importantly, they are agile—they allow companies to change quickly and respond to a changing competitive environment. Lean approaches eliminate waste and shorten delivery times. Who could argue with that? Agile and Lean ideas are good things for us IT leaders. The changes we are seeing are positive changes.

My fellow IT leaders, we must use these new Agile, Lean, and DevOps practices as a lever for changing the relationship between IT and the rest of the business. We have defined our roles and our goals in ways that are inconsistent. We simply cannot earn a seat at the table by doing the things we believe we need to do to earn that seat at the table; we simply cannot interact effectively with others at the table even if we have been given a seat. We are locked into a way of co-existing with the rest of the enterprise that is based on old stereotypes and assumptions—both about IT and about the business—and that destroys business value.

We can change this! The ideas behind Agile approaches are potent and compelling, and can help us reframe these business-IT interactions in a way that will create value—lots of it! Let us question the constraints, define the problem, brainstorm solutions, turn them into hypotheses, test them, and continuously improve how we practice IT leadership, as Agile thinking teaches us to do.

I believe that this is simpler than it sounds. It is about identifying the obstacles in our way and taking today's best-practice ideas—those found in the Agile Manifesto and in books like *Lean Startup*, *Lean Software Development*, *Lean Enterprise*, *The DevOps Handbook*, and others on today's management bookshelves—and applying them to IT leadership.

The news is good, colleagues. By the time you get to the last few chapters of this book, you will see that these changes in the IT world give you fairy dust and wizardry, new powers and influence that can be wielded for the good. What you must do now is open your mind, maintain your curiosity, and take on these new challenges courageously!

---

Obsessed with proving that it deserves a seat at the table, IT leadership continues to frame its problems in the same old ways—oblivious to the deep changes brought on by the Agile revolution—while the Agile world, ever suspicious of management, proceeds as if it can manage without the involvement of IT leaders.

---

2

# KEPT FROM THE TABLE

A picture held us captive. And we could not get outside it, for it lay in our language and language seemed to repeat it to us inexorably.

**—Ludwig Wittgenstein**, *Philosophical Investigations*

The almost insoluble task is to let neither the power of others, nor our own powerlessness, stupefy us.

**—Theodor Adorno**, *Minima Moralia*

In the beginning, there was technology. The company's technologists knew things that the rest of the enterprise didn't. They needed a leader, one who could communicate with the laypeople and yet represent the geeks. The CIO role was created—some 35 years ago as I write these words.[1] But the role was without form and void. It needed maturing and definition. It was not enough to say that the CIO was the geek who wears the suit; after all, that didn't help the other executives understand how to work with him or her, and it didn't really tell the CIO how to behave and what to spend time on, aside from hanging with the geeks and doodling FORTRAN code.

The truth was that the IT organization was filled with all manner of strange creatures walking upon the earth. Engineers, but not engineers who created product for the company to sell, your whiz kid inventor types. No, they were engineers who had something to do with actually making the company run. You had to rely on them so you could do your job. But, like most engineers, they were smart, quirky, and spoke a funny language. In the early days, you might even see them in breath-fogging, air-conditioned "computer rooms" wearing white lab coats and carrying reel-to-reel tapes.

They made you feel stupid. They were unpredictable. They were somehow *other*—while you were focused on business outcomes,

> It's not enough to say that the CIO is the geek who wears the suit.

they were focused on...what? They got all excited by making the computer do strange, seemingly useless little things. They took forever to get the simplest tasks done. They babbled away in acronyms and tossed cute but baffling little techie terms around, always with their peculiar sense of humor.* They were arrogant and looked down on people who didn't understand the difference between a linker and a loader. They cultivated aloofness. They were definitively *other*.

The CIO, then, was the executive responsible for *them*—the bridge between the worlds of the real business people and strange engineers. "It is commonly accepted that a CIO's value to an organization comes from the ability to bridge the gap between information technology and business."[2] Two obvious questions arise, since a bridge needs to be anchored on both sides. On the business side, what role should the CIO play? A provider of customer service to the business lines? An enforcer of policy and standards? A reassuring voice of technology familiarity? On the technology side, was the CIO a technologist leading technologists, a pointy haired management suit allocating budgets and blamed for schedule overages, an architect of the company's information function, or an accountant of IT chargebacks?

___

* For example, "GNU Unix," a recursive name where GNU stands for "GNU's Not Unix" Ha! Get it? Pretty funny, eh, business customer?!

The first of these questions begat a literature: advice books from experienced IT leaders and business authors telling senior IT leaders how to act like real business people to justify their role and importance in the company and to frame problems in business terms rather than technical terms. The advice to senior IT leaders sounded something like this: Get a seat at the table! Act like a C-level executive! Communicate the value of IT! Speak the language of the business, and only the language of the business! Drop all the techie stuff!

But it was on the second question that the CIO's real role became apparent. The CIO was there to keep them *under* control. Make them deliver business value, at a reasonable price, without any strange, geeky games. Maybe get them to wear freshly washed clothes now and then, and sleep at home rather than on their desks. *They* needed to be *controlled* because they were different, and thus untrustworthy. IT things—whatever you call that stuff—took much too long and cost too much: clearly, the IT people, instead of focusing on profits, were fooling around with the technology just because it amused them. They were out of control, or would be unless senior IT leaders could rein them in.

Honestly, the unpredictability and opacity of IT drove the other C-level executives crazy. It was easy for them to blame their frustrating lack of control on the technologists themselves, with their funny T-shirts and lack of business polish. Fortunately, the CIO would earn his seat at the table by showing that he could control *them* by making them deliver with predictability and teaching those arrogant folks to treat the rest of the company as their customers.

Thus, a distinctive way of thinking about IT was born, and has determined the course of IT since. First of all, we came to speak about "IT and the business" as two separate things, as if IT were an outside contractor. It had to be so: the business was us and IT was *them*. The arms-length contracting paradigm was amplified, in some companies, by the use of a chargeback model under which IT "charged" business units based on their consumption of IT services. Since it was essentially managing a contractor relationship, *the business* needed to specify its requirements perfectly and in detail so that it could hold IT to delivering on them, on schedule, completely, with high quality, and within budget. The contractor-control model led, inevitably, to the idea that IT should be delivering "customer service" to the enterprise—you'd certainly expect service with a smile if you were paying so much money to your contractors.

> We came to speak about "IT and the business" as two separate things, as if IT were an outside contractor. The business was us and IT was them.

IT and the business—two separate entities, with the poor CIO trying to keep one foot in each world while awkwardly struggling to gain a seat at the big table where the business executives sat. The business figured out business needs and handed them to the CIO, tapping its foot impatiently while it waited for him or her to deliver results. When IT (finally!) finished building or acquiring something to meet those needs, they turned it back over to the business, smiling and waiting for a pat on the head. If the CIO did well enough to get plenty of head pats, then perhaps he or she would have a place at the strategy table.

Stereotypes emerged, solidified, and remained unquestioned. If left to its own devices, IT would diverge from alignment with the business. IT people would play with the technology; do things that added no business value. IT people did not really understand what the business needed, and were incapable of making good business decisions and trade-offs. The business, for its part, was clueless, full of politics, and apt to point fingers. And, oh, yes: IT was just too damn expensive.[3]

How could you control a contractor? You asked for an estimate and pressured the contractor to deliver at or close to that estimate. Or you agreed on a fixed price. How could you control IT? Same model, but with the twist that the IT staff were your own employees who were paid a fixed salary—a bit awkward. Since their cost was fixed (at least in the short and medium terms), your biggest worry was that they would waste time on frivolous activities. How could you know that they weren't? Simple: you insisted that they deliver on schedule, and kept the pressure on them to do so.

Some of IT's work was *transactional*: user support, device provisioning, updates, and maintenance. In those areas, costs and lead times could be benchmarked and monitored. But a good deal of IT's work involved *delivering capabilities*—developing and integrating applications, rolling out ERP systems, installing collaboration tools, and so on. For IT to demonstrate that it was performing that type of work responsibly and for the business to verify that it was doing so, the scope of each task had to be defined precisely, bounded, and agreed upon in advance. The work had to be organized into *projects*, which are units of work with a defined set of deliverables, a beginning, and an end. You could establish control by making sure the project was completed within the bounds of its estimated cost and schedule. How perfect the Waterfall model is for this purpose! How perfectly it aligned with the business's need to know that IT was under control.

Of course, there are some problems with this way of organizing IT's work. In fact, when you really think about it, it makes as little sense as a semicolon terminator in a line of Python code. It could only have been born out of unease about the "black box" of IT and its seemingly uncontrollable costs.

For one thing, how does the idea of "project" fit with the idea of a "capability," an "application," or a "system"? Projects can be scoped, started, and ended; planned and measured against that plan. IT capabilities, on the contrary, are long-lived, granular, evolutionary, in constant flux, and future-oriented. After the project to build a system is finished, well, somehow the system keeps costing money! There always seems to be more work to do on systems that have already been finished. How many a frustrated CEO has complained that IT costs never end?

Aha! We found a way! We would fix the scope of the project all the more rigidly by defining some deliverable as the final operating capability (FOC), and then throw everything that happens after FOC into a bucket called operations and maintenance (O&M). Then we could try to minimize it. This in effect treats the system as a "product"—once the product is completed, it is done, and all that has to follow is the cost of "maintaining" or "operating" it. Like a car, right? But, alas, this is not how the world works. More or less secretly, the IT folks were actually enhancing and changing the product after it was finished—not just doing "maintenance" on it—to meet the business's needs as its competitive environment changed.

Unfortunately, the more rigid the scope was, the less likely the system was to meet actual business needs. A rigid scope resists change, while change in the business environment is constant. It also allows no room for errors in the original specification. While it might seem like a good way to manage contractors—that is, IT—it is also a good way to destroy business value. But at least it met the underlying goal—controlling the strange IT folk, who might suddenly burst into some peculiar, torpid yet manic activity bent on wasting the company's money.

IT was an island separate from the business; the CIO would need to control the natives, work the mines, and export the gold and silver. Or IT was the leper colony, and the business didn't want to get too close, preferring to communicate by tossing requirements documents over the channel that separated them.

*IT* and *the business*. To quote Martha Heller again, "Rather, the 'and' in 'IT and the business' connotes separateness and difference, an 'us and them' perception that has plagued IT organizations since the beginning of their existence."[4]

IT and the business have long known that they were in an uncomfortable, codependent, abusive relationship. To the business, Arthur C. Clarke's law holds: "Any sufficiently advanced technology is indistinguishable from magic."[5] IT stuff is alchemy—an esoteric art practiced by pocket-protector sophists who can run circles around anyone foolish enough to argue with them. And the IT folks—they knew they could turn on the gibberish and obfuscation any time they wanted.

When the business created a project, how could it know what a reasonable price tag for its set of requirements would be? Imagine yourself at a market in rural Codeistan trying to buy a fancy snowglobe souvenir or a Sergey Brin bobblehead, and there are no marked prices. You are sure you are being ripped off. The merchants can see that you are a tourist and have no idea what the prices "should be." You also don't quite get that there is no price things "should be"— prices vary depending on the circumstances.

> IT stuff is alchemy— an esoteric art practiced by pocket-protector sophists who can run circles around anyone foolish enough to argue with them.

Whatever price the vendor names, you cut in half and start the negotiation from there. Whatever price you wind up with, you still feel cheated.

The IT people were asked to estimate the cost and schedule for a project in advance. Since no one outside of IT had a good basis for judging whether the estimate was reasonable (putting aside the question of whether IT itself knew), the business folks felt that they had to negotiate the estimate—the cost was always too high, of course. The best the business could do was to refer to what seemed like comparable projects, possibly unrealistic quotes they had received from external vendors, a threat to outsource if the IT folks didn't reduce their estimate, and brute-force tactics like "let's cut it in half and then add a margin in our own minds because we know IT is always late."

Like the tourists in the Codeistan marketplace of the IT geeks, the business leaders left feeling ripped off. "IT is too expensive!" they said. Of course, even though it was "too expensive," they continued to buy it—as Tom DeMarco points out in *Why Does Software Cost So Much?: And Other Puzzles of the Information Age*—because they still expected to get enough value to justify the cost.[6] The tourists might complain that they are being cheated, but if you don't bring back a bobblehead and snow globe, no one will believe you've been to Codeistan. It still doesn't feel very good.

You know how this game goes: IT would learn to pad its estimate ("management reserve," "slack time," "contingency"), and the business would knock it down to something that made them feel like they were winning the negotiation. "No, we can't possibly wait a year for that capability. You have to do it in six months."

Unfortunately, these internal-to-the-company estimates are *estimates*, not prices. You don't get a better deal by knocking down an estimate. But it seemed so, because soon, the estimate would be accepted as the plan—the schedule, the budget. Control was achieved by telling the geeks to deliver on the estimate and holding them *accountable* for doing so. A project that didn't meet its estimates "by definition" must be out of control, troubled, and staffed with lazy or incompetent people. The distinction between an estimate, a target, a plan, and a measure of success disappeared behind the Waterfall— disappeared into an illusion of control.

Now that the estimate was locked in, it was time to begin the first phase of the project—gathering requirements. The requirements would be "specified" by the business without reference to what was possible, natural, or easy; specified, and then tossed over the wall to IT. The business learned a very important lesson: if the scope of the requirements increased while the project was underway, then IT would have an excuse for exceeding the planned cost and schedule. Demanding execution against plan, remember, is what gives the business control over the IT delivery process. The enemy of control, it follows, is *scope creep*: the gradual introduction of new requirements after the plan is created. Both the business and IT could agree that this is undesirable.

What behaviors does all of this incentivize? The business is motivated to get the requirements perfect at the outset; if they make any changes, then IT will force them to acknowledge that they are setting the project behind schedule and over budget. So the business tries to make sure that everything it *might* need is part of the requirements. Into the mix are thrown wish lists of features drawn from across the user base; features to support plans that the business has in mind but that might never get funded or executed; animated cats that stroll across the screen; ideas for things that plausibly sound like they *might* add value.

The result: *feature bloat*. Everything we *might* need rather than what we *do* need. More requirements than expected in the original estimates. Why not? The estimate had already been given, so the additional scope was "free" to the business representatives informing the requirements document. The geeks themselves made things worse by pushing the business folks to specify their requirements in ever greater detail so that there would be no ambiguity. Of course, with bloated scope, it also took longer to finalize the requirements, document them, and get them approved. The schedule and cost were already compromised even before work began.

Guess what: the results were not good. Somehow, despite the fact that IT Island was populated by brilliant, hard-working (okay, albeit strange) people, virtually every project was over budget, behind schedule, and filled with defects. IT's customer service skills weren't all that great, either—they liked to say "no" and insisted on using technical mumbo-jumbo. And wouldn't you know it—the geeks always had some excuse for this bad performance, especially the schedule slippage. The requirements had changed, they'd say. The hardware broke. The operating system had a bug. Memory was leaking. The jabberwocky had a slithy tove.

The geeks were still out of control!

"Knock, knock."
    "Who's there?"
    "CIO"
    "CIO who?"
    "It depends on your requirements."
    "Er, um—could you come back later? We're eating now."
    "Could I join you?"
    "Uh, no. We don't have any seats left at the table."
    Don't think this "control" attitude was one-sided. The geeks responded with all the tricks they knew for controlling the business so that they could deliver on their accountabilities. They "required"

the business to specify its requirements fully before they were willing to engage. To keep costs under control, they established standards—that is, they controlled what the business could do and could purchase. In other words, they said no. To deliver on their accountability to keep the company secure, they established security policies and controls. In other words, they said no. To maintain the integrity of the data in their databases, for which they were accountable, they "idiot-proofed" their systems, constraining what data could be entered and when. Even their software said no.

This last point is especially significant—the business folks are "idiots" to be talked down to and controlled in return. Mustn't use technical words, mustn't assume they know anything. If you want to control us, we will have to control you back.

These are interactions born of desperation, of deep-seated fear of the technologists that has been cultivated by the technologists themselves. That's why I called this a codependent, abusive relationship. Because of a cultural discomfort between the business and *them*, and the resulting dynamic of control and counter-control, a vicious cycle was engendered. But IT projects are—by their nature—not amenable to this sort of control. They are highly complex and unpredictable, influenced in a large way by small outside influences. In its desperation, the business evolved a set of practices that actually work *against* its best interests, leaving IT leadership in the middle of a mess of contradictory incentives and impractical demands.

As IT was incentivized to provide service with a smile, the business was disincentivized from learning and adapting to the new technology landscape. Consider technical jargon, for example: the IT staff was discouraged from using it because it would make business

ncomfortable. But should IT really refrain from using
___ terms any more than marketing should stop talking about
branding and finance stop talking about assets and liabilities?

> Isn't jargon, jargon
> because it is
> expressive and
> concise once
> understood?

Should we really assume that the non-IT folks are incapable of learning some of the important language of IT? Isn't jargon, jargon because it is expressive and concise once understood?

Perhaps these questions are moot—technology has become so central to everyone's lives and so consumerized, that most of the company *does* speak the jargon these days. People store their photos in *the cloud*, distinguish between Mac, Windows, and iOS *operating systems*, and might even know what a *domain name* is. The real problem is not the jargon, but the use of it for obfuscation.

To avoid making the non-IT folk feel stupid, IT responded, over and over, to password reset requests, questions about what button to push to make the phone vibrate, CD drives being used as cupholders,[†] claims that the internet is broken, difficulties in watching their porn videos, and mousepads alleged to be incompatible with the company's computers.

IT does so in a cheery, bright-eyed way, as if to earn tips. But these requests are a cost to the enterprise. As the world becomes more digital, shouldn't users be expected to become more sophisticated in their use of technology and its terminology?

When it comes down to delivering capabilities, a customer-service-oriented IT organization must give the business what it *wants*. In an Orwellian twist of language, we refer to what the

---

† May be apocryphal, but the story has been around for a while. In any case, I've seen worse.

business *wants* as what it *needs*. That's why we have *requirements*. Isn't this a strange way to speak to colleagues in your own company—"this is what we require of you" or "this here is what we need"? Never mind that IT might have deep knowledge of the business's needs born of its long experience, deep involvement, and ability to see across all lines of the business. The job of IT has been to deliver, not to decide what needs to be delivered. The business understands business value, and it's just a matter of translating it into terms the IT folk can understand.

While the IT organization is expected to develop standards and policies to reduce costs and keep the company secure, actually applying them—saying "no" with a frown—is bad customer service. Who wants to type a long password when they log in to a system? IT forces us to. Why do we have to standardize our desktop models and configurations? IT forces us to. The business might imagine features that would turn out to be prohibitively expensive to build. Is it IT's role to satisfy these "needs"? Why does the business have to accept systems that don't quite live up to their fantasies? IT forces them to.

According to Lyndon Tennison of the Union Pacific Corporation (as quoted in Heller), "The fewer tools I have in my tool kit, the more cost effective I can be. If I can force standardization through an architecture model, I should inherently be able to drive efficiency."[7] Note the word "force." The difficulty here should be clear: IT is expected both to enforce standards and to provide customer service—that is, fulfill the customers' desires while at the same time discouraging those desires. Enforcement with a smile. Perhaps this is something like the police breaking down a door and then distributing a survey to see whether the occupants are happy with the service they've received.

*The business*, of course, does not speak with a single voice. Different parts of the organization may want different things (or at least prioritize different things). IT is sure to disappoint some of these divisions of the organization, given limited resources. Sure, the company might set up governance processes to resolve these conflicts, but only at the level of deciding among projects—while IT will still have to deal with conflicting opinions and desires as the projects are being executed. And why can't IT do everything, or at least more than it is doing now? The more IT tries to control costs by limiting its resources, the more unhappy its customers will be.

A subtle problem with the customer service model, which will become important in later chapters, is the impossibility of adopting an enterprise view while being bounced about by individual customer service demands. Again, Hunter and Westerman nail it: "Over time," they say, "setting up IT as an order taker produces the complicated, brittle, and expensive legacy environments."[8] We can't have it both ways: we can't expect to build a set of Enterprise IT assets that have strategic value if we are drawn this way and that by demands for service.

In any case, Agile both demands and provides a new way for IT to interact with the enterprise. And while IT can no longer be held to an impossible standard, it also can no longer hide behind that standard.

The problems with the customer service model are legion. As Hunter and Westerman put it:

> Saying that "the business is IT's customer, and the customer is always right" seems like a good idea when there is deep dissatisfaction with IT that stems from a long history of unreliable service. But over the long term, this value trap sets up the IT unit for failure because customers are often wrong (especially

about matters in which they are not experts), and calling col-leagues "customers" puts a wedge between IT and the rest of the business.[9]

To Hunter and Westerman, the customer service model is a "value trap" because it sets up a frame of reference that actually prevents IT from achieving its potential value.

> Value traps create barriers between IT and the rest of the orga-nization, forcing conversations about IT into avenues that inherently reduce IT's value or place limits on how much IT can improve value. Value traps are often ingrained in the heads of IT leaders as well as business executives as basic underlying assumptions about the relationship between IT and the rest of the business.[10]

That is well put—this value trap is in the heads of both business and IT. Following this model, IT will get lost trying to find its seat at the table.

A customer service model presupposes an efficient market for services: the business would ideally benchmark its IT department against other offerings in the market to get some handle on what "good" performance looks like. You know, what prices they should be paying in the Codeistan craft market. Now, logically speaking, it should be difficult for the IT organization to lose a battle against outside providers: its incentives are aligned with those of the busi-ness; it has no need to earn a profit; there are no transaction or legal costs involved in transacting; the IT department already knows the business well and has no learning curve; and the IT department is fully dedicated to the customer's project. There is no *a priori* reason to think that the company's IT organization can't hire and manage people as well as a contractor. Yet somehow the IT department often comes up short in these comparisons.

Why? For one thing, we do not have an efficient market. There are no "identical" commodity services here. And besides, the comparison is also between estimates or predictions, not actuals. The internal IT organization has a good sense of what will need to be done, while an outside contractor probably does not—most likely, they are actually "bidding" on different services.

Why not simply fill the IT department with the finest people around, train them aggressively, and stop worrying about how they compare to outside firms?

Maybe we have it all backwards. Now that digital capabilities are so critical to the company's competitive strategy—to its value-creation activities—perhaps we should be designing business operations in a way that makes those digital capabilities more effective. Maybe the IT folks should formulate the company's strategy, and the rest of the business should do what is required as set forth by the IT folks to make that strategy successful. Perhaps the business should be providing customer service with a smile to the IT organization.

I jest. That was just the IT-savvy digital masters thing again. My point is that no part of the enterprise should be at arm's length providing customer service to the rest of the organization. Anyway, the business has no reason to smile: they are not having as much fun with the technology as we know the technologists secretly are, playing Warcraft and sunning themselves in LED light in those basement cubicles wherein they live.

If you are in a business environment today, look around. Try to do it with fresh eyes. Do you see IT people who are more interested in playing with technology than in supporting the business? Are the IT people still some mysterious fraternity (all men, by the stereotype) in white lab coats and super-air-conditioned rooms, speaking an obscure language that sounds suspiciously like Klingon? Is the business clueless about technology? Does the business always know what will create the most business value, and does it always follow through and harvest that value once a system is launched? Do IT projects ever really end? Do we build systems right up until we achieve FOC and then just do little bits of maintenance on them, like a car?

I might be moving in unusual circles—but it seems to me that most of the technologists I work with are human beings who are dedicated to the success of the company and eager to add business value. Not only that, but they have a deep understanding of what is valuable to the business. They know the details of the business's operations because they get to see operations and priorities across all of the business units. They know the business's challenges; they maintain relationships with all parts of the enterprise. They are more and more diverse; hailing from many cultures, they bring different sets of experiences and they have different types of communication skills. They often have political savvy, because they need it to do their jobs.

> It seems to me that most of the technologists I work with are human beings who are dedicated to the success of the company and eager to add business value.

You might also notice that the people who like to play with the technology, arguably, are now "on the business side." Subtly, without anyone noticing, it is no longer that IT needs to speak the language of the business, but rather that the business is coming to speak the language of IT.

In fact, the geeks have broken out; they've left their island and overrun the mainland. "The eruption of open source software into the mainstream in 1998," says Eric Raymond, one of the most eloquent theorists of the open source movement, "was the revenge of the hackers after 20 years of marginalization."[11] He continues "twenty years of living in a ghetto—a fairly comfortable ghetto full of interesting friends, but still one walled in by a vast and intangible barrier of mainstream prejudice inscribed 'ONLY FLAKES LIVE HERE.'"[12] By now, the mainstream world has become more comfortable with technology and has found common ground with the geeks.

Ironically, despite this convergence between IT folks and business folks, "the more your employees love technology, the more they dislike IT," as Heller puts it.[13] How could that be? "One of the reasons IT often gets such a bad name with other employees is that we always come up with complexities and barriers."[14] IT folks are no longer the *other* because they *love* technology; they are the *other*—and frustrating and annoying—because they *constrain* technology. They are the voice of the company's "control" over technology.

While the CIO and his IT legions have in many ways become the very barrier to agility, the company more and more needs to compete in a digital economy. Who should lead that effort? Clearly not the CIO. So companies have begun to create new roles for digital services experts—ultimately a Chief Digital Officer. The Chief Digital Officer's role (or that of the Digital C-suite or the Digital whatever) is to play the strategic role—the one that justifies the seat at the table—that the CIO had been vying for unsuccessfully. The CIO created a trap for him or herself: success, defined as controlling the iron triangle,[††] eliminating scope creep, taking orders from the business,

_____

[††] The boundaries of cost, schedule, and scope. Given the uncertainty in IT plans, it is axiomatic that one can't work within all three constraints simultaneously.

and keeping the lights on effectively and cheaply, meant not being qualified to lead the company into the digital era.

It turns out to be extremely difficult to stop thinking of IT as something separate from the business. It is built into the very way we speak, the terms we use every day. In Wittgenstein's words, "The picture holds us captive." To speak of "requirements" is to imply that the business is telling IT what it *must* do; to discuss "alignment" is to imply that IT is separate enough to become misaligned. Our entire discourse on IT presupposes a separation. There is nothing analogous to this when we speak of marketing, sales, or finance. "We're becoming essentially an IT consultant to the business, climbing the value chain," say Hunter and Westerman.[15] Really, we are struggling to become *part* of the business so that we can claim that seat at the table—while continuing to hold ourselves at arm's length.

But the old models are breaking down. IT is being driven deeper and deeper into the heart of the enterprise. IT *is* the business. The business *is* IT. We do not have a "telephone" department that is responsible for the company's telephone strategy, nor a paper-and-pencil department responsible for innovation around writing. These things have become normal, operational, quotidian. As the authors of *IT Governance* put it, "In the future, describing how much an enterprise spends on IT will be meaningless. IT will be imbedded in every process and budget, just like capital."[16] "In high-performance organizations today," say Jez Humble, Barry O'Reilly, and Joanne Molesky in *Lean Enterprise*, "people who design, build, and run software-based products are an integral part of the business. They are given—and accept—responsibility for customer outcomes."[17] Or, as Heller frames it, "CIOs who have broken the paradox do not think of their role as to support and enable the business; they—and their organizations—simply are the business."[18]

IT is no longer *other*, and the objective of "controlling" IT conflicts with today's objective: to derive business value from IT by using it to drive competitive strategy, profit generation, and mission accomplishment. The wall between IT and the business can no longer stand while requirements are being tossed over it and deliveries are being made through the door. Our metaphors are mingling uncomfortably.

Agile thinking gives us a way to escape from the old I-control-you-and-you-control-me-but-we-keep-smiling dynamic with supportive, positive, solution-oriented human interaction. IT is not about obsequious salespeople who bow to a customer's demands. I would replace "service with a smile" with "interaction with a smile," or maybe "partnership and teamwork with a smile," and we should all do it—IT, marketing, operations, and even the board of directors.

It will be a good topic of conversation at the table when we claim our seats there.

---

The relationship between IT and the rest of the business has been defined in the same terms as that of a contractor to its customer, where the business negotiates terms with IT and then frets about its ability to control IT's delivery and customer service. This model is also called the *Waterfall*.

---

# A NIMBLE APPROACH
# TO THE TABLE

How many are the things I can do without!

**—Socrates**, quoted by Diogenes Laertius

If you wish to make Pythocles rich, do not add to his store of money, but subtract from his desires.

**—Epicurus**, *Fragment 28*

The essence of Agile approaches is simply this: we should inspect and adapt frequently rather than slavishly following a plan. We can express this in terms of learning: rather than avoiding or punishing learning, we should learn constantly and incorporate what we learn into what we do—even if what we learn is not consistent with our original plan. This might sound obvious, and it is, but it is also fundamentally opposed to the way we have always managed IT system delivery.

My friends, this is all there is to Agile delivery.

How can we best inspect and adapt? The answer lies in Lean thinking. We must create fast feedback cycles where we can see results often and reflect on how effective they are. The shorter our cycle time, the quicker we can get feedback, analyze it, and incorporate it. Lean thinking tells us that we can minimize cycle time by eliminating waste in our process, working on fewer things at a time, reducing handoffs between teams, building in quality rather than catching and fixing errors, and various other ways that have proven effective in manufacturing and product design. Fellow travelers, this is all there is to it—Agile and Lean thinking complement each other elegantly.

I mentioned reducing handoffs, continuously improving, and gathering feedback rapidly. This is where Continuous Delivery and DevOps come in. All Agile approaches recognize the importance of working in small teams: a small team can communicate effectively through face-to-face contact; it can brainstorm improvements and make them quickly. DevOps simply adds the idea that small, cross-functional teams should own the entire delivery process from concept through user feedback and production monitoring. By bringing together development and operations on the same small team, we can eliminate handoffs and speed up feedback by letting the team observe its work in production and react to what it sees. The techniques of Continuous Delivery provide the automation framework that makes frequent deployments possible, thus allowing the team to quickly get work to production, where it can get valuable feedback. Brother and sister revolutionaries, this is all there is to changing IT from the ground up.

> Agile thinking simply says that we should empower small teams to inspect and adapt rather than stick to a plan.

Having reduced the Agile world to three paragraphs, I can't resist the temptation to now try it in a single paragraph. You with me?

Agile thinking simply says that we should empower small teams to inspect and adapt rather than stick to a plan. Lean thinking gives that small team ways to speed up its inspecting and adapting process to maximize its impact. Continuous Delivery and DevOps place the entire value stream in the hands of that small team so that it can "optimize the whole" (a term of art in Lean thinking) and be empowered as a team to own the entire value delivery process.

<Bow/><Applause/>

Of course, I have over-simplified. For example, I have emphasized the process implications rather than the importance that Agile, Lean, and DevOps principles place on empowering and motivating people. As the Agile Manifesto puts it, we attach importance to "people and interactions over processes."[1] A strong theme in DevOps is that of eliminating the inhumane position that operations teams are placed in when systems are "tossed over the wall" from development to operations. These are very important aspects of Agility; they also follow nicely from the basic concept I have outlined: an empowered, energized team can best inspect and adapt.

I have also neglected to mention that Agile approaches try their best to deliver business value quickly and frequently. An Agile project will try to make its initial delivery as soon as possible, and then add incrementally to that minimum viable product. This is different from the old, plan-driven Waterfall approach that often didn't deliver product until the project was complete after testing and deployment phases. This is indeed a very important part of the Agile approach. It also fits well with the "short feedback cycles" I have emphasized. Getting product quickly to users generates fast feedback; it also adds immediate business value.

I have chosen to present Agile approaches from the viewpoint of feedback and adaptation for several reasons. One is that it emphasizes the business motivation: agility is simply about changing plans quickly as circumstances change. A second is that this way of framing it focuses on the hardest part of Agile approaches for people to accept, which is also the part that has the greatest implications for senior IT leadership's changed role. I am speaking of the idea that we should plan *not* to follow our plans. The true contribution of Agile thinking is the idea that plan-driven approaches to IT don't work well and should be discarded.

When I say that Waterfall approaches are plan-driven, I mean they place a high value on planning and then delivering according to plan. Agile approaches also involve planning, but value outcomes much higher than delivering according to plan. So the difference is really in values, or how success is determined. "Plan-driven" to me means that the plan drives the process; Agile means that adjustments are constantly made to the plan to maximize value based on what is learned during execution. Or, to put it another way, does the team trust the map or the territory that they actually encounter?

I also want—and, yes, I know that this is Agile heresy—to de-emphasize the idea that Agile teams "deliver" value. The term can be misleading—it gives the feeling of a contractor relationship where IT delivers to the business. I would rather think of the process instead as a joint adventure of learning between the business and IT. I am also not sure that the Agile team delivers "value"— perhaps it is more accurate to say that they deliver product that helps the business achieve value. Scrum, XP, and other Agile frameworks don't talk about how value is harvested—just how user stories are delivered. Or, to put it differently, I am not sure that the Agile approach fully accounts for how the Agile team can deliver value— and I think it should.

> I want to de-emphasize the idea that Agile teams "deliver" value.

The key characteristic of a plan-driven approach is that we begin it by organizing the delivery of capabilities into a *project*, with milestones and a planned scope; we then try to execute the capability delivery as closely to that plan as possible. The most common plan-driven approach in IT is the aforementioned Waterfall approach, so-called because of how it appears when drawn on a Gantt chart. Waterfall is a phased or stage-gate approach: the plan is laid out as a series of phases that follow each other linearly, with defined handoffs between them. The phases typically include requirements-gathering, design, development, testing, and deployment. Because Waterfall—though probably never used exactly in practice—was how we used to think about software delivery, we often compare Agile thinking to it, but the truth is that Agile thinking questions *any* plan-driven approach, or the idea that valuing adherence to plan makes sense for a complex, empirical process.

Success in the Waterfall model means hitting the schedule milestones for each stage while remaining under budget and completing exactly what was specified in the initial scope of requirements. Nothing more: that would be scope creep. Nothing less: that would be poor quality. Teams are accountable for delivering according to plan.

What is wrong with plans? Nothing. Agile approaches also encourage making plans. They discourage measuring success by adherence to those plans, arguing that business value cannot be maximized by sticking to plans that are made at the beginning of a project, when the least amount of information is known.

The Waterfall adherent would probably advance two counter-arguments. First, adherence to a plan gives the company predictability; it allows other projects and investment planning to be synchronized with the delivery initiative. That is true, say the Agilists, but because of the uncertainty and complexity of large IT projects, schedules are almost never met, so that predictability is never obtained. If synchronizing other corporate activities is the goal, wouldn't it be better to constantly reassess the project's status and adjust plans accordingly?

The Waterfallers would further argue that adherence to plan is how we control a project. The team executing the project must be held accountable, and if they agree to deliver the project on a particular schedule and budget, then they should be held to doing so.

That is the crux of this book.

The Waterfall approach, I say, is focused on controlling the techie IT folks, whom we still assume require controlling. The idea that they "agree" to deliver on a schedule and budget is drawn from the world of contracting, but the truth is that the techies have no choice but to "agree" because they are employees. The CIO, angling for a seat at the table by demonstrating control, is an agent of the non-IT folk in perpetuating this model.

> The true meaning of the Waterfall approach is actually about control, and melds beautifully with the contractor-control model of IT.

The true meaning of the Waterfall approach, then, is unmasked <flourish/>: it's actually about control, and melds beautifully with the contractor-control model of IT. The CIO wants to earn the seat at the table through demonstrating control over the chaos of IT delivery. But in an uncertain world, that sort of control is impossible, and trying too hard to achieve it destroys business value, ultimately denying the CIO that very place at the table.

What we really want from the techies is not that they slavishly obey a plan, but that they harness their skills, creativity, and hard work to achieve the best outcomes possible for the company just like any other employee of the company. Well, would they achieve the best outcomes for the company by following a plan? Yes—under conditions of low uncertainty, and where the predictability of delivery is valuable. But under conditions of high uncertainty—the conditions under which most IT projects operate—the best value to the company comes from adaptation, flexibility, and responsiveness...in other words, changing plans.

But if IT teams are not accountable for delivering according to plan, then we have chaos, don't we? If you are an IT leader reading this, you are undoubtedly wondering how you can do your job in the Agile world. Does the Agile approach say that you should just let your teams deliver whatever they want, whenever they want?

The answer, in short, is that when we bring Agile thinking into our leadership practices, it gives us something that is like control, but better and more effective. It is something more akin to shaping behavior rather than controlling behavior—but it works, and the rest of this book is about how to practice it.

Agile approaches use fast feedback cycles to make course corrections. Developers and users work together—face to face if possible—so that the users can answer questions and comment on what is being produced and the developers can incorporate their feedback. To make this fast feedback possible, developers build entire features at a time; they take a valuable unit of functionality, develop it in collaboration with users, test it, declare it complete, and move on to the next unit of functionality.

Feedback is accelerated in another critical way: code is deployed to production frequently and incrementally. Users can use it right away. Based on their feedback and on quantitative, objective assessments of how the features are performing in meeting business objectives, the developers can improve the features. Any mistakes in the requirements will be discovered quickly and fixed.

The development teams also give themselves feedback: they retrospect periodically on their process and find ways to improve it. They become better and better at creating the product as the product becomes better and better through user feedback. Keeping teams small helps accelerate feedback—the members of a small team can actually talk to one another!

How could we ever have thought that the plan-driven approach is actually effective for IT system delivery? Honestly, once you get the Agile concept, it is hard to go back.

For an IT leader, here are the key advantages of the Agile approach when it comes to managing IT initiatives:

- **Learning:** In the Agile approach, we learn as we go and incorporate what we learn. In a plan-driven approach, we can only learn to the extent that it doesn't change our original plan. Which is better: To adjust as we learn, or to reject learning for the sake of the plan?
- **Nimbleness:** In the Agile approach, we harness change to the company's advantage. As a project proceeds, circumstances change. Competitors introduce new products. The government introduces new regulations. New technologies appear. Our choice is between changing the plan to accommodate new developments or ignoring new developments.
- **Course Correction:** In the Agile approach, we adjust course based on feedback—from users, from a product owner, from objective measures of system performance, and from management. The alternatives are to get less feedback or to ignore feedback.

- **Delivery:** In the Agile approach, we deliver quickly and frequently to users. In the plan-driven approach, delivery often comes at the end of the project. Early delivery lets the business get value earlier (and there is a time value of money) and checks to see whether the product actually works in an operational setting.

- **Risk:** In the Agile approach, we reduce risk by testing and delivering in short increments. At any given time, we risk only the small increment being worked on. In the plan-driven approach, on the other hand, risk increases until delivery—the more we do without finishing and delivering, the more is at risk from defects, operational problems, or our inability to finish.

- **Salvage Value:** In the Agile approach, we can terminate a project at any time without wasting money, since all the work to date has been delivered and is in use. In a plan-driven approach with delivery at the end, terminating the project before completion generally means that nothing has been salvaged.

- **Budget Adherence:** In the Agile approach, we can ensure that we work within budget. We simply adjust scope as necessary to fit within the given resources. With the plan-driven approach, we must keep working until we complete the plan—the defined scope—even if that means we run behind schedule or over budget. Or we can terminate the project without delivering anything.

- **Technical Practices:** The Agile toolset is powerful, and technical excellence is highly valued. Agile techniques include zero-downtime deployments; A/B testing; and clustered, containerized microservices for high availability. Tools such as burndown charts give us the most accurate way to gauge the status of an initiative; task boards bring teams together with a common picture of the work in progress; cumulative flow diagrams help us pinpoint process flaws; and value stream maps help us diagnose the underlying sources of waste.

These are the reasons you are rolling out Agile approaches for projects within your IT organization. But what is the impact of these Agile ideas on how you lead, how you oversee the IT organization, and how you interact with the rest of the business? How can you provide the organizational context in which these techniques will have those wonderful advantages over the Waterfall? How can you avoid placing impediments in the way of these Agile teams? These questions will be addressed and explored in the chapters to come.

Let's be clear about the implications of this Agile way of doing business. Requirements are allowed to change during the development process. More than that: they are encouraged to change as the users are better able to define what they need and as business needs change. I draw attention to this because I have heard many IT leaders, with one foot still in the Waterfall world, say things like, "Well, of course, *some* change is acceptable." Not "some" change—as much change as results in a better outcome. Not "acceptable"—encouraged. Agile approaches, simply, are agile!

Even if your company has adopted "Agile methodologies," the ideas behind the plan-driven framework are probably still with you, deeply and quietly embedded in your company's way of thinking. You might be using Scrum, doing daily standups and sprint reviews, writing your requirements in a user-story headline format. You might be doing continuous integration and pair programming, and even automating some of your tests. But the ideas of project-based, plan-driven delivery are likely still with you; you are not yet Agile.

I'm just guessing, but perhaps you are beginning projects with a large backlog of user stories that you are expecting a team to implement—in other words, a fixed scope. If you are doing that, you are not alone, and you are not yet agile.

The sections above describe the logic behind the Agile way of thinking. The history of Agile methods is the history of finding better and better ways to practice it. This is important to keep in mind; many people confuse the Agile approach with the particular frameworks that implement those Agile concepts. The next sections are intended to help IT leaders who are less familiar with this history understand the evolution of Agile frameworks—that is, ways of systematizing Agility—and can safely be skipped by those already familiar with these frameworks. The important thing to remember is that the Agile principles and values are constant, while ways of implementing them come and go and build upon each other.

In 2001, a group of software development gurus got together at Snowbird Ski Resort near Salt Lake City, Utah, to record their ideas on new and better ways to develop software. When they descended from their mountain, they announced the Agile Manifesto, articulating four values and twelve principles.[2] The manifesto proclaimed the importance of small, self-organizing teams receiving constant feedback from users and the frequent, rapid delivery of working software that adds business value. That the manifesto's principles have continued to guide Agile thinking is probably due to the coherence of the initial vision: the principles suggest an entire worldview, a way of thinking about software delivery that is radically different from the old way.

Several Agile methodologies were introduced based on these values and principles. *Extreme Programming* (XP) had already been described in print by Kent Beck in 1999 in his book *Extreme Programming Explained*.[3] XP called for small development teams working with "onsite customers." Requirements were not documented in advance; instead, the team created a set of "story cards" with a brief description of an intended capability. The story card served as a reminder to the team to have a conversation with the onsite customer about the feature it described. The conversation itself was the requirement, and could be refined through feedback from the onsite customer as the feature was developed.

XP advocated several technical practices that may seem strange. One was *pair programming*, where developers worked in pairs, one of them at the keyboard and the second looking over his or her shoulder and contributing ideas. Periodically, they would switch places. This might seem to cut productivity in half, but the typical result is an increase in productivity. One explanation for the increase is that quality dramatically increases through the constant vigilance of the partner, thereby reducing the necessity for rework. In a way, pair programming shortens the feedback cycle of having a peer code review, which has been found to be an extremely effective way to find defects.

A second practice introduced by XP was *test-driven development* (TDD). A developer using TDD would write an automated test for his or her code before writing the code itself. The developer runs the test, watches it fail, and then begins coding. The developer knows it's done as soon as it passes after periodic test runs. Why is this effective? First, it ensures that the developer understands the requirement before building. Second, it forces the developer to structure code in a way that facilitates testing. Third, it provides an objective way to know when the code is done, preventing endless fiddling. Think of this as an extreme reduction in feedback lead time: not only is the code tested soon after it is written, but it is tested even before it is written!

Actually, and importantly, the fiddling continues a bit after the tests pass. The third practice of XP is *refactoring*: After the tests pass, the developer improves the innards of the code to make it more maintainable and to improve its design. As he or she does so, he or she makes sure that the tests continue to pass; refactoring means improving the code without changing what it does. This practice ensures that the developers attend not only to the functions the code performs, but also to the quality of the asset they have created.

XP promoted four values: communication, simplicity, feedback, and courage. The importance of communication and feedback should be clear from my explanation of Agile and Lean concepts above; the importance of simplicity will become clear in the discussion of Enterprise Architecture; and courage will be the topic of the concluding chapter of this book.

*Scrum*, created by Ken Schwaber and Jeff Sutherland and based on some ideas from a 1986 Harvard Business Review article by Hirotaka Takeuchi and Ikujiro Nonaka,[4] is less focused on technical practices and more on how the project is organized. Development is still accomplished by small teams who work in iterations of fixed length (generally two to four weeks). A representative of the business, the product owner, maintains a prioritized list of requirements, called a *backlog*. At the beginning of each iteration, the team commits to developing a subset of those requirements from the top of the backlog; during the iteration, they self-organize to code and test that set of requirements. The iteration ends with a demonstration and review of the work completed, feedback from stakeholders, and a retrospective for the team to improve its processes. The product owner may reprioritize, add to, or subtract from the backlog at any time—the only rule is that he or she may not change the portion of the backlog that the team is working on in the current iteration.

Scrum ensures that the team can inspect and adapt by requiring continuous production of features accompanied by feedback from users and stakeholders; through constant involvement of the product owner and other users; through testing that takes place within the sprint; and through retrospectives. You can think of Scrum as fixing the cycle time for development of features at the two to four weeks that are its chosen iteration length. This is a shorter cycle time by far than traditional methods, but is not necessarily as short as possible. It is Lean and flow-based development principles that place the focus on reducing cycle time to its absolute minimum.

The Toyota Production System for manufacturing automobiles has been tremendously influential in management thinking, spawning the Lean Manufacturing movement and the ideas behind Lean Six Sigma. In their book *Lean Software Development: An Agile Toolkit*, Mary and Tom Poppendieck showed how the concepts of Lean thinking could be applied to the software development process. The Lean approach is to map out a production process and then find steps in the process that are waste—defined as work that does not add value to the finished product. These sources of waste are then systematically eliminated to reduce lead time (the time it takes for a single unit to make its way through the production process). Lean thinking can be stated in seven principles:[5]

- Eliminate waste
- Amplify learning
- Decide as late as possible
- Deliver as fast as possible
- Empower the team
- Build integrity in
- See the whole

These principles fit together to help an organization keep lead times short. "Decide as late as possible," for example, means making a decision when the maximum amount of information is available to support it, thereby avoiding waste. "Build integrity in," where integrity is a concept related to quality, is important because poor quality causes rework (fixing), which is waste. "See the whole" is important because sometimes optimizing one part of a process can add waste to another part of the process.

One of the most interesting aspects of Lean thinking is its analysis of the sources of waste, some of which are subtle. The Poppendiecks list the classic Lean sources of waste and their interpretation of these in the software development process (I've noted the software equivalents in parentheses below):[6]

- Inventory (partially done work)
- Extra processing (extra processes)
- Overproduction (extra features)
- Transportation (task switching)
- Waiting (waiting)
- Motion (motion)

• Defects (defects)

Some of these might require explanation. Clearly, unnecessary processes and extra features are wasteful, and as we've already noted, *defects* cause rework, which is also wasteful. Partially done work has a less obvious but still severe impact on lead time. Imagine it as stuff that clogs up the production process—stuff that either needs to get finished before other things can be produced or that sits in process for a while, thus increasing the average time items need to make their way through the production process.

A corollary of Little's Law tells us that the more work that is in process, the longer the lead time—or, more exactly, that wait time = queue size/processing rate.[7] In a software delivery context, large batches of requirements reduce throughput, since requirements are a kind of work in progress. An example of *waiting* is the time papers are sitting on someone's desk waiting to be approved. This takes calendar time (though not effort time) and therefore lengthens lead times. *Motion* is the time it takes to hand off tasks between one person and another; reducing handoffs is a goal of the DevOps approach, which combines different skill sets on a single "full stack" team.

Donald Reinertsen's book *The Principles of Product Development Flow: Second Generation Lean Product Development* is particularly helpful in understanding how Lean principles apply to the software development process. It contains an extensive discussion on the evils of large batch sizes. Reinertsen calls excessive project scope, "one of the most dangerous of all batch size problems."[8] Reducing batch sizes, he shows, leads to shorter cycle times, lower variability, accelerated feedback, reduced risk, reduced overhead, increased efficiency, and better motivation. Large batch sizes, on the other hand, cause exponential cost and schedule growth and lead to a death spiral where scope becomes larger and larger.[9]

*Kanban* is David Anderson's approach to bringing Lean principles into software development while driving fear out of the transformation process through incremental change.[10] It is based on the Kanban principles formulated by Taiichi Ohno of Toyota as a way of managing Toyota's supply chain and arriving at "just in time" inventory.

Anderson provides four rules for implementing Kanban:

1. Start with existing processes
2. Pursue incremental, evolutionary change
3. Respect the current process, roles, responsibilities, and titles
4. Encourage leadership at all levels

Teams using Kanban maintain a Kanban board—a visual representation of the status of requirements in process, which is similar to the value stream map used in Lean methods. Requirements flow through categories on the map, such as "In Development" and "Testing." When they reach the last column, they are ready. Requirements are "pulled" from one category to the next when the destination category is ready to receive them.

There is one critical rule, though. Each column—that is, each step in the process—has a limited capacity (called a work-in-progress limit, or WIP limit). If a step in the process has reached its limit, then no new work can be pulled into that step. It causes a traffic jam that can percolate back to the first column. This forces the team to put all of its effort into finishing work. When a step hits its maximum, team members may switch roles to help out with that step. If this is not possible, then they will figure out ways to reorganize to address the bottleneck. Decreasing WIP reduces lead times, as the corollary of Little's Law demonstrates.

Since Kanban is flow-based rather than iteration-based, it does not have the arbitrary imposition of a fixed-iteration cycle time (the two to four weeks that Scrum adopts).

*DevOps* represents the maturation of these approaches combined with an emphasis on automation. In a DevOps approach, teams are truly cross-functional: in addition to skills in development and testing, DevOps teams have skills in operations, infrastructure, and often security as well. The teams use a Continuous Delivery process—a highly automated system for building and deploying code into a virtual environment, generally in the cloud.

It looks something like this: A developer writes code and automated tests for that code and checks them in to version control. A Continuous Integration server notices that new code has been checked in and automatically rebuilds the system with the new changes. It runs automated tests on the new build—both the developer's new tests and a large number of old tests—which function as a regression test suite that ensures that the new changes didn't break any previously created functionality. If the build passes its tests, an automated Continuous Deployment process can be used to deploy it into production, perhaps also standing up new infrastructure automatically.

Teams using a DevOps approach often deploy changes to production many times per day. Since each change set is small, risk is low and problems can be addressed quickly.

Let's look at what this does to lead times. The time from code to test is tiny, as the Continuous Integration process gives the developer near-immediate feedback on his code. The time from test to production is reduced—deployments occur many times per day—so the developer gets feedback on how his or her code operates in production quickly. The time from concept to code to production can be minimized—lead time is reduced by a Lean development process, so the team can get fast feedback on whether it has built the right feature or needs to make changes.

The inclusion of Ops expertise on the team means that it can observe the behavior of the code in production and immediately make improvements that can cross boundaries between development and infrastructure. DevOps is the approach that goes furthest toward eliminating the sources of waste in an IT delivery process.

These Agile and Lean techniques fundamentally change how we think about IT projects. When I say that, what I really mean is that we should stop thinking about "projects." Although Scrum, for example, provided a powerful way to be project-oriented—the ability to plan for a fixed commitment of time and resources and then juggle scope to make sure it fits within that commitment—it also introduced the idea of a continually groomed, prioritized backlog, where some of the items toward the end of the backlog would always still be available for future work. In this way, Scrum began to blur the line between delivery and maintenance: delivery is simply producing the highest value items in the backlog, while maintenance is just the continuation of pulling items from the backlog. Scrum moved the focus from the *project* to the *product*.

As we implement DevOps and Continuous Delivery, the idea of a project becomes even blurrier. We come closer to single-piece flow, where we accept one requirement at a time into the development process, have the team "swarm" on it until it is finished, deploy it, and move on to the next requirement. The "continuous" in Continuous

Delivery need not refer just to the technical build and deployment process, but to the way we organize, prioritize, and fund our work.

Continuous Delivery, you might say, makes it hard for us to keep talking about *discrete* delivery—delivery based on chunking requirements into things we call projects. As I will show in later chapters, the technical practices that have emerged to support Agile delivery also make it hard for us to keep talking about discrete *systems* or *applications*. Similarly, good governance practices should make it harder for us to keep talking about discrete *investments*.

The Agile world is a *continuous* world more than it is a *discrete* world. But I may be exaggerating a bit. In the Agile approach, we still want to deliver discrete units of value-adding capability—that is the notion of a user story. But we want to work as close to that level of granularity as possible rather than at the coarse granularity of projects or investments. As in calculus, we can think of the continuous as the limit when the size of a discrete interval becomes smaller and smaller. We need to align our governance, our architecture, and our investment strategy to support this level of granularity.

> We need to align our governance, our architecture, and our investment strategy to support this level of granularity.

Poor CIO! DevOps moves him or her even further away from a model where he or she can try to earn a seat at the table by "proving" that he or she can deliver business value through control of *projects*. Instead, the notion of a project seems more and more like an arbitrary grouping of work—a way of creating a large batch of requirements—which in turn is a way of destroying business value. That is a heavy price to pay for giving the CIO a way to demonstrate control.

The Agile team finds the world around it to be in flux. The competitive landscape changes, tools change, company politics change, and its understanding of the task changes. To deal with this flux, the team allows its own work to change.

Jean-Paul Sartre argued that consciousness is not a fixed "thing," but that rather it chooses, at any given instant, what it is. In his way of thinking, this is an extreme sort of freedom, the ability to choose oneself—and therefore change oneself—at any time. For this reason (and others), he labeled consciousness "nothingness"—I know, that depressing, pseudo-profound-sounding existentialist mumbo-jumbo. But Sartre, in many ways, was an early Agilist. An Agile initiative is an initiative that chooses itself at each instant. Its existence precedes its essence, as the existentialists say—meaning that it defines itself as it proceeds rather than being defined in advance. At the same time, it creates itself in such a way as to succeed in its "projects"—yes, that is actually the term Sartre uses (in French, of course).

I'll be honest: when I was a philosophy student, I didn't think much of the existentialists. They were the philosophers of cliché, full of themselves, careless with logic, exhaling pseudo-profundities with their cigarette smoke. But now that I've learned about Agile delivery, it's fun to think of our IT delivery initiative as radically free, at any moment choosing what to be in order to deliver the maximum business value. It has a history, which is acknowledged and part of its decision-making process. It has a "project"—that is, an objective that is future-directed. But at the same time, that history does not constrain it. In order to accomplish its projects, the team chooses itself and its actions at every instant. Agile delivery is existentialist IT.

The Agile team is nothingness. Has anyone ever said that before?

---

In the confusion of all the different ways of practicing Agile and Lean, it is easy to forget the underlying principle, which is simply that, in an uncertain, constantly changing environment, we must continuously learn and adapt. That principle applies not just to how we run an IT project, but to how we lead IT.

---

# Part II

## *Earning the Seat*

# PLANNING

Life can only be understood backwards; but it must be lived forwards.

—**Søren Kierkegaard**, *Journals*

Let us not make random conjectures about the greatest matters.

—**Heraclitus of Ephesus**, *Fragments*

You cannot be agile while rigidly following a plan. This, I'm sure, is obvious by now. Though we desire agility—who doesn't, really?—we have difficulty following this simple principle because we have built so many of our IT management practices around following plans. Of course, there are very good reasons we used to think that planning was so important. IT is extremely complex—with so many dependencies to worry about, so many different resources that need to be coordinated, and so large an impact if some minor point is overlooked, it is tempting to try to think of everything in advance.

Planning always seemed extremely inexpensive compared to execution—so to avoid waste in execution, we naturally put extra effort into planning. And, of course, planning and then executing according to plan were how we tried to demonstrate trustworthiness to the non-IT parts of the business, and how they tried to feel like they had control over something they didn't understand.

When Agile proponents claim that the plan-driven approach hasn't worked well in the past, their argument is always vulnerable to the response, "Well, it hasn't worked because you are not doing it right—you just have to plan and execute better." Fine; the real reason we should reject the plan-driven approach to IT is that it espouses all the wrong values. Even if it were wholly successful at what it tries to do, it would be accomplishing the wrong things. After all, what is the value of rigidity and executing according to plan if you could be improving on the plan or responding to changing circumstances instead? What is the value of hitting your spending target if you could be spending less, or if a marginal dollar of unplanned spend will bring a return of much more than a dollar? What is the value of telling knowledge workers to follow a plan when you are hiring them to use their brains to figure out how to do things best? What is the value of adhering to a plan that was made at the beginning of a project, when uncertainty was greatest?

> The real reason we should reject the plan-driven approach to IT is that it espouses all the wrong values.

This is not to say that we shouldn't plan. But there are a few things we have to keep in mind as we do. The first is that planning costs money and time. The time it takes to plan is time that could be used to get a simple product in front of users and learn from how well it meets their needs. The second is that plans are *necessarily* unreliable, because they are made under conditions of tremendous uncertainty. We cannot act as if a point estimate of a future resource need is likely to be accurate, and we cannot know for sure that a planned initiative will have the business outcomes it intends. Finally, we must remember that plans are different from *targets*, and also different from *projections*. To use the plan as a way to assess performance is—at best—to direct performance to the wrong goals.

Plans are good. They get people communicating and help align people around a common goal. They set a vision that knowledge workers can use to frame their creative work. They help everyone see dependencies and risks. They initiate a conversation about what is possible, and reveal assumptions that must be tested as the project proceeds. Plans can be used to get a sense of what resources might be needed to accomplish the work of the project, which can be important if there is a long lead time for procuring those resources. Agile approaches are in no way opposed to planning, and in fact place a high value on communication and feedback. Business value is destroyed only when we substitute extensive planning for execution and when we substitute execution according to plan for thinking and adapting.

> Business value is destroyed only when we substitute extensive planning for execution and when we substitute execution according to plan for thinking and adapting.

In the Agile world, as we add salt to the soup, we keep sticking a finger in and tasting. It doesn't matter how much salt the recipe called for; we adjust our salting based on whether it tastes good to us or not. A project plan, like a recipe, should be written on a fading index card in Grandma's handwriting, and ignored if Grandma's instructions make the soup unpalatable.

One of my former managers liked to say, "Plan the work and work the plan." The expression's symmetry and brevity gives it a ring of truth that is quite unjustified. Perhaps, "Plan the work and work the plan, if you are in a domain where sticking to a plan is valuable," would be a more apt—though less beautiful—construction. I like the alternative proposed by Jeff Patton in *User Story Mapping: Discover the Whole Story, Build the Right Product*, "Plan to learn, and learn to plan."[1] Plan to learn: learning is valuable if we use it to adjust our plans, so we should tailor our process to maximize learning. Learn to plan: find out through experience what plans are actually valuable for, and optimize the planning process to derive that value.

What beliefs underlie the principle "plan the work and work the plan"? I offer the following as the articles of faith of the PTW-WTP religion:

- *I believe* that even if we discover we are doing something silly, we should persevere, because the plan says so.
- *I believe* that we should try not to learn anything during the project that might lead us to change the plan.
- *I believe* that assumptions we make before we start the project are more important than actual facts we learn during the course of the project.
- *I believe* that responding to changing circumstances is not valuable if it leads us to diverge from the plan.
- *I believe* that spending time creating a plan is more important than spending time delivering outcomes.

A bit pointed, right? Let me be gentler. We can all agree that what creates value for the business is actually *executing* the project—building the capabilities or whatever it is we are trying to do. The plan does not provide value *per se*: it is valuable only to the extent that it results in better execution of the project. Or, to push that a bit further: if we spent a lot of resources planning but only made a slight increase in the effectiveness of execution, that still would not be helpful.

Well, then, we should also be able to agree that we should limit our planning and our adherence to plan to what actually results in the best outcome. Now, the more we expect that circumstances will change during execution, and the more valuable stuff we expect to learn during execution, the less valuable planning and conformance to plan will be, right? Did I hear an assenting grunt? All right, then, I will just add a teeny-tiny assumption without trying to prove it: IT projects are generally those kinds of projects.

Our poor CIO has a dilemma. He or she has bought into the idea that to get the seat at the big boy table, he or she needs to show that he or she can make IT projects stick to plan. I love this scientific-sounding gem from Weill and Ross:

> One other way to assess how IT savvy your firm has become is to do the following calculation for each major IT project: ROI business case—ROI post-implementation review. Total the results for all of last year's major projects. In IT-savvy firms, this total approaches zero.[2]

This says that if you are good at IT, you will make sure that the ROI you plan for a given project will be the same as the ROI you actually *achieve* for the project. In other words, your execution will be so close to your plan that even ROI—a distant, lagging outcome from what you are doing—will match your plan. Aside from the fact that ROI is not generally a good metric to use for this purpose,*

---

\* See my book, *The Art of Business Value*, for an explanation of why this is so.

the idea that success is judged by a metric that is so vulnerable to uncertainty—I have to say—is truly crazy.

If the savvy IT organization could really do this, sure, the CIO would deserve a seat at the table—and in the Business Hall of Fame, and probably in the pantheon of the gods who foretell the future. But there is some good news. That seat at the table is not being held for someone with superhuman powers. Who says that to win the chair the CIO has to show that unpredictable IT projects are predictable? The table is for executives who can inspire valuable outcomes for the company.

Let's do away with the idea that the plan-driven approach is better for predictability, control, and efficiency. These supposed advantages are brought to life in that showpiece of the plan-driven approach: the Gantt chart, the Waterfall of legend. Reassuringly precise timelines, and the frigging thing even captures dependencies and milestones. If one task takes longer than expected, then the whole chart automatically readjusts!

That's good, because the labor involved in juggling the lines on the chart can be considerable. As soon as the project starts, the re-jiggering begins. I worked on a project where we had a team of more than ten people who did nothing but maintain the Gantt chart as circumstances changed. We needed that many people because the Gantt chart had ten thousand or so tasks on it. I'm sorry to report that the Gantt chart gave neither control nor predictability—the lines on the chart did not cause development to speed up, and the status of development was well-known to everyone—unless they looked at the Gantt chart, which generally was still in the process of being updated, and anyway, who can read those things when they get to have ten thousand lines?

A deeper problem is this scenario, which I'm sure we have all experienced: the project team is running behind schedule, but they have been told that they *must* follow the schedule—there is no choice. Here are some likely outcomes: (1) The team becomes vague in its definition of whether something is "done," and declares milestones accomplished even when they are only *sort-of* accomplished, (2) the team reports what they are instructed to report—that the project is still on schedule—in contradiction of reality, or (3) the team admits that they are behind schedule, but says that they will "make it up" in the next phase and "get back on track."

Option three is the most insidious and quite common. At the instant when this phrase is uttered, all objective evidence says that tasks are taking longer than projected. Despite this evidence, the team is saying that the next phase will take *less* time than projected. Management takes this dubious claim seriously, because it is what they want to hear: the team is stepping up and "dealing with the problem." But if we are serious about *predictability*, if we really want to objectively make projections about when the project will be completed, we have to assume that the next phase will take more time than projected, not less.[†]

In "Why the FBI Can't Build a Case Management System," Jerome Israel describes the FBI's troubled eight-year project to build their Sentinel system. For the first three years, he says, senior managers received regular briefings from the contractor on the status of the project. The managers just wanted to know

[†] Not that we *should* be all that serious about predictability. As David Evans of Neuri Consulting has pointed out to me, you can make a bus more predictable if it doesn't stop to pick up passengers. What were we talking about again?

"the bottom line," so the contractor prepared a high-level summary for each briefing. "At the top of the first chart was a horizontal thermometer, which expressed the project's overall status in red, yellow, or green. From meeting to meeting, the temperature never changed—it was always yellow, trending toward green."[3] So much for predictability.

Nor is the plan-driven approach effective for *control*, simply because the time it takes to code something does not depend on what is in the plan. There is no causal link between the paper and the real world of action.

But perhaps meeting plan milestones demonstrates efficiency and productivity?

Nope. Any planner is going to pad the estimate to give him or herself "slack." Anyone reviewing the estimate is going to say that the estimate needs to be reduced. The baseline plan, in the end, will be a compromise between guesswork, gaming, and wishful thinking. So if the project happens to hit the estimate exactly, how could that mean that it was efficient? Perhaps the estimate was leisurely and the team just succeeded in taking its time. Or perhaps the team passed up good opportunities to add value so that they could stick to the schedule. Very likely they spent a lot of time saying "no" to anyone who thought of ways to improve outcomes.

What if they exceed the schedule? Does that mean they were inefficient? Who knows? The schedule might have been too aggressive. Things outside of the team's control might have gotten in the way. Perhaps an original estimate was correct, but then in the negotiation process it was reduced. If a team did not deliver on schedule, it means one thing only: the scheduled time and the actual time were different.

An Agile approach can offer the predictability, control, and efficiency that the plan-driven approach cannot, and has the additional advantages of delivering good value and making sense. I know that the Agile community will flinch at my use of those words, but I don't mean any harm, I promise. I am simply going to say that if we define those terms in the right way, the way that is most meaningful to us in a business context, then all our wishes can be answered—because our wishes are fundamental to Agile practice while only notional for plan-driven practices.

> An Agile approach can offer the predictability, control, and efficiency that the plan-driven approach cannot.

**Predictability:** Predictability is the ability to know, to the best accuracy and precision possible, based on the information available at a given point in time, when certain results will be achieved and what outcomes will be derived from them. Is that not what we want? I know that some of us have a different definition in mind. I think it goes something like this: predictability is the ability to know, before a project starts, exactly what it will accomplish and when it will accomplish those things, even though we are operating in an environment of high complexity and rapid change. But that is a definition of omniscience, not predictability.

In contrast to the plan-driven approach—which, as we have said, pressures the team to continue to affirm the original schedule despite evidence that it is wrong—an Agile process re-adjusts its estimates frequently based on reality. A great tool for this is the burndown chart—or sometimes a burnup chart—which shows, given historical trends in velocity and given the current scope, when that scope will most likely be completed. It can be adjusted every day based on the latest information. *That* is predictability.

**Control:** Control is the ability for management to influence or make decisions that will affect the course of the project, including its actual cost and timeframes. Some people think that control is the ability of management to compel behavior of employees, but this is the plot of a science fiction movie (never turns out well for the mind-controlling villain), the *modus operandi* of the brainwashing cult (usually just accomplishes getting people out on the street wearing mindless smiles and handing out leaflets), or the strategy of a dictator (okay, it often turns out well for them, but arguably not effective as a business strategy).

In the plan-driven approach, managers can only make decisions about what to write in the plan; once the plan is launched, their influence ends. In an Agile approach, the manager has continuous transparency into the status of the project and can adjust the plan to get the best result. Based on changing circumstances and learnings to date, the manager can—for example—make sure that the work is delivered on schedule by adjusting scope as the project unfolds, or can act to remove impediments to make things move faster. The manager can also stop the project if he or she thinks it has delivered enough value and wants to move on to something else; change the requirements if the competitive situation has changed; or mold the team's solution-creation by giving feedback on what the team produces. Management has true control.

**Efficiency:** Efficiency means that waste is minimized—that is, the minimal product is delivered that accomplishes the business goals, and it is delivered as quickly as possible and with the minimum expenditure of resources. While the plan-driven approach seeks to deliver the project that was planned, the Agile approach seeks to "maximize the amount of work not done"—in other words, to find the smallest set of features that delivers the business value. Agile and Lean projects promote continuous process optimization through retrospectives and Lean tools.

Predictability, control, efficiency. Strange as it might sound, if you want them, you must be willing to toss out the plan. The better way to achieve them is through fast feedback cycles, which also preserve flexibility and agility.

From Lean thinking, we learn that "just in time" planning is more effective than holding plans "in inventory," so to speak. A Lean principle says: "Decide at the last responsible moment." It's a clever principle, with the word "responsible" in there instead of, say, "possible." It doesn't say decide at the last moment; it says you should put off decisions as long as you can before it starts to cost you something.

The principle offends our moral sense; it sounds like laziness. We've been brought up with the saying, "never put off until tomorrow what you can do today," but Lean thinking seems to be telling us, "never do today what you can put off until tomorrow." It just doesn't feel right.

But it more or less *is* right. As Donald Reinertsen shows, we have to tweak the principle a bit to make it exact.[4] He points out that there is an *optimal* moment for making each decision; a moment when the value of any new information you can gain becomes less than the cost of deferring the decision further. The idea that decisions should be deferred is closely related to the idea of optionality—there is value in keeping options open until you are forced to close them off. Yes, if you are going to choose Option A next week, then you could choose it today. But keeping open Options B and C has value; it mitigates risk (you have other options, after all!).

The financial value of options can be quantified, but it is not generally necessary to do so in our context. As long as we know the value is positive, we should put off making decisions. If the value is negative, we should make a decision right away. Additionally, option value can be increased through clever management. If I do things that give me information that will lead to a better decision, then I have increased the value of waiting. Good management is about managing learning; that is, about doing things that generate information that will help inform decisions.

> Maximizing business value is sometimes indistinguishable from laziness.

Who knew? Maximizing business value is sometimes indistinguishable from laziness.

Another seeming virtue of the plan-driven approach is that it appears to give us a way to gauge the success of a project: projects should be on time and within budget while completing the requirements specified in the original plan at a high level of quality. But in what universe is this truly what success looks like? This definition of success says nothing about value to the company, nothing about accomplishing strategic goals, and nothing about accomplishing desired outcomes. Or, to put it another way, if the CIO somehow could deliver this type of success, would it mean that he or she deserves a seat at the strategy-makers table?

Perhaps this measure of success is meant to be a *proxy* for business value, or a necessary condition for it. Perhaps the argument is that IT can only add business value if it delivers pre-planned requirements on schedule and on budget, or that doing so *maximizes* business value. Simple thought exercises show that this is not so. What if the requirements are that the system endlessly display a message saying, "What if the requirements are that the system endlessly display a message saying"? In that case, on-time and on-budget delivery— in every case I can imagine—would have destroyed business value. What if the plan was overly leisurely? What if it left plenty of time for thumb-twiddling—I mean management slack? In that case, on-time and on-budget delivery would have left value on the table—true success would have been to deliver well ahead of schedule. At best, plan adherence delivers only the value that was in the plan.

I think we have to face the fact that adherence to plan is our definition of success only because it is measurable and clear (at least on the surface). It is a lazy definition of success, and laziness only sometimes leads to business value.

So, what is a better definition of success? How can we gauge success if we don't measure against plan? Jim Highsmith tells us that, "Agile projects are not controlled by conformance to plan but by conformance to business value...If they [the results] don't conform to the plan, the plan was wrong. If they delivered business value, then whether the plan was 'right' or not is immaterial."[5] Business value seems like the thing we are after, not milestone adherence. But as I demonstrated in *The Art of Business Value*, it is hard to know when you have delivered business value.

You can devise your own definition of success, including some quantifiable aspects and some qualitative. Mine would be: (1) short cycle time for delivery, (2) frequent deployment of 100%-complete and high-quality capabilities, (3) a measurable business outcome (different for each project), and (4) contribution to the overall Enterprise IT asset, which I will discuss in a later chapter. These things are more important to me than adherence to a predetermined schedule.

Nevertheless, planning is important. In my role, I need to decide whether to allow an initiative to begin, which of course depends on whether I am satisfied with its plan. I might ask these questions when I review a team's plans:

- What are the business outcomes the team is trying to achieve? What kinds of activities do they think will achieve them? Why are those outcomes valuable to the business? I want to make sure that the team has a clear vision, that they understand the business's intent, and that they will make decisions within the context of that intent.
- How will the team determine the specific requirements—that is, determine what work they will do? Note that I am not asking what the requirements are, but rather *how* the team will discover them. I want to make sure the team has a good basis for making value decisions.
- How is the team planning to work together? What skills are on the team? How will the team communicate? How do they plan to retrospect and continually improve their process? I want to make sure they can operate as a team and learn together, and that they are committed to continuous improvement.
- How will the team seek feedback on its work? How will it solicit feedback and guidance from management? How frequently will it engage management? I want to make sure that we have an understanding on how *my* input and feedback will enter into their process.
- What are the key risks to delivery? What assumptions are contained in the plans? How will the team move quickly to

test those assumptions and gain information to manage the risks? I want to understand their plan for learning.

- What can I do to help them accomplish their objectives? I want to remove impediments.

You will notice that the plan implicitly includes a business case—I am asking questions about the expected outcomes and why they are valuable to the business. Let's assume for the moment that the business case has already been vetted through a governance process—the subject of a later chapter—so my concern here is to make sure the team understands the business case and the thought process behind it so that they can make good decisions in line with it. As Humble, O'Reilly, and Molesky explain in *Lean Enterprise*, there are two important factors to consider in a business plan: the sensitivity of key metrics to variables in the business case,

> Plans establish learning objectives; they give the team and oversight a shared basis for communicating as the project is executed.

and the level of uncertainty in those variables.[6] Given that the business case is based on uncertain assumptions, I cannot fully approve a business case, only provisionally approve it and assess the team's plan for dealing with uncertainty.

"Don't just make one plan," Humble, O'Reilly, and Molesky advise.[7] I would add this: make sure you are ready to adapt as you learn by choosing the right plan. You will need to have indicators that tell you which of the plans to apply. Plans establish learning objectives; they give the team and oversight a shared basis for communicating as the project is executed.

Which brings us to the ultimate plan: the annual budget.

It's easy to see that there is tension between an annual planning exercise and the desire to be agile. How can we know in advance how we will want to spend our money if we want to be responsive to change? How can we inspect and adapt if we lock in something as important as spending even before we start the year? Actually, the budgeting process typically requires us to predict our activities well more than a year in advance, since the budgeting process—or negotiation—itself takes time.

The Beyond Budgeting movement advocates a change in how we think about budgets. Its techniques have been implemented by companies in many industries (banks, car manufacturers, telecommunications companies) ranging in size from a 250-person charity to a global industrial organization with thousands of products.[8]

In his book *Implementing Beyond Budgeting: Unlocking the Performance Potential*, Bjarte Bogsnes describes how he rolled out Beyond Budgeting at Borealis, Europe's largest petrochemical company, and at Statoil, Scandinavia's largest company, and the reasons why he did so. Interestingly, many of the problems Bogsnes sees with budgeting echo those we have seen with the contractor-control model of IT. Underlying the budgeting process, as Bogsnes sees it, is an attempt to use pre-planning as a way to establish control in the face of uncertainty. "We have costs under control, have we not? Yes, we have, if this is how we define control, if the goal is to spend no more than decided 15 to 16 months ago. But is this really what we aim for?" he asks.[9]

The problem with control through planning—in IT projects no less than in budgeting—is that "we are almost overwhelmed with uncertainty."[10] I like the way he says that; it is important to understand that there is not just a small amount of uncertainty, but that the amount of uncertainty is *overwhelming*.

Just as in IT delivery, rigid adherence to budget imposes the cost of opportunities foregone. Managing under uncertainty is not just about avoiding risks, but also about seizing opportunities:

> Is it always good performance to hit the budget number? What if great value-creating opportunities were turned down because job number one was no budget overrun?....What if value-adding scope changes were dropped because they would have meant cost or time overruns?[11]

Although budgets give us the feeling of control, this control is illusory—the budget is the product of negotiation, gaming, and prediction—something like our tourist in the Codeistan market. In Bogsnes's view,

> There are, however, two other types of control that we want less of. The first one is controlling what people shall and shall not do, through detailed budgets, tight mandates, detailed job descriptions, rigid organizational structures....The second type of control, we probably never had to begin with. That is the perceived control of the future, the one we think we get if we only have enough numbers and details in our plans and forecasts.[12]

Bogsnes and others have replaced their companies' budgeting processes with something more responsive and agile. Of course, most IT leaders do not have that option, but within the scope of the IT budget, it may be possible to gain some flexibility and apply some of Beyond Budgeting's principles.

A first stab at improving the planning cycle might be to use a plan based on a "rolling" cycle. Intuitively, we know that the early part of the year is something we can see clearly, while the latter part of the year is more uncertain. Perhaps at any given moment we make a plan for the next five quarters, regardless of the annual cycle. The plan is relatively detailed for the quarter to come, less detailed for the quarter after that, and less and less detailed for later quarters. This would give the company some degree of predictability, but still give flexibility to adjust based on new information and new decisions.

Another key to increasing flexibility is transparency. What if we constantly reported on the key metrics that will drive spending and made that reporting available to everyone in the company, or at least in the IT department? Everyone could then self-organize, spot potential issues, and find possible solutions. We would be crowd-sourcing. We could make decisions on the fly because we would have information on the fly. We could make decisions that maximize our ultimate goals (let's say maximizing earnings per share) while changing our intermediate goals (let's say reducing datacenter costs).

Perhaps some budget items can be allocated at a higher level. For example, rather than budgeting for datacenter costs, we can budget for infrastructure costs as a whole. This approach effectively creates a portfolio of cost buckets, and thereby reduces risk through diversification. Even if datacenter costs cannot be reduced, other infrastructure costs might be amenable to reduction. Adjustments can be made during the year by transferring funds between different infrastructure categories.

The IT organization can begin by identifying the assumptions that drive its budget. As with other requirements, it can treat those assumptions as hypotheses and work to confirm or refute them, adjusting plans as indicated. We can incorporate risks into this process, as well: execution risks, changes to the business needs, unproven hypotheses, and goals that have no plans yet. Say, for example, that the budget calls for us to reduce our datacenter costs by a certain amount. We can identify the assumptions behind this plan: perhaps that we will be able to renegotiate our hosting costs and that our infrastructure requirements will remain more or less the same as the previous year. Based on the analysis, we can identify uncertainties: power costs may rise or we may get sidetracked from our negotiations by other urgent initiatives, for example.

We can then test the assumptions and see—early in the year if possible—whether we will have to make adjustments to the plan. We can even plot scenarios and make allowances for each. In one scenario, we imagine that the datacenter providers increase their prices. In another, we imagine that the migration to a new datacenter turns out to be more expensive than expected. For each scenario (and I suggest keeping them simple), we figure out what the indicators would be that would tell us we were in that scenario, and when we would know. Finally, we decide on adjustments to the budget if we wind up in each of the scenarios that would still accomplish the overall budget goals. In a way, we are planning our flexibility to change the plan.

Plans can be used to control behavior when there is relatively little uncertainty; even then, controlling behavior is not the right goal when you care about harnessing the creativity and problem-solving skills of employees. In the Agile world, plans are a tool for thinking and communicating, for framing problems and encouraging discussion, for establishing visions and values. But they are no longer tools of the contractor-control model.

The idea that we should make a plan and then stick to it is a terrible idea in an environment of uncertainty and change. It has dominated the IT world because it appears to offer predictability, control, and efficiency, the key values of the contractor-control model. But it doesn't.

# 5 REQUIREMENTS

If I were to wish for anything, I should not wish for wealth and power, but for the passionate sense of the potential, for the eye which, ever young and ardent, sees the possible. Pleasure disappoints, possibility never.

—**Søren Kierkegaard**, *Either/Or: A Fragment of Life*

We do not desire a thing because we judge it to be good; on the contrary, we call the object of our desire good, and consequently the object of our aversion bad.

—**Baruch Spinoza**, *Ethics*

Requirements simply don't exist. A requirement, by definition, is something *required*: the basis for a contract, a way of managing an external service provider, part of a deal where a buyer promises money and a contractor promises to deliver something well-defined. But within an enterprise, what does it mean for something to be "required"? A requirement purports to express a necessity, but where could this necessity come from? In a publicly held company, maximizing shareholder value might be a necessity, but how could a particular feature of an application be *necessary* when there might be many other ways of maximizing shareholder value?

A requirement is a *constraint*. It is a way of saying "create value *this* way, rather than other ways." Really, a requirement is a constraint masquerading as a *decision*. When the business stakeholders talk among themselves, their discourse is about making decisions:

among the possible IT functions, *these* are the ones they want. But when the decision is relayed to IT, it is worded as a requirement. "You are required to do *this*, not to fool around with the other stuff you would otherwise do."

Is a requirement required when there is no money to implement it? In that case, will the company have to shut down, since something required is absent? Is the requirement required if it turns out to be very costly to implement? If it has unintended side effects? If the company finds better ways to spend its money rather than implementing this requirement?

I thought not.

Requirements are not *required except* in an arms-length contractor relationship where you want to make sure you get what you were promised.

It is equally misleading to speak of business *needs*. Does the business *need* a particular capability? *Need*, as with *requirement*, would imply that the business would have to shut down if the need is not met. Such would be a rare case—after all, the business is already operating without the "needed" capability. I would suggest that what we call a *business need* is really just an idea someone has that they believe will improve the business in a way that is meaningful given its ultimate objectives (creating a return for investors, accomplishing a nonprofit mission, etc.).

We have become so used to the terms requirements and needs that we fail to see this important implication. It is normal to state your requirements when you are ordering a cut of meat at the butcher; it is strange to go to colleagues in another part of your company and tell them what you "require."

Working with requirements is inefficient. If the requirements are truly required—if they are needs—then it doesn't matter when in the process the business states them. But if, as I say, the business is actually making decisions rather than expressing needs, then it should make those decisions at the optimal time: that is, when it has the most information available, and is willing to forego the option value of entertaining multiple possibilities. Making decisions when it is time to "specify" requirements is making them too early; it is leaving potentially valuable information on the table.

Specifying requirements constrains the solution space without taking advantage of the experience and knowledge of the team that will be implementing those requirements. Development teams are experts in creating value through information technology. In many cases, they also know the business well, often having experience across multiple product areas and enterprise functions—knowledge that is left unused when they are constrained by a pre-ordained requirement.

Stating its "requirements" is simply the business's way of communicating with IT. But, unfortunately, the term *requirement* is one that closes off discussion: if something is required, we cannot discuss whether it is sensible. On the other hand, if we are dealing with *an idea* for improving the business, others can weigh in, costs can be measured against the benefits, and colleagues can try to suggest better ideas that will have even better impacts on the business. As Spinoza says at the beginning of this chapter, we call the object of our desire good—the item in our requirements document then becomes the thing we value rather than the ultimate outcomes those requirements are supposed to provide.

> The problem with Waterfall is not that requirements are defined in advance; the problem is that there are any requirements at all.

Agile thought leaders often say that creating a set of requirements in advance—as in the Waterfall approach—is not effective because circumstances change, because the team learns as it goes, or because no business is great at figuring out all of its requirements in advance. They rarely point out that requirements are a bad idea simply because they are wrongheaded—they are based on the old contractor-control model. The problem with Waterfall is not that requirements are defined in advance; the problem is that there are any requirements at all. There should just be a team working together to figure out how to maximize business value.

Unfortunately, I have no better term to use than requirement; "proposed work item" is awkward. We are bound by the language that has been in place for decades, created when a very different model of IT was in place. For now, we will just have to accept it.

Requirements are formulated by *the business* and delivered to IT, which then in turn delivers the capabilities ordered. IT might map those requirements into a more detailed or more technical formulation, but the requirements are the guide; they *must* be satisfied. When the business takes possession of the delivered capabilities, it must judge whether they are acceptable; that is, whether they satisfy the requirements as originally stated.

Sometimes, the business folks realize that the capabilities will not lead to the results they desired. At that point, the IT folks say that the system is "working as designed"—that is, it does what was originally required. If the business users are unhappy, they will have to formally request a change and allow for extra effort and time to accomplish it. It is interesting, by the way, that we can even talk about changing a requirement: Isn't it *required*? I mean, isn't the original requirement a business *need*?

What unfolds is the game of control that I described in chapter 2. The business tries to control the IT team by telling it what it must do;

the IT team tries to control the business by forcing it to specify and stick to its initial set of requirements. Both sides want to lock down scope and forbid it to "creep."

But as Jeff Patton points out in *User Story Mapping*, "Scope doesn't creep; understanding grows."[1] As they execute the project, the business and development team together learn more about the application and the business's needs, and can thus find the best way to accomplish the business goal. Not the best way to "satisfy" a requirement—the best way to *accomplish an objective*. Whatever was required ceases to be—instead, the team uses its creativity, experience, and understanding to determine what is beneficial.

What we have traditionally called a *requirement* may better be thought of as a *hypothesis*. It is the "passionate sense of the potential" to which Kierkegaard refers. Although the purpose of the requirement is to add business value, there is no way to know with certainty at the time it is formulated whether it in fact *will* add business value. In *Lean Enterprise*, the authors cite a Microsoft study that found 60–90% of ideas do not actually improve the metric they were intended to improve.[2] In fact, about a third of the ideas actually had the opposite of the intended effect.[3] Yet, in our old practice, these ideas, in order to be implemented, must be framed as requirements and tossed over the wall to the IT developers.

*Hypothesis-driven* development is a very different way of thinking about . . . um, proposed work items.[4] It begins with a story like this: "We believe that <building the feature> <for these people> will achieve <this outcome>. We will know we are successful when we see <this signal from the market>." Humble et al. suggest that, instead of building a set of requirements, we build a backlog of questions[5]—in other words, admit that we do not know everything we need to design the product and organize our process to learn what is most critical.

The requirement to build feature X holds risk: we don't know for sure that it will add the value expected; we don't know for sure that it will be used in the expected ways; and we don't know for sure what the cost will be to build the feature. That is a lot of risk, and it adds up over the complete scope of requirements. We must manage this risk—ideally by conducting low-cost experiments to gain information. If it turns out that the hypothesis is not confirmed, then we can pivot and work with a more promising hypothesis. The feature is in no sense required; it is proposed as a route to accomplishing an outcome, and the true requirement is that we achieve the outcome to the extent that it turns out to be possible.

We can think of the project team and its sponsors and stakeholders as embarking on a voyage of discovery and innovation, during which they begin with a goal in mind* and empirically find and test hypotheses. Eric Ries describes such an approach in *Lean Startup*[6]. A company has an idea about what will make for a profitable product. It formulates two hypotheses: a *value hypothesis*—what product features will add value for the customer—and a *growth hypothesis*—what will allow the company to sell more and more of the product. The company then conducts "validated learning" experiments to confirm or refute these two hypotheses. It finds the quickest, least-effort—that is, lowest-cost—way to gain information about whether the value and growth hypotheses will hold. Sometimes, this means developing the absolute minimum product or feature that is useful and putting it out in the market. Sometimes, such development is not even needed—just advertising the non-existent product might yield information

---

* Let's put aside for a moment where this goal comes from; I'll get to that.

about who is interested. By executing a series of experiments, the company can learn whether its hypotheses are sound—in which case, it should persevere—or unsound—in which case, it should pivot to a new approach.

The same thinking can be applied to IT projects within the enterprise. We no more know exactly what set of requirements will best satisfy the company's business needs than a startup knows what product will be best for consumers. More than that, we have little idea how much of our desired outcome will be achieved when we deliver the "required" functionality.

Project proposals often include a target—"We will decrease the time claims processors spend on each case by 25%"—and a set of requirements to attain it. In the governance process, senior leaders weigh the benefit of the 25% gain against the total estimated cost. But how much uncertainty is built into the analysis that shows the potential 25% reduction? A more meaningful business case would attach a confidence range—something like "we are 40% confident that the reduction will be between 20 and 30%."

> We no more know exactly what set of requirements will best satisfy the company's business needs than a startup knows what product will be best for consumers.

So, our "green light" decision is likely to be as risky as if it were based on intuition and gut feeling. And that is fine—there is little value in overanalyzing the future when we could get even more certainty by proceeding in small increments and learning as we go. In other words, at the time we make the governance decision, we have to consider not only the proposed costs and benefits, but also what the first learning increment will cost. The business case is also a hypothesis: "We believe that if we do X, Y, and Z, it will reduce processing time by 25%." The hypothesis, we hope, is plausible enough that we are willing to buy an option: to invest a small amount to conduct an experiment to validate the hypothesis. Not to *prove* the hypothesis, but to reduce uncertainty.

To compound the challenge, we need to consider the business case for each requirement "just in time" as we come to it. At any given point in development, a given requirement might have become more or less valuable than we originally thought. We must think about the hypothesis and the extent to which it has been confirmed; we think about the incremental business value of the feature given what we already have built; we think about new opportunities that have presented themselves and which might yield more return for the investment; and we think about any new information we have on what the feature will cost.

In place of requirements, Agilists often substitute user stories, story cards, or some variation on them. IT leaders new to the Agile world often make the mistake of thinking of these user stories as requirements, but Agilists have something different in mind, they call these things stories because they are meant to be just that, narratives about how someone using the system might derive value through a proposed capability.

It is tempting to focus on the wording that is used in story headlines: "As a someone-or-other, I would like to something-or-other so that I get some-value-or-other." This predefined format sounds comfortingly like the "shall" format of requirements in the Waterfall world: "The system *shall* notify the user that a number has been entered in the incorrect format." But the choice of the wording "I would like" in the heading is deliberate; it is a challenge to find better ways to create the value desired rather than simply fulfilling the user's wish. It is deliberately tentative.

The story is a reminder to have a conversation—to explore a scenario, a proposal. A user or user representative explains to the team why the story would be valuable. The team asks questions and proposes changes. The team and the story's "owner" agree on a set of acceptance criteria, which are the true constraints around the solution. The process of arriving at the acceptance criteria has sometimes been called "negotiation" in the Agile world[7]—an unfortunate term, since it implies two sides with different objectives. The acceptance criteria are then turned into tests by the team. When the system is able to pass the tests, the developer has delivered...well, not quite. The developer continues to work with the user to make sure that the system *really* does what is needed. They might be able to improve the solution when they see it working in a demonstration or in practice.

Yikes! Scope creep alarm! What if the user keeps adding more stuff or the developer makes more stuff? Well, yes, it does open the levees to a scope deluge in a sense. If the product owner and team discover something that is valuable but that wasn't included in the user stories, they may add it. The deluge is more likely a trickle, but hey, sometimes the company needs a bit more drinking water.

In any case, the company does have ways to control scope. First, resources are limited: the project may be allowed a fixed timebox or budget. This in turn forces the product owner to make trade-offs. A high-priority feature that is added may force a low-priority feature to be cut, or at least put off until it can be justified in another request for funding. Second, the product owner must act as a trusted agent of the company—he or she must take seriously the responsibility to make good decisions with the company's resources. We trust other people in the company to do so—why not the product owner? Third, the product owner receives frequent feedback, at least through sprint reviews and demos, where other stakeholders can rein the product owner in if he or she is over-building the product or flooding the feature fields (capability crops?).

As we have said, the enemy of Agility and Leanness is not scope creep, but *feature bloat*—the inclusion of features that do not add enough value. Feature bloat not only represents wasted investment, but also gets in the way of delivering the real value—the more bloat the team delivers, the longer the cycle time for delivering the important features. An Agile team adds business value by *not doing* the stories that represent bloat. But scope creep—the addition of new features—is neither good nor bad in and of itself.

Why do we feel that there must be more to requirements than this? I think it is again about *control* of the solution-creation process. We are willing to accept something less than the optimal result in order to have a feeling of control. It is less than optimal because we are deciding upon the requirements too early. We focus on the wrong things: instead of aiming at the business goal, we organize the initiative in a way that gives us a feeling of control.

The closest analogy to requirements in an Agile process is tests. Tests are often automated, especially in a Continuous Delivery/DevOps environment. All tests must pass, so if the requirements as understood by the team change, the tests must be changed as well. They therefore necessarily reflect the most up-to-date requirements. Tests are *executable* requirements—they not only document and convey the business intent, but they also check that the intent has been met. Or, alternatively, the requirement tells us what the feature needs to do in order to be considered finished at a high level of quality.

In the Waterfall world, we often thought of tests as "gotchas"—in order for the testing to be "independent" of development, it was best if the developers did not know how the code would be tested when they were writing it. In the Agile worldview, the test is simply a way of describing what the code needs to do. The developer *should* know what the test is beforehand so that he or she can make the code do whatever it needs to do to be successful.

This is the idea underlying test driven development (TDD), where the developer writes tests before he or she writes the functional code. When the tests finally pass, he or she has achieved the required functionality. Actually, TDD usually involves unit tests—tests of small modules of code—so the "requirement" expressed is really the developer's interpretation of how the business outcome will be implemented. But with acceptance test driven development (ATDD) and behavior driven development (BDD), users themselves define the requirements by writing tests or by creating illustrative scenarios and stating the results they would expect in those scenarios. As the developer develops, he or she can run those tests to make sure the code produces the right results.

I like to apply the same approach to non-functional requirements: security, performance, code quality, accessibility needs for users with disabilities, and compliance requirements, for example. A good suite of security tests can serve as a security requirement for the developer and can let him or her know if the requirement has been met. This is much more efficient than writing security requirements into a document, letting the developer write code, and then later running security tests based on the document and informing the developer that he or she has done something wrong.

But this equation—tests = requirements—still does not really tell us where requirements come from in the first place and how best to discover them. The answer is, I think, one that should cause the IT world to slap its collective forehead and say, "Why didn't I think of that before?" It is this: we must replace the notion of *requirement* with that of a *desired outcome*. What gets tossed over the wall for the team to solve should not be a set of requirements: it should be an objective, an envisioned outcome that would add business value. Requirements are not part of that desired outcome; it is better to think of them as part of the solution. The team is empowered to figure out the requirements—that is, the tests—that is, the output from the development process—that it believes will best achieve the envisioned outcome.

> We must replace the notion of *requirement* with that of a *desired outcome.*

The best framework I have found for working with desired outcomes as requirements is Gojko Adzic's *Impact Mapping: Making a Big Impact with Software Products and Projects*. Essentially Adzic makes the point that we make IT investments in order to accomplish desired results, or impacts, for the business.[8] These impacts always involve a change in behavior on the part of *someone*. That someone might be a customer, a marketer, a senior executive—anyone. To accomplish the change in behavior, we first decide what change in behavior we want, and then find ways to obtain it.

Instead of jumping immediately to requirements, then, we begin Adzic's exercise by framing the desired impact or strategic objective. As a team, we then conduct a brainstorming exercise where we begin to map out whose behavior might change and in what ways in order to accomplish our objective. For each of those ways, we brainstorm a set of "hows"—capabilities we might provide that would drive that particular behavior change. We can draw the results of the exercise as an impact map—a mind-map sort of diagram—showing *why* we are doing something (what impact we want), and a number of options for *who* (whose behavior should change), *what* (what behavior change we want), and *how* (what capabilities can we give them to elicit that behavior). This impact map is not static, but is expected to change as we begin experimentation and delivering.

Seen correctly, the impact map is simply a set of hypotheses about what capabilities might produce the desired outcome. These capabilities are like product attributes in Eric Ries's *Lean Startup*—they must be validated.[9] With an impact map in hand, we choose a path—a capability and its expected impact—and begin development and release. Ideally, we begin with the smallest piece of capability development that we can use to test the hypothesis implied by a particular branch of the map. How will we know if the experiment is successful? We will know because it will have a positive impact on the stated outcome, or at least the hypothesized change in behaviors.

We continue trying branches of the map—that is, new capabilities—until the desired outcome is achieved. And then we stop. No scope creep, no feature bloat. We do exactly what is necessary to accomplish the outcome we set out to accomplish.

Where do the desired outcomes come from? In other words, how do we start the impact mapping exercise? An easy answer would be that we start with whatever "the business" says will add business value. But, as I said in *The Art of Business Value*, this is not as straightforward as it sounds. There is unfortunately no universal currency of business value. The best we can say is that business value is the current hypothesis of executive leadership of what will best accomplish the aims for which the organization is chartered—increased shareholder value for a publicly traded company, mission value within liquidity targets for a nonprofit, mission value with continued appropriations for a government agency, and whatever the owners want for a closely held private company.

So, let's create an Agile framework for acquiring requirements. It starts with the enterprise and its ultimate mission—increasing shareholder value, let's say, or eradicating malaria, or preventing terrorist activities within the country's borders. Based on that, its competitive position in the market, its current assets and competencies, and many other factors, the company's senior leaders set a direction—a set of outcomes or impacts that they believe will best help the enterprise accomplish that ultimate mission. We can call this defining what business value means for the enterprise.

We can also call it strategy setting, whether the strategy is explicit or not. Each company has a way of being-in-its-industry,[†] a competitive approach, a vision of itself in the future, an attitude, a spirit. Whatever it is, it is what drives the company forward. Perhaps, for example, the executives believe that a cost leadership strategy, one of economist Michael Porter's generic competitive strategies,[10] will yield the best results. In that case, its desired outcomes will involve cutting costs to reduce its prices.

Of course, the executives do not know for sure that these outcomes will actually lead to the desired ultimate goals—they cannot be certain that strategic goals A, B, and C will lead to increased shareholder value. That uncertainty means that the enterprise must set up feedback loops to test whether accomplishing those goals will in fact result in the ultimate objective, or whether it needs to pivot and try a different set of goals. Perhaps other entrants into the market have advantages that let them reduce costs even further. If so, the executive team might decide to pivot to a focus strategy, which will drive a different set of desired outcomes.

---

[†] Nod to Heidegger.

The company will then take each of the desired outcomes and attempt to achieve them, attaching to them a tentative spending plan. The spending plan will later be adjusted as new information is gathered. For each desired outcome, a team is assigned. The team then performs an impact-mapping exercise with the desired outcome, generating a number of possible paths it believes will lead to the desired impact. These paths are uncertain, and also require validation through feedback, as we discussed above.

The team—and by "team" I mean the IT folks together with the business folks—tests a path by quickly creating and deploying a capability. Here is where something like "requirements" finally enters the picture. The team hypothesizes a piece of product—a piece of software, a piece of value delivery—that it thinks will satisfy the chosen path. Acceptance tests and unit tests are created for that piece of capability. The team develops, gets feedback from each other and the onsite business representatives, deploys, and gets feedback from users (preferably objective measures of user behavior) to see if the desired impacts were obtained, and adjusts course accordingly.

This process as I have described it consists of one feedback loop within another feedback loop, which in turn is inside another feedback loop. The pace of these feedback loops differs. The developers rely on super-fast feedback from their automated tests. Feedback from product owners and users occurs in a slightly slower loop. The feedback loop that tests different paths through the impact map happens at yet a slower pace. Finally, the feedback loop that tells executives whether their strategic direction is working is slowest of all. Faster feedback loops are embedded in slower feedback loops.

Basing their work on desired impacts turns the team into outcome owners: they are responsible for the entire value stream of accomplishing the desired outcome. This differs from the classic formulation of IT's role—and even the typical Agile formulation—where the team builds the features requested by the business or its product owner and then hands things over to a business lead, who might or might not be effective at harvesting business value. Agile writers often imply that the team is responsible for value creation, but in their formulation, the team enters the picture too late—after the product owner has decided what will be valuable—and leaves too early—before the value is harvested—to truly have ownership of value delivery

Conversely, with the impact-ownership approach, the team takes charge of the outcome from the beginning. Upper management need not "control" the team because the team's progress can be seen in changes to the core metrics—the impact—as they deliver, with frequent checkpoints. Jim Highsmith says in *Agile Project Management*:

> The traditional rationale goes that development teams have no control over outcomes or value, therefore they should not be held accountable for them. However, when a development team is divorced from outcomes they become fixated on requirements, requirements that should change as projects progress, but often don't because they are deemed a critical piece of performance measurement. When teams are focused on outcomes they are more apt to deliver true business value.[11]

Humble, O'Reilly, and Molesky reach a similar conclusion. The enterprise should, they say, describe, in measurable terms, the business outcomes it wants to achieve. "It is then up to the teams to discover ideas for features which will achieve these business outcomes...Thus, the responsibility for achieving business goals is pushed down to the teams, and teams focus on business outcomes."[12]

The business and IT—or better, the thing that is the business and IT together—is engaged in a voyage of discovery, generating and testing hypotheses and adjusting course as necessary. As I write these words, it occurs to me that some senior leaders might think that this is an overly tentative, weak-willed, wishy-washy way of running a company. But it is not. To use this model, one must boldly formulate hypotheses and pursue them without overanalyzing them. An executive's job is to creatively define strategic parameters, align the organization behind them, and boldly implement them—boldly, but not stupidly. Feedback cycles tell the executive when to pivot and try a bold, new plan.

The age of IT organizations hiding behind requirements—"just tell me what you need"— is gone. IT leaders must instead take ownership, responsibility, and accountability for accomplishing the business's objectives. The IT leader must have the courage to own outcomes.

---

Requirements are a way of controlling the development team by constraining their creativity. Instead of requirements, we want to charge the team—the joint business/IT team, that is—with delivering business outcomes, and let them find the capabilities that deliver these outcomes best.

---

# TRANSFORMATION

This world…always was and will be: an ever-living fire, with measures of it kindling, and measures going out.

—**Heraclitus**, *Fragment 30*

Life is the continuous adjustment of internal relations to external relations.

—**Herbert Spencer**, *Principles of Psychology*

Transformational projects are evidence that a mistake has been made. The worst of these transformational projects are so-called "modernization projects"—transformational projects undertaken to bring technology platforms up to date. But whether these projects are to transform business capabilities or their technological underpinnings, they are the result of poor stewardship of IT assets and old ways of thinking about IT governance and execution.

I have come to this conclusion after participating in a number of such projects. They are a lot like New Year's resolutions. I'm sure that you know this syndrome: You have in mind a change of behavior that you know is a good idea but that will be difficult to adopt. Maybe you need to start exercising more, so you resolve that you will start going to that SteakFit class offered by the local deli. But you do prefer watching that Real Opera Singers of Poughkeepsie reality TV show to working out, so you decide to put off doing anything about your resolution until after January 1. All of a sudden, it's March, and you haven't been to a single SteakFit session. That is what we call a New Year's resolution.

We know how well these resolutions tend to work. They are set up to fail, because by waiting until the new year, you have already made your decision not to act on the resolution. You have increased the risk of your initiative by deciding to do it in one big effort instead of taking incremental actions. You have framed the problem in a way that shows that you have no urgency around solving it. Essentially, by finally deciding to attend SteakFit class, you are about to embark on a costly, risky, painful initiative without any true sense of determination, no matter what you might tell yourself.

> A transformational project occurs when the amount of debt has become too much to bear.

How do IT modernization projects come about in a business organization? Over time, IT systems begin to diverge from what the enterprise really needs. The divergence widens and widens, and at some point, the company decides to take action to close the gap. A business-generated transformation follows a similar logic, where divergence from the way the company wants to compete in the market or the way the nonprofit wants to fulfill its mission leads to a sudden attempt to remedy the situation and realign capabilities. An effort is transformational to the extent that this gap has become wide. The gap widens with time, just as atrophying muscles will get worse the more days there are until New Year's.

If there has been a divergence of IT systems from what the company needs, then the company has been paying for that divergence. It might be paying in actual dollars, or it might be paying in opportunity costs. Perhaps the gap is making it harder for the company to close on sales opportunities or forcing it to forgo them entirely; perhaps it is causing the company to hire more employees than necessary. It gets harder and harder to find COBOL programmers: costs go up, systems are failing more often than they should because the technology is getting old, and it is taking longer to repair IT components when they do fail. New code is taking longer to write because the old code has become a panoply of pappardelle* Customer service may be suffering. Employees may be creating costly workarounds. As the divergence widens, business value is destroyed.

An example of this growing divergence is *technical debt*. Technical debt arises when the development team takes a shortcut to release a feature more quickly, leaving known imperfections in the code. This debt will need to be paid off sooner or later by improving the code, but for the moment, the feature works in production and users cannot tell the difference. As with any other debt, though, the company will need to pay interest until it is retired. Perhaps the code is poorly organized—future modifications will be difficult and costly until the debt is retired by reorganizing the code. This is neither an argument against pappardelle nor against incurring technical debt—companies often properly take on debt to finance activities. But too much debt can sink the company.

Similarly, an operational debt arises naturally over time if the company does not invest in keeping its systems closely aligned with its operating needs, its potential opportunities, or its competitive strategy. Until the debt is paid off in a transformation or

---

* I'm riffing on "spaghetti code," but an interesting topic of research might be the use of other pasta names as analogies for code filled with technical debt. Macaroni code—filled with holes? Ravioli code—tight at the edges but stuffed with filling? Barbina (little beards)—code that keeps getting fuzzier? Vermicelli (worms)—those bad practices that worm their way through your code? Strozzapretti ("strangled priest") code? I'm not touching that one.

modernization investment, the company will be paying some form of interest.

Transformational projects demonstrate waste in a governance process. If the governance process is unable to approve incremental changes to a system to keep it synchronized with business needs and technology trends, then that inability is costing the business money.

A transformational project occurs when the amount of debt has become too much to bear. It is a painful lump-sum payment at a time when the company has been paying so much interest that it may already be frail and tottering.

Now that the company has been paying interest on its debt, it embarks on its New Year's resolution to pay off the debt in one big project. *Big* is an important word here, because studies have shown that the larger the project, the riskier it will be.[†] This makes sense, because large projects have more things that can go wrong, more interacting pieces, and more cultural and process change that will need to accompany them. But because of the complex interactions and the requirement for change on so many dimensions, the risk increases non-linearly with the size of the project. Large batches of requirements, as we have seen in the content on Agile and Lean software development, lead to longer cycle times and slower feedback cycles. By saving up all of our work until the transformation project, we have increased risk and effort substantially.

---

[†] Studies vary so much it is hard to know what to trust. Of the studies available, two seem relevant. McKinsey: Large IT projects run 45% over budget and 7% over time, while delivering 56% less value than predicted. Gartner: The failure rate of large IT projects with budgets exceeding $1 million was found to be almost 50% higher than for project with budgets below $350,000.[1]

We have also—paradoxically, perhaps—reduced incentives and motivation to make the changes. If the transformational changes are truly important, then why haven't we made them already? Instead, we have encouraged a culture where workarounds are considered normal. We have also made the changes as painful as possible by delaying them, so business leaders and users of the system have no urgency to see the changes implemented—the changes can only cause disruption and uncertainty. They will want to wait until the software has been tested to "perfection"—that is, tested beyond the level appropriate to mitigating risks.

To make matters worse, transforming is not in itself a business objective. How can we make good decisions about what should be in or out of scope? In the worst-case scenario, everyone in the organization seizes on the large transformation effort as a way to get their pet projects done. But even with the best intentions and focus, it is hard to make good business-case decisions when your goal is "transforming" or "modernizing." Is this particular feature or technology something that will make us "more modernized" or "more transformed"? Transformations stimulate risk-averse behaviors and encourage feature bloat.

Yes, it is possible that the business itself has suddenly decided to "transform," in the sense of adopting a new strategy or building a new basis on which to compete. Perhaps there hasn't been any accumulating debt. Perhaps there is new management, or perhaps leadership has been sold on a new idea by a change agent. In that case, there is no choice but to do a transformational IT project to match this new strategic change, right? Wrong. An IT transformation, even if it is intended to support a sudden business transformation, is still a large and risky project. Better to move to the transformed state incrementally, taking advantage of learning opportunities along the way.

Then there is the final irony: by the time we finish a large transformation effort, it is time to start transforming again.

There is a deeper problem at the root of this dysfunctional transformation cycle. It lies, I believe, in our distinction between the *development* of a system and its *operation and maintenance*. This distinction permeates the way we organize our investment decisions, the way we budget, the way we measure success, and the way we do our accounting. The underlying assumption is that, after some point, we merely perform maintenance on an IT system the way we perform maintenance on a car. All we need to do is have it checked every 5,000 miles, move the tires around, and put in new oil and wiper fluid now and then. There is the cost of the car, and then there are the recurring maintenance costs. But this metaphor is misleading and, ultimately, inaccurate.

In the Waterfall model, we called the moment when we moved from development to maintenance final operating capability (FOC); that is, the moment when the entire *required* scope had been completed and the point at which the system was finally released to users. Our accounting model is based on this distinction: the work up to FOC is capitalized because it is considered to be building an asset; after that point, the asset is depreciated, since it is being used to generate profits.[††] Any new expenses then become "run the business" or "keeping the lights on" costs.

These distinctions have largely broken down with Agile and Continuous Delivery techniques. After all, there is no fixed set of

---

[††] Recorded as expenses over time to reduce the value of the asset on the balance sheet.

requirements, so how can we gauge when we have reached FOC? What's worse is that we start releasing product to users early in the project and continue releasing it in tiny increments. Should we start depreciating the asset as soon as we have launched the initial deployment? And what makes the final capability final? We maintain a backlog of requested incremental features, and we will continue to add to the product over its lifetime. So the system is never finished, nor should it be—assuming that the business wants the agility to accommodate change.

What is "maintenance" of an IT system, anyway? Sometimes it is fixing defects (which presumably means improving the value of the asset that has been created, though strangely, these costs do not get capitalized), but most of the time it means changing and enhancing the system as the business changes and develops new needs. How is that different from the "initial" development effort? In the Agile world, and especially when we release code in tiny increments, it is more accurate to say that we have a continuous flow of investment that continually adjusts the value of the asset that has been capitalized.[§]

To confuse the accountants more, the current system of capitalizing and depreciating the value of the system requires gauging the expected life of the system—the period in which we will use it to generate profits. But if we continue to "maintain" the system in a way that avoids a Big-Bang transformation, then its lifetime is effectively endless. All the more so if we never replace the system, just slowly change it piece by piece until it no longer resembles the original.

---

[§] Again, I realize that this is not currently generally accepted accounting practice. I am thinking of this as an economic asset rather than a financial asset—more on this later—and pointing out a place where I think financial accounting practices are misleading us in our investment decisions.

Dividing our IT spending into development and maintenance buckets leads to some ineffective ways of making decisions. According to Weill and Ross:

> All IT spending falls into either the new or sustaining category. Sustaining expenditures keep the current systems running and include regular maintenance and updating—often called keeping the lights on. Sustaining outlays are typically viewed as nondiscretionary spending in firms. As a result, the sustaining spending can be a source of frustration. In 2007, the average firm spent 71 percent of its total IT spending (operating expenses plus capital) in the sustaining category.[2]

Maintenance spending is viewed as a painful necessity that interferes with innovation and value-adding activities: organizations try to do as little of it as possible. "High-performing IT units can reduce the run-the-business expense to 50 percent," say Hunter and Westerman.[3] By throwing the operations and maintenance of our IT systems into this bucket of "keeping the lights on" costs, we are throwing it into a cost-control bucket, making it a line item that IT leaders try to minimize.

> IT leaders who are successful in keeping maintenance costs low may actually be doing their companies a disservice.

But, ultimately, the distinction between directing money toward "maintenance" and directing it toward new system delivery is specious. Both create or refine capabilities that the business uses to generate business value. An incremental dollar invested in an existing system is probably worth even *more* than an incremental dollar invested in building a new system. The dollar in the existing system can take advantage of other functionality that has already been built into the system; it is also a small increment added to what is already there, so it doesn't involve as much risk or training costs. IT leaders who are successful in keeping maintenance costs low may actually be doing their companies a disservice by creating technical or functional debt and making a risky transformation project inevitable.

Back to Weill and Ross's statement, the idea that maintenance costs are non-discretionary is really a disguised sunk cost fallacy. Because we have already spent the money to deliver a "legacy" system, we assume that we have to keep spending money on its continued existence. But why? Shouldn't we be deciding whether the incremental spending is worthwhile in itself, or whether a different approach to delivering the needed capabilities are in order? Even if we are just "fixing" or "maintaining" the system?

It is a decision-making mistake to treat as unavoidable costs that you are not actually committed to. People tend to view themselves as committed because they have already "sunk" money into something, but good decision-making requires ignoring the sunk cost and only considering the alternatives for future spending. For example, if a business has already spent $10 million on building a new plant and requires another $5 million to finish it, but because of new advances in technology they can scrap the work they've already done, start over, and only spend $4 million to build the plant, then the $10 million already spent is irrelevant to the decision. The choice is between spending $5 million or $4 million, and the decision should be obvious. In the case of run-the-business IT costs, we might have already spent a lot to buy licenses for a software product, and now consider paying maintenance fees for that product to be non-discretionary. But they are discretionary—the fact that we paid a lot for the original licenses is not relevant to the decision. We should just consider the maintenance costs versus whatever alternatives exist—perhaps even discarding the product.

The model that distinguishes between development and maintenance costs is rooted in the idea that the IT system is a *product*; something that has clear boundaries and attributes for which you pay a fixed price and that you eventually stop paying for. But the product metaphor, like many others in this book, has outlived its usefulness. We maintain a car to make it *continue* to function as if it were new. A piece of software, on the other hand, does not require lubrication—it continues to operate the way it always has even if we don't "maintain" it. What we call *maintenance* is really making changes to keep up with changes in the business need or technology standards.

Our governance systems are more or less designed around this product concept. We govern at a coarse level: we decide to invest in an entire system or product, but we don't generally make decisions at the level of features or requirements within that product. As a result, the governance process wants to know "how much it will cost" and "how much it will cost to maintain in the steady state." Of course, there is no such thing as the steady state—the needs of a company change constantly. The only real question is how much we will spend now and how much we will spend later. Even further, there is no fixed amount we will spend later—it depends on how much the business will change and how much the company chooses to spend on new features and enhancements.

> What we call *maintenance* is really making changes to keep up with changes in the business need or technology standards.

Systems are in a state of flux. To paraphrase Heraclitus, you can never log into the same system twice. Systems are software models of dynamic business systems—how *could* they be static? By pretending that they are fixed products, we destroy business value.

For the product and maintenance metaphor, let me substitute one that is more apt, with a nod to the ancient Greek philosophers, who apparently thought a lot about Agile software delivery. When we talk about change, they realized, we are also implicitly talking about identity—that is, something that stays the same. For example, if I say, "The boy got taller" (a statement about change), I am not saying, "The short boy was replaced by a taller boy." I am asserting an identity (that the short boy was the same boy as the tall boy). To the ancient Greeks, there was something challenging about this. What makes it the same boy? What does it mean to preserve identity through change?

To illustrate the problem, they proposed the paradox of the ship of Theseus. Here's my version: Theseus, a great hero, is given a ship as a present from the Greeks. After a few years, Theseus finds that one of the ship's wooden planks is becoming a little worn, so he has it replaced. At this point, we ask, does Theseus still have the same ship, or is it now a different ship? Most of us would say that it is the same ship. Can we agree that replacing one plank in a ship doesn't make it a whole different ship? Good.

Over the next few years, one plank after another starts to wear out, and each time Theseus has it replaced. Finally, one day, Theseus realizes that he has now replaced every plank in the ship—there is not a single material thing in the ship that was there when he was first given it. And he wonders . . . is this still the same ship? Or does he now have a different ship? And if so, when did it become a different ship? If it is the same ship, then what makes it the same?

It could never have become a different ship. Each time Theseus replaced a plank, it was still the same ship it was before he replaced the plank—remember that we said that changing a single plank does not make the boat a different boat. Therefore, the boat could never have become a new boat. But how is it the same boat if it has nothing in common with the original boat?

In the eighteenth century, Thomas Hobbes added another twist to the paradox.[4] As Theseus throws out each worn plank, his neighbor gathers it up. The neighbor reassembles the discarded planks into a boat, putting each plank right where it had been in Theseus's original boat. In the end, he has a complete boat that is "identical" to Theseus's original boat. Now which boat is Theseus's original boat—Theseus's or the neighbor's?

That's the thing—when you study philosophy, you often feel like the ancient Greeks had already figured everything out. Now it turns out that they already understood IT.

Theseus's activities fall into what the software world now calls the strangler pattern: a way to incrementally modernize a legacy system as defined by Martin Fowler.[5] Instead of building an entirely new system, we take a small piece of the legacy system and rebuild it in a way that lets it interoperate with the rest of the legacy system. We launch that piece into production and have users use it seamlessly as if it is part of the legacy system. Then we take another piece out of the legacy system and do the same thing. And another. And another. Until eventually there is nothing left of the legacy system—it has vanished, piece by piece, like *Alice in Wonderland's* Cheshire Cat. Or has it? To use Fowler's term, we have strangled the poor cat—I mean the IT system—without ever replacing it; modernized it without ever modernizing it. It is possible to transform without undertaking a transformation project.

The strangler pattern overcomes a critical problem many of us have faced in applying Agile techniques to modernizations. In the absence of the strangler pattern, we would develop a new system on the modernized architecture and then move the users over to it. The problem is that the users cannot begin using the new system until its capabilities at least match those of the legacy system. Because this usually takes a while, the first release of the new system doesn't come for quite some time, which works against the Agile principle of delivering value quickly and frequently. Legacy modernizations cannot be done in an Agile way without the strangler pattern.

Using the strangler pattern takes some thought and creativity. Usually, it is done through some reorganization of code to encapsulate the part of the system that will change, and then the use of web service interfaces to integrate the new code. It might require single sign-on so that users can move seamlessly between the legacy code and the new code, but there are techniques that work pretty well for all of these things.[6]

Similar techniques can—with some creativity—also be used to accomplish business transformation. A particular business function

> We have strangled the poor cat—I mean the IT system—without ever replacing it.

> This ability to change business and IT capabilities as the world changes is what we call Agility. To be Agile, in a sense, means to always be transforming.

can be carved out, encapsulated, and "loosely coupled" with the other business processes. It can then be transformed without much effect on the other business processes. The technique is then repeated with the next process, and the next. In parallel with the business process strangulation, the company can execute its IT system strangulation.

This ability to change business and IT capabilities as the world changes is what we call agility. To be Agile, in a sense, means to always be transforming.

Everything that resists continual change imposes economic costs. When a software designer makes a decision that will be hard to change later, he or she is imposing a cost on the company. When the company imposes bureaucratic overhead on IT changes, it incurs a cost. When a feature is created that is constraining rather than enabling, it imposes a cost. In the next chapter, we will look more closely at the advantages and disadvantages of standardization, but for the moment, let's just consider the fact that standards need to change over time. They become more and more constraining, until—whap!—we have to transform. It is the familiar pattern, yet another growing divergence from the optimal, on which we pay interest and eventually must make a sudden adjustment.

Even our traditional way of dividing IT capabilities into discrete systems or applications impedes agility and necessitates transformational projects. Systems tend to persist until replaced whole heifer—an expensive proposition. So, what do we do? We avoid replacing them until the business case becomes strong enough to justify a large investment. Suddenly, we find ourselves with a modernization project.

Interestingly, academia has also come to believe that continuous transformation is a way that businesses can generate superior profits. In their article, "Information Technology and Business-Level Strategy: Toward an Integrated Theoretical Perspective," Paul Drnevitch of the University of Alabama and David Croson of Southern Methodist University propose that one way IT can support business strategy is through "commanding Schumpeterian flexibility rents," or the ability to "preserve or improve value and position through superior adaptation."[7]

Joseph Schumpeter, the economist referenced by Drnevitch and Croson, was a mid-twentieth-century thinker who focused on entrepreneurial aspects of strategy. Economic "rents," referred to by Drnevitch and Croson above, are profits that a company is able to earn above what would be expected in an efficient, competitive market. Agility, adaptation, continuous innovation, and creative destruction, in the Schumpeterian sense, are all ways that a firm can stay ahead of competitors and thereby earn those better-than-normal profits. Schumpeter, it would seem, was an early Agile proponent, a Theseusian transformer. As Drnevitch and Crosan put it:

> Flexibility can improve efficiency through enabling the firm to minimize the costs of adapting to a new situation (i.e., increasing producer surplus through reducing the total costs of creating a product or service that delivers a given level of consumer value). Flexibility can improve effectiveness through enabling the firm to seize an opportunity for extraordinary profit (i.e., increasing producer surplus through creating a new or improved product or service, thereby increasing value to the consumer and repricing to capture it). The flexibility perspective

originates from Schumpeter's (1934, 1950) classic concept of creative destruction, in which old practices, businesses, and industries are continually replaced by new ones that are more efficient or effective at value creation and capture.[8]

They attribute these flexibility rents to two sources: evolution of capabilities and real options. Evolution of capabilities, they explain, means altering processes and organizational structure over time, "with the final configuration accomplished through experience and trial-and-error rather than ex ante optimal design."[9] The options view is focused on uncertainty: "real options is the strategy concept perhaps most directly applicable to the valuation of IT investments under uncertainty...a characterization of the immanent flexibility in the firm's stock of resources, the financial results of which mimic options contracts."[10]

All of this sounds curiously like the Lean-Agile approach, doesn't it?

As the economy churns and turns, booms and bursts, as memes travel at the speed of light through the vastly connected Internet of Things and Thoughts, spaces open up momentarily where entrepreneurs and entrepreneurial firms can dive in, earn Schumpeterian rents, and move on to the next open space. In order to do so, the firm's IT assets and processes must support rapid change, and the firm must use them to change rapidly. It must transform continuously rather than in fits and starts. New Year's resolutions are signs of a death spiral, a disconnect from the changing market.

It is the job of senior IT leaders to avoid transformations and modernizations by keeping the enterprise's IT assets aligned with the business's current and future needs. The strangler pattern is more than a coding tactic—it is an IT strategy meant to maximize business value through true alignment between business needs and technology. Modernizing and transforming should be as easy as stripping a worn-out board from Theseus's ship and replacing it with a fresh one. Agility, as we have seen, requires continuous, not discrete, transformation.

---

Transformation and modernization projects are exactly what IT leaders must avoid; continuously transforming and modernizing the company's IT systems makes Fowler's strangler pattern into an IT strategy rather than just a coding tactic.

---

# 7

# ENTERPRISE ARCHITECTURE

Many neckless faces sprouted, and arms were wandering naked, bereft of shoulders, and eyes were roaming alone, in need of foreheads.

—**Empedocles of Acragas**, *On Nature*

It is right both to say and to think that it is what-is: for it is the case that it is, but nothing is not: these things I bid you to ponder.

—**Parmenides of Elea**, *Fragments*

Enterprise Architecture, the domain of the IT bureaucrats, is the place we must look for the solution to our Agile challenges. For it is in Enterprise Architecture, or EA, that we can attempt to "optimize the whole," as Lean theory advises. EA is the place where we can view IT capabilities for what they truly are—an economic asset. We shall journey to the land of the template zombies to retrieve our golden asset, careful to carry mirrors to avoid petrification. Good luck, Agile fellows.

That's the way EA has always seemed to me. It's not fair, of course, to the many talented people who practice the EA craft, and not their fault that they have been used as tools of the contractor-control paradigm of IT. I believe that many Agile thinkers have stumbled over the question of what EA means in an Agile paradigm. In this chapter, I'm going to try to show that the idea of an EA asset is actually central to our Agile practice. Later, in chapter 12, I'm going to propose a new community-centric role for the EA folks within IT, one which I believe aligns elegantly with Agile and DevOps practices.

I have said that we need to stop looking at IT delivery in terms of projects and products. With what, then, shall we replace them? I'd like to suggest that the enterprise architects have had it right all along. We manage an enterprise-wide asset with an "as-is" state and a "to-be" state. We groom this asset in perpetuity—as the company changes and develops—by adding, removing, and improving its capabilities. We try to build into it agility and options, risk mitigations, and usability. The totality of our IT capabilities is an economic asset that will be used to derive profits or accomplish mission, and we might as well just call this the Enterprise Architecture.

> The total of our IT capabilities is an economic asset that will be used to derive profits or accomplish mission.

I hesitate to use the term only because EA has meant something very different in the contractor-control model. It was given the uncomfortable role of trying to impose order on something that is naturally chaotic, where *impose* is the critical word. It was easy to think of EA folk as office-dwelling trolls who manufacture constraints—I think they call them *standards*—to confine people who are trying to be productive. A conservative wing that tries to keep everyone in line with old values. The guardians of the traditions of how to build stuff. But as they have been trying to tell us, the EA folk are up to something quite different.

In the past, we viewed EA as primarily concerned with standardization, consistency, planning, and cost reduction. In other words, EA was responsible for many of those concepts we have traditionally associated with the Waterfall model. It documented as-is and to-be architectures, demonstrated alignment of systems with business needs, and did the "rigorous" up-front analysis and centralized planning that could then be used to set boundaries for developers when they began a project. In other words, a vehicle for control.

Standardization has always been an obsession of IT departments. It has had to be so in a model focused on control and cost containment. As one of the CIOs in Heller's study says, "The fewer tools I have in my tool kit, the more cost effective I can be. If I can force standardization through an architecture model, I should inherently be able to drive efficiency."[1] Please notice the use of the word "force"—do you see how deeply embedded the idea of control has been in the way we think about IT? Sometimes, instead we talk about "compliance." Weill and Ross advise us that "…information technology does two things well: integration and standardization"[2] and that, therefore, CIOs should "develop technology standards and compliance and exception processes."[3]

We know why standardization has been such a concern for IT leaders, who have often been burned by its absence in the past. Business users might have bought products based on whim, incomplete understanding, or persuasive sales pitches, leaving IT with a mess of costly products that were difficult and expensive to maintain. The products might not have interoperated, causing additional work for IT and maybe throwing projects behind schedule. Economies of scale and procurement leverage come from standardization.

But standardization also imposes costs by limiting agility and adding bureaucratic waste: exceptions must be put through an approval process, and in some organizations, every purchase has to be vetted to be sure it conforms to standards. Standardization limits the space of possible solutions to a problem. When it comes to consumer technologies, standardizing means telling users that they can't have devices they are used to using at home, that they have seen used successfully elsewhere, or that they are comfortable with. Frustration is a predictable response. Werner Boeing of Roche Diagnostics tells Martha Heller:

> When it comes to consumer technologies, many CIOs have not found a way to define their contribution in this new environment, and the business perceives us as standing in their way. Our traditional mantra of standardization and consolidation does not work anymore.[4]

Or, to put it more bluntly, "The more your employees love technology, the more they dislike IT," the guardians of standards.[5]

Standards that constrain IT delivery teams—standards that IT imposes on itself—have more subtle costs, the most insidious of which, in my experience, is the process to ensure standardization. For example, if we mandate that projects reuse code whenever possible, each project may have to spend time searching archives of available code to find something that is a near fit, and then deal with the question of whether it is a *near enough* fit. Perhaps the project then needs to document its search through the archives and justify why none of the existing code was adequate, and someone will need to review the justification. As another example, standardized lifecycle processes— SDLCs—push all projects through a uniform process even when some of its steps may be unnecessary for that initiative. The cost is in dollars, time, and frustration.

We often take a knee-jerk approach to standardization. "Of course," we think, "standardizing on one programming language for the enterprise is essential; it will let us focus our expertise and move developers from one project to another." This is valid, and in some cases standards can even improve agility. If everyone uses the same brand of laptop, then we can provision it quickly and make sure we have the skills to support it. Absolutely—standardization can have substantial economic benefits.

So we standardize on Java or INTERCAL or DonaldDuck* across the enterprise. But perhaps for lightweight, front-end development Ruby on Rails would be better. Perhaps for high concurrency, super-efficient back-end services Go or Node might be better. We can agree that there is a cost to breaking from the standard—but there is also a benefit, and the two must be weighed against each other. Perhaps allowing developers to work in their favorite language will give them extra energy: developers love to try out new things. Perhaps it will help the company recruit more great developers. But once an organization has bought into the standardization-or-death dogma, this conversation is less likely to happen—standardization is accepted as an end in itself.

Let me suggest that the obsession with standardization is related to the desire to control the geeks—the fear that they will go off and waste the company's money, which is a fear that we've touched upon in previous chapters. The idea that a programmer might choose to work in Erlang is precisely the sort of thing that fostered that fear in the first place: the non-IT folks' perception was that the geeks were just playing with the company's money irresponsibly. The control-oriented reaction to this perception was to draw boundaries and declare that the programmer must stick to standards. Today, we have to consider the possibility that the programmer has valid reasons for working in Erlang or LOLCAT or what have you; perhaps reasons

---

* Alas, I can no longer find any references to this wonderful language anywhere. It was a dialect of LISP, invented by my professor, Drew McDermott, for a computer science class at Yale; and its name stood for something like "Drew's Own Algorithmic Language…"

that are not clear to those without the technical skill. The conversation must be had.

I don't mean that standards are bad. Let's just agree that they might be overrated.

Standards are imposed on projects as they enter a design phase, and are thus easily aligned to a Waterfall-based model. The alignment is less clear for an Agile model, where designs "emerge" in an evolutionary way and where—as we have said—projects are a misleading way to think about the continuous transformation of IT capabilities that is Agility. When we instead think of IT capabilities as assets that we must keep in alignment with the business as it changes, or better yet as a single, large asset where the synergies and relationships between the capabilities are a map of the enterprise's operations and strategic intent, we can see that standards are a kind of stickiness that impedes adaptability—goo gumming up the gears.

When we add all of our current IT capabilities together, we arrive at an asset that enables the enterprise to earn future revenues and reduce future costs—that is, an asset in the classic economic sense. Not always exactly in the financial accounting sense—based on generally accepted accounting principles, some parts of this asset will have been capitalized, some expensed, and some capitalized and then depreciated. The asset does not appear—or appear in the form, I mean—on the company's balance sheet. Much of its value is hidden; its ability to support Agility, for example. But it is an economic asset nonetheless.

This asset I will refer to as the EA, which could just as well stand for *Economic Asset*. I will try to stay consistent in my language: An *investment* is a commitment of resources to develop, improve, groom, repair, and/or build this asset (or any other). A *project* is a bad thing—a control-oriented, defined-scope, and/or defined-start-and-end type of an initiative. I'll just use the word *initiative* when I'm talking in a loose way about a set of activities.

What I have in mind with EA is something like the asset Drnevitch and Croson refer to when they say:

> IT investments can, on their own merits, comprise a tangible resource…or an intangible capability…Such IT investments can influence a firm's strategy through affecting both its efficiency and effectiveness, as well as providing critical information that either increases the value of making investments in other resources or capabilities or steers management toward more effective decision making.[6]

The capabilities that make up the EA are resources, endpoints, off-the-shelf software, tangled and dusty cables, Y2K-surviving COBOL punch cards, little code hacks no one understands anymore, commented code full of bad geek-jokes, and those last two Windows 2003 servers no one got around to replacing, still grinding away in happy, vulnerable, if-it-ain't-broke-don't-fix-it denial. In the best of cases, the EA matches the business's needs; it is an image, in software, of what the business does. Sometimes, it is a distorting mirror image—it has either diverged over time from what the company does or it has had lots of extra capabilities that are not useful piled onto it. Sometimes, the EA asset is elegant, artistic, and clearly expresses a vision and a style. Other times, it is a formless mess of manicotti and macaroni. Or, in Empedocles's cosmology, "arms bereft of shoulders, and eyes roaming alone, in need of foreheads."

But there is more to it: the EA has intangible, *latent* capabilities—potential that is, for the moment, hidden. To see this, we need to look more deeply into how the asset is constructed, the vision and values that hold it together, and the quality of its workmanship.

The EA might promote agility—it might be flexible, simple, and easily adaptable to new needs. Or, it might inhibit agility through a tightly coupled, inflexible design. It might be a poorly managed and confusing mess that will easily breed or hide nasty bugs as the enterprise tries to respond to change. It might be highly performant, scalable, and secure; it might be none of those things. It might even be *more* scalable than the firm could ever need, and thereby demonstrate a history of bad investments or wasteful risk aversion.

> The EA has intangible, *latent* capabilities—potential that is, for the moment, hidden.

The EA asset evolves over time through incremental investments. IT leaders must invest wisely with the goal of managing it. Grooming it. Stewarding or cultivating it so that it can easily adapt to meet tomorrow's needs. Their goal should be to evolve it so that it continues to support the company's strategies. No one else in "the business" will have this strategic intent. Since transformation is the normal, day-to-day Agile progress of the enterprise's capabilities, an EA asset is always evolving.

Technical debt is a liability that represents flaws in the EA asset; the stuff that will cause future work to be non-agile, slow, and expensive. When we speak of "paying interest" on technical debt, we are simply saying that continued development work will cost more until we groom our EA asset to make it more productive, which increases its latent value. In *The Art of Business Value*, I called this process "polishing the hairball," though here we might call it trimming the tagliatelle.

Managing the EA asset is an art, just as all strategic management is an art. An art informed by science. There are well-known design patterns, testing practices, and security features that can support IT leadership's vision for the asset. But formulating the vision and managing the manifold of trade-offs and tactical decisions that must be made to cultivate the asset is the domain of the artist, the finesse-meister, the inspired. Just as the CMO must sense market opportunities, weigh tactics for communicating with that market and encouraging it to purchase, and manage creative talent to present the message compellingly, the CIO must similarly steward the EA. IT leaders practice their art just as marketing does, at the level of, well, the CMO—the person with the seat at the table.

The EA asset embodies the history of the company and all of its learnings to date. It is how the company competes and how it manages its daily operations. In their book *Enterprise Architecture as Strategy: Creating a Foundation for Business Execution*, Ross, Weill, and Robertson speak of the EA as the principles behind the company's *foundation for execution*—the IT infrastructure and processes that automate the company's core capabilities:[7]

> Enterprise architecture directs the digitization of the foundation for execution ... [it] is the organizing logic for business processes and IT infrastructure reflecting the integration and standardization requirements of the company's operating model.[8]

Though they speak in terms of standardization, they are really talking about the choices IT makes in digitizing that foundation for execution. EA is not just a technical structure, but a business vision. "[It] begins at the top—with a statement of how a company operates—and results in a foundation of IT and business process capabilities on which a company builds its competitiveness."[9] As the title of their book suggests, the authors see the EA as expressing the company's strategy.

The EA evolves through the company's projects. "The alternative to the 'big-bang' implementations is to build the foundation one project at a time. To do so, every business project must not only meet its short-term business goals but also help implement (or at least not undermine) the company's architecture."[10] This is where I think they have it backwards: "Not undermining" the architecture is too weak a formulation. The EA is built through those initiatives; there is no separate investment in EA. The challenge for the CIO is to ensure that each investment dollar actually moves the EA forward in the direction of his or her vision.

> The challenge for the CIO is to ensure that each investment dollar actually moves the EA forward in the direction of his or her vision.

The authors, perhaps, are thinking that each project must deliver "business value" according to its own business case, and they may be having trouble reconciling that goal with the goal of advancing the EA. In my view, the two are the same; what is valuable to the business is moving its current set of IT capabilities to a new set of IT capabilities that delivers more revenue, lower costs, and future agility. Locked into the view of IT as a series of projects, I think Ross and co-authors miss the fundamental point that it is the movement toward the ideal EA that delivers the business value. But that is perhaps a quibble, as Ross et al. also seem to see the EA as a hairball in need of polishing:

All companies have entrenched legacy systems that are the accumulation of years of IT-enabled business projects. Intentionally or not, the resulting capability locks in assumptions about the internal and external relationships and business process definitions.[11]

To get the most economic value from our asset, we need to groom it carefully, attending to its ability to support future directions and not just letting the goals of individual projects tug it in this direction and that. This is hard to accomplish when our governance and planning, and especially the business cases we create, are based on the goals of individual projects. Does this project develop code that will be reusable by other projects? Does it help us learn things that will be useful in other contexts? Will it let us retire some technical debt that has been cluttering up our asset? Will it bring to light security risks in other parts of the system? Will it give us flexibility to take on additional work in the future—in other words, does it create investment options for us? Or are there opportunities to take on bits of incremental work within this initiative that will improve profitability in ways that are not in our business case?

> When we see the CIO's role as controlling projects to deliver on time and on budget, we are missing his or her most critical responsibility.

All of this *could* be incorporated into the business case for a project, but it would be difficult to do so because we are dealing with proverbial apples and oranges—we have no common currency in which to measure and add together all of these different types of business value.

When we see the CIO's role as controlling projects to deliver on time and on budget, we are missing his or her most critical responsibility: that of stewarding the EA asset to maximize its agility, quality, and fit to business needs.

The trick is to think of EA not as a way to impose constraints through standardization, but rather as a way to empower the business to evolve and transform. Standardizing means constraining—decisions are made centrally and imposed to control the decentralized actors. Reuse is empowering; it helps teams achieve their goals more quickly by putting decision-making in the hands of the teams, who can see best what reuse makes sense. As we shall see in chapter 12, reuse can serve as the foundation for a community-centric IT approach.

The EA asset can be flexible not just in regard to future changes, but also in regard to how it can be used in the present. It can include tools that can be used in innovative ways; tools that empower business users to find creative new solutions not foreseen by the planners and developers. Yet we often design features that unnecessarily constrain the user by directing the user into only a single way of using them. We build systems as if the user is an *operator*—someone who simply follows the manual. We "idiot-proof" our features. But users can gain value from being able to innovate and, well, think. Of course, there are trade-offs—we have to worry about data integrity, for example. My point is simply that we should not have a knee-jerk reaction that says that we must control how our systems are used. Agility has two dimensions: flexibility over time and flexibility in the present.

> Agility has two dimensions: flexibility over time and flexibility in the present.

Business intelligence tools and visualization software are examples of tools that can be used flexibly. Consider, for example, Microsoft Excel: it can be used for almost anything. Some would say it is too flexible, but consider the value that that flexibility has added to the business world!

IT is trying to control the business, I say, through standardization and enforced data integrity, rather than empowering the business through reusable services, up-to-date technical capabilities, and user-centric design. I know, this is a book about how the business has been trying to control IT. Didn't expect that plot twist, did you?

It is in this context that we need to consider the next chapter's discussions on building versus buying. Imagine the EA asset as a ball that we mold and polish. If it is built as a collection of individual products, it is lumpy rather than smooth. The products don't quite fit together; they have excess capabilities that we don't really need; the ball has strange gaps where it is unexpectedly hollow and missing needed capabilities. We want a smooth ball of EA, an EA shaped to facilitate change and reuse, something you can easily roll in any direction you choose. That is its latent value; the inverse of the cost of implementing changes in the future.

What does such an EA, brimming with latent value, look like?

It has little technical debt. It is built according to good, extensible design patterns and uses well-accepted standards. It is loosely coupled—pieces of it can be easily exchanged for newer pieces without requiring changes to the whole ball of EA. It is well documented—not too much (which would impose costs of keeping all the documentation up-to-date), not too little (which would impose costs of developers trying to figure out how things work when they make changes), and tailored to the right audience (the people who will be making changes later). It has a robust, automated regression test suite, so that new development does not cause expensive break-fix activity. It has good monitoring tools in place. It is coded in a way that resists hard-to-find defects like concurrency errors.

Who, in the business, is going to look after the EA asset *qua* asset? Right—only IT leadership. The quality of the EA asset is not just a side concern or an incidental, necessary, but unfortunate worry. No, it is agility itself. The EA asset is the embodiment of a strategic IT vision; the CIO's strategy written into the company's IT systems. Stewarding the EA asset is IT's way of being future-directed. "More and more, we expect CIOs to be held accountable for a firm's strategic agility—at least the IT infrastructure components, but perhaps some part of process agility also," say the authors of *IT Governance*.[12]

> The EA asset is the embodiment of a strategic IT vision; the CIO's strategy written into the company's IT systems.

The role of IT leadership is not, as we thought in the contractor-control model, to govern, manage, and deliver IT projects and programs. It is rather to steward *assets*—assets that allow the company to best attain its goals today and that will enable the company to attain its goals in the future with minimal investment of time and money. Assembling and keeping those assets current does not require us to distinguish between *new development* and *maintenance*; some combination of the two is optimal, and neither is good or bad per se. Even *divesting* parts of the assets has value.

The difficulty here is that in the contractor-control model IT can only invest in this asset through projects generated by *the business*. The artistry that goes into sculpting an elegant EA is achieved only as a side effect of deploying capabilities that are determined through some process of demand generation (project proposals from the business), supply setting (budgets and hiring plans), and some kind of governance to reconcile the always-present imbalance between the two.

In the contractor-control model, IT is a production capacity—a vendor in the marketplace for projects tasked with providing a service to its "customers," i.e., the business groups demanding attention. In a true market, IT would be able to grow freely, scale up its resources, increase its prices, and develop a competitive strategy so that it could stand out among its competitors. But IT in an enterprise can do no such thing. It is constrained by a budget and other corporate policies. It has to accept responsibility for the results the business achieves with the products it delivers. Imagine if Ford had to accept responsibility for the way people drive its cars.

As IT is jerked this way and that by whatever customer demand makes it through the governance filter, the design and quality of the code for that particular project can be optimized, but how can the whole—the enterprise asset—be optimized? We have seen many times that, "over time, setting up IT as an order taker produces the complicated, brittle, and expensive legacy environments."[13] We will address this problem in the chapter on governance and oversight, but we will just note the connection here.

There are at least two other intangible economic assets that should matter to IT leadership: what I will call the *IT skills* asset and the *enterprise data* asset. The IT skills asset is the abstracted sum of all the skills—the human stuff—that will determine how agile the enterprise can be in the future—that is, how well it can meet the changing needs of the enterprise. Like the EA asset, it can impede agility or promote it; it can raise or lower the costs and time needed to get a change to market. Like the EA, it can carry debt that will continue to command interest until it is retired. If we don't have a great performance engineer, for example, then performance will suffer until we find one.

I think of the skills asset as something much broader than human capital in its usual sense. Sure, it includes the people we have on hand and the skills they have. Its value is enhanced by investments we make in employee training and development. But it also includes our corporate and IT cultures, which may promote or inhibit agility. It includes our processes, policies, standard operating procedures (SOPs), organizational structures—what you might refer to as our bureaucracy. It includes institutional knowledge, relationships, and facilities design. IT leaders must groom this asset as well as the EA and build an agile skills asset that is directed toward the future.

The enterprise data asset is the information that is contained in the company's databases—and the company's ability to use that information. Our IT systems are barely transactional anymore: for

> EA is more than strategy; it is the values of the IT organization.

every piece of data that is written into the database once as the result of a transaction, we read or examine that piece of data many times over in our analytics processes. Eighty percent of users only read information rather than adding or updating it.[14] This suggests that the data make up a very valuable economic asset, oozing latent value that sometime later we may be able to harvest by extracting, analyzing, and making actionable.

The data asset does not just consist of the data—it includes the tools we make available to analysts to work with said data. It includes the information-access policies we have in place; the ability of the analysts to get at the data they need to work with. It includes the skills of the data analysts; the company's ability to articulate the questions it wants to pose to the data.

We can have debt here, as well. Data may be inaccurate or may lose referential integrity within a database. Perhaps the wrong data are collected; perhaps the right data are collected but stored in a form that is unusable or inaccessible. Perhaps, on the contrary, the data are exposed to the wrong people, creating risk.

The seated CIO is no longer sitting on a "data processing" transactional environment; he or she is sitting on an information asset whose value is large and unbounded (transactional data is useful for processing transactions; this information asset is useful for...well, who knows what?). You might say that the CIO makes good conversation at the strategy table.

The CIO is the person at the table who supports the company's strategy by creating an aligned IT vision, not by aligning individual projects. The vision is dynamic—at any moment, the EA asset includes experiments that will determine its future evolution; it grows out of itself, with guidance from IT leadership. "Architecture is a belief system," says Ralph Loura, CIO of Clorox, cited in Heller's book. "Architecture is defining what you truly believe in."[15] EA is more than strategy; it is the *values* of the IT organization.

The job of IT leaders is not to execute projects on behalf of the business; it is to steward the asset that is the total of all of the enterprise's IT capabilities—an asset that has functional capabilities (how it is used today) but also latent capabilities (how it will support future agility and how it will offer options in the future).

# BUILD VERSUS BUY

Everyone knows that in every case under the sun, in any example one can imagine, when rational human beings are making decisions, if an IT product can be acquired "off the shelf," it is better to do so than to build it. After all, building IT capabilities is expensive and risky, and custom capabilities can take a long time to get to the keyboards of users. A third-party product's vendor may have special expertise in the relevant domain, and can take advantage of the collective learning of all its customers. An off-the-shelf product can be brought in-house quickly, configured rather than coded, and launched into production in no time.

This obvious fact is neat, plausible, and in most cases, wrong. I know this will make some of my readers gag, and it certainly is hard to swallow for those of us trained in the corporate table manners of the last few decades, but please hear me out. First of all, the economics of software development have changed in a way that now favors "building" over "buying." There are now ways of custom-developing systems that preserve many of the advantages of buying off the shelf. The risk of developing a system incrementally and altering it based on user feedback is often lower than that of buying a finished product that is hard to change. The advantages of the agility that can be gained through a flexible, changeable, custom system—a smooth rather than a lumpy EA, as we put it in the last chapter—are becoming more compelling, and the disadvantages of proprietary products, always evident, are becoming harder to accept.

Although we might think otherwise, there is evidence that about 95% of code is still written in-house.[1] Why? Not only because we often recognize what I say to be the truth, but because when we buy off-the-shelf products thinking that they will reduce in-house coding, we turn out to be mistaken. Buying rather than building might even be increasing the amount of building we have to do.

We make this mistake a lot. We organize our business around a product rather than creating IT capabilities to fit our business. Or, we acquire a product that does not fit our business and customize it until it does. Even worse, sometimes we hide the lack of fit by quietly developing workarounds—workarounds that, over time, we come to think of as normal. We offer our business users a user interface that is clunky because it was designed for users in the abstract across many possible companies and usage situations, rather than being designed for the particular needs of our employees. We scope IT projects in terms of what is possible given the limitations of the COTS (consumer off-the-shelf) product with which we're working. We take on the language of the COTS product, and it comes to control our way of thinking.

Off-the-shelf systems are more expensive than we expect, and take longer to roll out. We pay for features that we don't actually use. Although they allow for configuration rather than customization, the configuration is so complicated that we might as well write custom code, or it is so limited that we have to add custom code to get the results we want.

Sometimes, we frame the purchase decision in terms of product categories that don't really apply. Not surprisingly, these are often product categories promoted by the software vendors as part of their marketing strategies. For example, just what is a case management system? Almost every company has some need that can be thought of as case management, but there are so many different types of cases and ways of managing them that an off-the-shelf system needs to be impossibly general. When you go beyond the buzz terms, a case management system is a system that does whatever the company needs to do to manage its cases. And that is different for every company.

As Martha Heller says, "All enterprise software providers have the same fundamental flaws: poor quality, a lack of innovation, and no incentive to change."[2] Eric Raymond, in his book *The Cathedral and the Bazaar*—a classic work of the open source software movement—explains why this is so. According to Raymond, our usual way of looking at the software industry is deeply flawed. "Software," he says, "is largely a service industry operating under the persistent but unfounded delusion that it is a manufacturing industry."[3]

We assume that we are buying *products* when we buy software, but we are actually buying *services*. "People have a strong tendency to assume that software has the value characteristics of a typical manufactured good,"[4] but "when a software product's vendor goes out of business (or if the product is merely discontinued), the maximum price consumers will pay for it rapidly falls to near zero...the price a consumer will pay is effectively capped by the expected future value of vendor service."[5] We keep confusing ourselves by acting as if we are dealing in products rather than ongoing activities.

> We assume that we are buying *products* when we buy software, but we are actually buying *services*.

When we compare an off-the-shelf software product to custom development, we are comparing apples to washing machines. The true costs of IT are in the integration of the product, the custom development to make it fit our processes, and the costs for the vendor's ongoing development, improvement, and fixes. Or, as Raymond puts it, by far the greatest portion of cost and effort that goes into IT systems is "use value"—the costs of making the software work and continue to work in a particular usage scenario.[6]

The problem is that incentives in this model work against a vendor's offering good service.[7] When you buy a proprietary product, you necessarily put yourself at the mercy of a supplier monopoly since there is only one possible provider of support, bug fixes, and enhancements. For Raymond, this is an argument for open source software, but it is equally an argument against buying off-the-shelf products.

As we saw in the last chapter, an IT leader's goal is to groom the EA asset to enhance its flexibility and agility. The leaner the asset is, the more flexible it will be. We don't want to carry extra baggage in our asset—it adds weight that makes it harder to roll. It presents more surface area for technical and functional debt. It has more defects.

Incorporating a proprietary product into our architecture adds weight—it surely has features we will not use, and its architecture is complicated by those excess features. It resists change—we can't even change it ourselves, but have to get the vendor to change it. Furthermore, we have to expect that the direction the vendor takes the product will, over time, diverge from our particular needs—thus requiring a transformational project that generally involves the purchase of a new off-the-shelf product. Our IT Skills Asset also becomes less flexible when we acquire an off-the-shelf product, since we will have to employ people with skills in that product.

Buying off-the-shelf is essentially another way of saying that we know all or most of our requirements in advance. It assumes that we can put together a request for proposal (RFP) or a set of evaluation criteria and then search for a product in the market that comes close to meeting those requirements. The closer it comes, the less customization is required and the more favorable the economics are. But requirements, in our Agile world, are purely hypothetical; they will evolve, and will only become known empirically.

> Buying off-the-shelf is essentially another way of saying that we know all or most of our requirements in advance.

In cases where we don't expect much change or where we understand our needs well, Raymond's argument doesn't hold—we *are* buying a product rather than services. Arguably, such is the case when we buy something like an accounting system. Our generally accepted accounting principles do not change much and are well defined. Information architectures and user interfaces have become standardized. Our requirements are essentially the body of literature that describes accounting standards and rules.

But how often do these conditions hold elsewhere? In all other cases, we are buying a vendor's promise to provide the services we need—a risky way of doing business.

At the same time, the cost of custom development is falling. More and more logic is abstracted away by frameworks and design patterns. Incremental delivery and staged investments reduce cost and risk. Virtualization reduces complex dependencies between software and hardware. Security concerns—arguably—favor custom development, which at least gives the enterprise more control over its security posture rather than putting it in the hands of a vendor, who may have other business priorities.

Software development has changed. New programming languages make it easier to build the kind of complex systems we now require. Programming languages are designed to avoid common types of defects. Scripting languages are concise and clear. REST APIs and messaging-queue standards make it easy to combine and orchestrate software services. Languages like Go are highly performant and designed to support concurrency. There are supporting APIs, platforms, frameworks, and tools that take care of much of the grunt work of development and that standardize design patterns.

In fact, custom code is almost not custom these days. A developer incorporates open source frameworks, uses standardized design patterns, and orchestrates services that are already available. That developer might release some parts of his or her work to the open source community and get support or help from others outside the company. There are "cookbooks" available with templates for deploying systems, code snippets that handle common tasks, and well-known and well-studied algorithms for solving typical problems.

Development takes place on automated pipelines that help the developer move frictionlessly and quickly from requirements to deployment. The developer uses a powerful integrated development environment (IDE) that centralizes the tools that help him or her do the job. The code is built automatically using Continuous Integration, and it is tested automatically through scripted tests. It is deployed automatically with automated deployment tools onto infrastructure that can be automatically provisioned.

These techniques, if we use them correctly, enable a fast try-and-learn cycle in which developers can produce something, get feedback, and then adjust what they have produced. As a result, the code can be developed in a user-centric way and match the enterprise's needs precisely. Changes are easy to make with automated regression tests that allow experimentation without fear. Risk is low, because the team is constantly adjusting.

Compare that to the risk of buying a vendor's product, where the investment is one large lump sum—and a commitment to future maintenance payments. Then, of course, there is the risk of the vendor going out of business or discontinuing the product. It seems strange that back in the Stone Age (yesterday) we believed that it was riskier to develop custom code.

So, today's choice is no longer really between build and buy. It is between quickly assembling best-practice frameworks with continuous user feedback and then continuing to adapt the system over time as the business changes versus buying an undefined stream of future services from a vendor who doesn't know your business and doesn't have financial incentives to support you. Text "1" to @obvious if you like the first option, or "2" to @/dev/null if you prefer the second.

There is something deep going on here. For a long time, we have lived with a model where business processes and the changes we wanted to make to them were first translated into requirements or specifications, and then those requirements were translated into code. This is odd, when you think about it—why have this additional step of requirements between the process and the code that automates it? In a contractor-control world, requirements are necessary: they are a way of telling the contractor—the geeks—what you want them to do. In a world where we wish to consider buying off the shelf, we also need to elaborate requirements. But if you think about it, code is simply a way of precisely expressing a business process, and adding a requirements step in between is like setting up that children's game of "telephone," where the message just becomes more and more garbled as it is passed along.

> Agile development is a kind of brainstorming and process improvement performed by a single team composed of users and developers, thinking in both code and conversation.

Building IT systems is about abstracting business capabilities; about finding the rules underlying business processes and competitive strategies and expressing them in code. A software developer looks at a business process—something done in the physical world by physical bodies—and turns that process into thought, then expresses that thought in code. Or, more precisely, he or she imagines a digital world that interacts with users in a sort of dance; an interaction that results in a business process being accomplished. Developing an enterprise IT system means imagining into being the IT system that will be an effective partner for the human in accomplishing the company's business. Agile development is a kind of brainstorming and process improvement performed by a single team composed of users and developers. It is thinking together—in both code and conversation.

When we think of our software as an embodiment in code of our company's ever-changing business processes, the idea of pulling a product off the shelf seems much less sensible. At best, it will be a clumsy partner.

It would have been impractical to brainstorm in code in the early days of IT. Each idea would have to be translated into CPU instructions, hardware interactions, network cables, and ASCII code pages. What has changed is that we now compute in ever-higher levels of abstraction. The raw materials of our trade, the thingies we mix and match and build from, are now closer to the concepts we combine in our thoughts. Layer upon layer of abstraction and virtualization have brought our solution domain closer to our problem domain. We can virtually think in software. Three major trends have dramatically altered the tradeoff between building and buying: *virtualization*, *abstraction*, and *scriptability*.

## Virtualization

We used to have server computers—pieces of hardware that slid into a rack. Now, most of our computing is done on virtual machines. The cloud operators who provide them presumably have some sort of hardware—maybe even those same servers that we used to slide into racks, but for all we know, it could be bits of fairy dust assembled by techno-sprites—Who cares? Who knows?—that somehow make us believe they are providing us with a server. The cloud operator gives us the things we expect a server to have—computing capability, storage, "ports" to communicate with other devices—so that we can't tell the difference between what they are giving us and an actual server.

That is the key: I can't tell the difference, because in every detail I care about, the techno-sprites have made sure that the cloud service provides what a physical server would provide. When I am using a physical server, I do not normally care about what the circuit boards look like; I don't care where the fan is located...there are lots of things that I don't care about and very few that I do care about. The genius of virtualization is that it takes those few things I do care about and provides them in a way that hides their actual implementation behind pixie dust.

It turns out that a lot of things can be virtualized. That is interesting in and of itself. It turns out that much of the infrastructure of our IT lives doesn't really matter—there are only a few salient characteristics of each thing that we rely on. Storage, for example: we tell it something, and then later we ask it what we previously told it. Anything that can do that is storage. Of course, different "storages" can have different performance characteristics— we primarily care about capacity, speed, reliability, and sometimes transience (we sometimes want to make sure that things are "forgotten" by the storage). But storage is the thing with those characteristics, not the boxy things with the whirring disk drives.

We have virtual private networks, virtual LANs, virtual switching fabrics. Through software-defined networking (SDN), we have come to intuit the very idea—or form, or essence—of switches and routers, and then implemented that essence as a tool for ourselves. As the humans in Plato's cave allegory, we were condemned to look only at the imperfect shadows of these essences on the wall of the cave until now, when we have managed to turn around despite our chains and look at the things themselves.[8]

The amazing thing about virtualization is that we can provide ever-higher layers of it in a sort of Hegelian dialectic that moves toward the true idea underlying all of the concrete "stuff" we started out with. For example, we have not just virtualized our servers—now cloud providers are virtualizing our virtualized servers by providing server-less computing capabilities (such as Amazon's Lambda). It turns out that even "virtual server"—a "device" persistent through time and maintaining its own state—is one of those incidental things that we don't really need. The important abstraction, we have learned, is "compute power" not "server," and all we really need is something that "executes" code, or allows the code to do whatever it does.

## Abstraction

Software has always involved abstraction. The critical concept is that of an API—an abstraction of the services that one piece of software is willing to provide to another. In the object-oriented programming paradigm, interfaces were separated from implementations so that dependent pieces of code should never have to be concerned with how the interface was implemented. A programmer could change that implementation as long as the code continued to provide the same interface—that is, abstraction of salient characteristics—just as the cloud provider could change from disk storage to solid-state storage or a single disk to pieces of multiple disks as long as our abstract notion of "storage" is satisfied.

Software engineers have also abstracted design patterns from their code—in some cases, vendors or the open source community have provided these design patterns out of the box. Spring Cloud provides an implementation of a circuit breaker pattern, as Spring itself provides an implementation of dependency injection. These implementations of design abstraction not only save developers time, but also allow the developer to think through problems at a higher level: "I need decorator pattern here" rather than "I need to figure out a dynamic way to add responsibilities to this object without changing its interface."

## Scriptability

IT used to be about software and hardware. Increasingly, it is just about software. This causes me joy—my background is in software development, and I can't say that I've ever felt entirely comfortable with the blinky boxes and cables with the dust that gets under your fingernails. Many of us CIOs grew up on one side or the other of this hardware/software divide, and I am proud to say that my team won.

> IT used to be about software and hardware. Increasingly, it is just about software. This causes me joy.

We used to outsource software development. Now we outsource hardware to cloud providers. It makes more sense: software takes up less space in the closet.

How did this happen? Back when—before we evolved from sludge to tadpoles to site reliability engineers and full-stack, T-shaped humans—systems administrators used to set up physical computers and do the magic stuff that configured them. Those sysadmins learned how to automate some of their manual work through scripts. Eventually, virtualization and the cloud made it possible to provision a server without touching metal. Then the scripts for configuring those servers became more sophisticated, and even included provisioning the virtual machine in the first place. Ansible, Chef,

Puppet—infrastructure scripting platforms—became available and powerful. As with many technology stories, this one ends with a buzz term: we now have *infrastructure as code*.

Well, why not? We could now *think* our infrastructure and write our thoughts down as software. It was a great use of an abstraction layer: as long as we wound up with something that had the characteristics we specified in our provisioning and deployment scripts, it didn't matter what that thing really was. An infrastructure script had all the advantages of code: we could test it, put it under version control, and guarantee that it would work the same way every time. We could treat our servers as cattle rather than pets*—every time we ran our scripts, we'd get a server that was exactly like all the others rather than a work of art created by Brent,[†] the sysadmin somewhere off in an infrastructure department cubicle.

By the way, speaking of testing—we no longer are. Tests, for the most part, have become code as well. In a Continuous Delivery environment, most of our testing is automated; simply another kind of code. As code, it is an abstraction—an abstraction, in this case, of requirements. Tests are a kind of introspection, or reflection, where the code turns on itself and asks itself whether in fact it meets the requirements. If the test passes, then it does. In the source code repository, the tests are the superego that makes sure the rest of the system behaves. Tests are the self-consciousness of code.

So, code is code; tests are code; requirements are code; infrastructure is code; build and deployment instructions are code. There is a final frontier—the network itself often still requires wiring and

---

* The expression is credited to Joshua McKenty of Pivotal Labs. The idea is that we should not get attached to our servers, as we would to a puppy, but be perfectly content if one server is killed off and an identical one replaces it.

[†] Brent is the bottleneck of bottlenecks in *The Phoenix Project* by Gene Kim, Kevin Behr, and George Spafford.

plugging in and configuring devices like switches and firewalls. This is the problem that is being solved by SDN. Once the promise of SDN is fully realized, we will be able to check our network description in to version control, include it in our build process, test it along with all the other code, and deploy it all—network included—through some more code.

Sorry, hardware folks. The seated CIO can stay seated: he doesn't have to get up and connect any cables. Software has won. The seated-at-the-table CIO is a thinker, a philosopher, and a dealer in abstractions that have been given compute power.

Ultimately, the build-versus-buy distinction is evaporating. We build our EA asset by assembling pieces that might have been developed in-house or sourced elsewhere. The chunks that we assemble need not be products—they may just as well be frameworks, components, snippets of code, or code libraries. When they are products, what matters is how they are stitched into the EA as a whole, which will include integration patterns, supplementary custom code, and an ongoing stream of services.

A product is a marketing concept—it is a set of capabilities grouped together to be saleable, an abstraction of features to which a price can be attached. In the old world, custom-developed applications were sort of like that, too: grouped sets of capabilities that were bound together as single executables. That is no longer the case. Our application is probably web-based and divided into several tiers with separate process spaces and separate server infrastructure. It is probably built from a number of web services that communicate with one another. We group these together and label them an application, even though the application is increasingly porous—those same services can be used by other applications. Our capabilities are just REST endpoints and message bus consumers—they are not really "in" any particular application—and we are implementing single sign-on so that users do not have to log in to any particular applications. So, to which application do our capabilities really belong?

We have forced our users into talking about applications, as well—it is buried deeply in their way of thinking about IT. We give our systems cute names (I used to use cartoon character names—Casper, Nemo, etc.) or we teach users to refer to the product name ("then we look them up in Salesforce"). But why should users care about system names? Why should they even care what "application" or "system" a particular capability is found in? We live in a world of hyperlinks, where people move seamlessly from one site to another with a click of the mouse.

> A product is a marketing concept—it is a set of capabilities grouped together to be saleable, an abstraction of features to which a price can be attached.

Yet this idea of grouping capabilities into systems or products or applications persists. One reason for this is that we continue to think of the capabilities as something we have to make build-or-buy decisions on. If we can buy the capabilities, then they make up a product in the vendor's eyes and an application to us, organized and bounded based on the vendor's marketing approach. Or perhaps we talk about applications to satisfy the template zombies, who have organized their change control and security processes around applications. Or for the finance folks, who need to identify an asset and capitalize it. The one thing I'm sure of is that this notion of an application is getting farther and farther away from the actual architecture of our capabilities.

A seated CIO presides over an architecture of resources, tiny building blocks that can be composed into different Lego-like constructions, and the units we used to deal in—applications or systems—are no longer meaningful. This is good: in the Agile world, we want to work in small units.

We know that our EA asset is our company's strategy and capabilities writ in software. Buying a COTS product is essentially taking a part of someone else's essay—on a related but not identical topic—and copy/pasting it into your essay. It is unlikely to fit—both in terms of style and content—and you are going to have to pay for the rights to use it as well. You won't be allowed to make changes to it yourself. If you are doing lots of this copying and pasting, we have to ask whether you really have a sustainable company—how is it possible that your thoughts are expressed so well in everyone else's essays?

It comes as a surprise to those of us who grew up in the IT world of the last century to find that software is cheap. But think about it. I, as a software developer, can produce product that is essentially just my thoughts brought to digital life. I sit down at a keyboard and code flows out of my thoughts and onto the screen. Each character I type costs nothing.*

Compare that to hardware and other physical products. After I have the ideas that define the product, I still have to set up a factory, buy materials, and ship stuff around. The total cost is the cost

---

* By the way, did you know that a memory location that stores a one weighs slightly more than one that is holding a zero? The more ones there are in your binary code, the heavier your computer is? So, perhaps there is additional shipping cost from that weight increasing as you type?[9]

9of my ideas plus all that other stuff. One of the joys of developing software is that you can start with nothing and make things purely with your ideas.

Perhaps more importantly, you can *change* things at no cost other than the cost of your thoughts. In a world of change, physical products are strange artifacts: The words of a book stay the same every time you pick it up. Okay, it collects more dust, and your furniture wears out and the upholstery develops tears and coffee stains. But that sort of change is only about entropy: it is not the result of deliberate introduction of new ideas that address changed circumstances. Wine can age and improve, but a cabernet cannot easily be changed into a chardonnay when your tastes change. But code is infinitely pliable. Add a few modules to an accounting package and it might help send a rocket to the moon. The difference between World of Warcraft and a piece of software to automate actual warfighting is just some differences in their bits. Switch some ones and zeros and Facebook becomes Oracle.

We used to think of the enterprise as something that ran independently of its software; we could build or buy IT products to improve or supplement the business's processes. But now, our approach to IT needs to be inverted: IT is the business, or runs the business, rather than being a set of tools that we can buy off the shelf like a typewriter.

In a world where IT capabilities were delivered as a single "product" at the end of a project, a "product" that then only required a bit of maintenance now and then, the economics of IT delivery often favored buying a product off the shelf. But when we view IT capabilities as being in a continuous state of transformation, when we see them as tightly integrated into an EA, and when we realize that the costs and risks of custom development have been radically reduced, the economics often now favor custom development.

# GOVERNANCE
# AND OVERSIGHT

I have to admit we are mired in the most exquisite mysterious muck. This muck heaves and palpitates. It is multi-directional and has a mayor.

—**Donald Barthelme**, *City Life*

A thinker sees his own actions as experiments and questions—as attempts to find out something. Success and failure are for him answers above all.

—**Friedrich Nietzsche**, *The Gay Science*

*G*overnance is the process by which IT is excused from playing a strategic role in the enterprise. Through governance, IT becomes *aligned* with business strategy by applying a decision strategy to select among various investments proposed to it by other parts of the business. This decision strategy may consist of deferring the decision to a steering committee drawn from the business, or it might involve applying objective decision criteria based on the company's priorities. Either way, IT leaders are excused from actually making the decisions that drive strategy.

In an environment where IT has a limited capacity and the company's needs for IT are insatiable, governance provides a way to say no to proposed projects, absolving IT leaders from having to take personal responsibility for such decisions. And yet, while sidestepping this critical responsibility, IT clamors for its seat at the table.

Our governance approach often separates concerns that, in reality, are part of a continuum. The *governance* decision is a decision about how to apply the firm's investment dollars, and this generally means investing in a portfolio of projects. *Oversight* and *management* are concerned with a project once it is underway, with management primarily focusing on making the project successful and with oversight terminating projects that are not. *Budgets* are annual plans that focus on spending by categories, and usually on "keeping the lights on" costs rather than investments. All of these have to do with optimizing the use of the firm's scarce resources—money and people, primarily—and in the Agile world, it becomes harder to tell these things apart.

On the other hand, our governance processes often mix together concepts that are quite distinct. First is the idea of an *investment*; an allocation of resources to develop an asset. The second is the idea of a *project*, or a program; a set of work tasks with a beginning and an end. The third is the idea of a *system* or *product*; a collection of capabilities that we group together for convenience and which, in theory, is the asset we are creating by the investment. The fourth is the idea of a *business case*, or business goal, that we are choosing to fund.

We govern by allocating resources to a thingamabob that is a mishmash of these four things. We fund an investment to create an asset that is a system or application, by means of a project, based on a business case whose goal we want to accomplish. In this soup, we blend many of the topics I have discussed in previous chapters, so here we will bring together the mirepoix and savories we have accumulated up to this point, and stir vigorously. To wit:

- A project includes a bunch of activities. Usually a big bunch. Are we making our governance decisions at the right level of granularity? Big clumps of requirements are not Lean—they will lead to long cycle times and get caught in your teeth. Are they all equally important?

- Will the bunch of planned activities actually lead to the business outcomes as stated in the business case? Even if this is a brand new recipe? How certain are we (if we are honest with ourselves)?

- Why is a *system*, or an *application*, or an *executable* the right asset to associate with our investment? Today, we architect systems as a bouillabaisse of loosely coupled microservices. Is there some product-like system—the asset—that will be "finished" at the same time as the project, or indeed at any time during the project?

- How can we attend to "optimizing the whole" when we are funding individual projects based on individual business cases? When we approve a business case because it has a good ROI, how do we know that an alternative business case couldn't be created that would have an even better ROI? What if there are synergies or discrepancies between projects? Do we really want pickles and jelly beans in the same soup? Are there too many proverbial cooks stirring the ROI?

In our Agile way of looking at the world, what we really want is to fund the outcomes we desire, while understanding that there is real uncertainty in our ability to achieve them. We want to approve the smallest experiment that will let us test the business case and our approach to achieving it, and then revisit the proposed investment. We want to make decisions at the finest practical level of granularity so that we can continue to make priority trade-offs and decide at the last responsible moment whether to fund each feature. And we would like to maximize and make good use of our learnings. In this chapter, I will try to show how we can do all of this.

Governance decisions are a big deal in IT circles. I think this is because (1) we (mistakenly) organize IT investment decisions into initiatives and projects that are large, expensive, and risky; (2) IT is relatively scary to the rest of the business, and a governance process is one way the business tries to feel in control; and (3) IT investments are so central to corporate initiatives that it is hard to make any other investment decisions without first making IT decisions. This last point is interesting, right? Perhaps it suggests that IT governance decisions should be made together with or in advance of other business governance decisions. Instead, in our traditional model, we think first about "business" decisions, and then try to "align" the IT decisions with them. But in our digital world—if we are truly committed to the idea that that's the world we live in—IT should not follow business decisions but drive them.

> The governance process is a filter through which proposed ideas can be dripped, with only the purest flavoring the waters of execution.

Here's Hunter and Westerman's traditional view of governance:

> The basics of the [governance] process involve project sponsors (1) developing a formal proposal that incorporates estimated benefits, risks, and resource requirements and (2) submitting the proposal to decision makers who select preferred investments from the proposals…the first question to be answered in assessing a proposed initiative is this: exactly how, and how much, will the investment affect and improve business performance?[1]

In a transparent investment process, opportunities meet a well-defined prioritization process designed to identify winning proposals.[2]

The governance process is a filter through which proposed ideas can be dripped, with only the purest flavoring the waters of execution. Or, closer to Hunter and Westerman's description, I imagine a sort of Star Chamber*—a dimly lit group of serious, hooded faces ("decision makers") seated around a table, passing judgment on each "formal proposal" presented to them.

Notice how passive this approach is. The decision makers play golf or shuffle papers on their desks until they receive a "formal" proposal—and then they render a judgment and return to shuffling papers. Can this really result in investments that are aligned with corporate strategy? What if none of the proposals they receive happen to touch on an important aspect of the strategy? How do we know that the particular set of proposals offered is the *best* set of proposals to advance the company's strategy? Shouldn't governance start from what the company is trying to accomplish, and then *produce* investment themes that support those goals?

Notice how judgmental the process is. It feels funny to me. We want the creative minds in the company to come up with good ideas, and then we make them do a bunch of work to document those proposals "formally." Then we tell them "no." It's got the feel of a reality TV show—*American Idol*, *The Apprentice*, or maybe *Survivor*—we had to vote one of the proposals off the island, and I'm sorry, kid, but it's

---

* I had to look up "Star Chamber"—it was one of those terms I vaguely knew of and that felt like it applied here. It turns out that the Star Chamber was a British court from around 1487 to 1641, which became known for its arbitrary and subjective judgments, as well as its secrecy.

yours. Perhaps it's the use of the term "winning proposals" in Hunter and Westerman's description that irks me.

"Star Chamber" has the right eerie feel to it, but maybe this is more like a king and his court, allowing subjects to come and petition him for—whatever people petition kings for. Then the king, I don't know, decides to chop the subject's head off, or rules that the subject can chop his neighbor's head off, or whatever it is kings rule on. Project sponsors are already in an abject position when they propose a project and beg for funding, and the dynamic is not likely to improve when they later report to the king that they are behind schedule. Off with his head! It just doesn't seem motivating to me.

That last piece of Hunter and Westerman's quote gets me every time. *Exactly* how and how much will the investment improve the business's performance? Are they serious? Do we know *exactly* how many consumers would buy our new product? *Exactly* what price they would pay? *Exactly* how much it would cost us to design and produce it? Will our competitors launch a competing product? Will our market be wiped out in a dramatic fireball from space, or will the Four Horsemen ride in just as we start our TV commercial campaign?

I will turn off my sarcasm engine for a moment. Look—it turns out that the future involves lots of uncertainty. No one knows *exactly* what the benefit of an investment will be—no one even knows *approximately* what it will be—in fact, I doubt that anyone could agree exactly on what they even *mean* by "benefit" and how they would measure it. Yeesh. What a basis for making such important decisions!

Even Hunter and Westerman agree that it is not easy. "That means understanding what matters most to the business. In many organizations, that's a nontrivial task."[3] Nontrivial, indeed—I wrote an entire book about that subject.

The Star Chamber approach, I believe, is based on an assumption that there is a common currency of business value that can be used to compare benefits across different types of proposals. That, of course, turns out to be harder than it sounds. We may have in mind some common measure like ROI, or NPV, or shareholder value added. But these are problematic measures when making investment trade-off decisions.

For example, suppose the IT organization notices a need to invest in grooming the EA asset—perhaps it needs some security enhancements or some polishing of the asset to enhance agility. IT, we are told, should create one of those Star Chamber proposals, making clear the business value of the initiative in terms such as ROI. When the initiative doesn't get funded, it is easy for us to blame the IT folks' inability to express their ideas in business terms.

A better explanation might be that there is no good way to express their ideas in business terms—at least, not a way that will allow the Star Chamber to compare them to functional enhancements. How much value does a new firewall have? Well…let's see…the cost of a typical hacker event is X dollars, and it is Y% less likely if we have the firewall. Really? How do we know that it will be the firewall that will block the next intrusion rather than one of our other security controls? How do we know how likely it is that the hackers will be targeting us? For how long will the firewall protect us? Will the value of our assets—that is, the cost of the potential hack—remain steady over time? Or will we have more valuable assets later?

The number of assumptions we have to make to arrive at a business value here is daunting, and the decision makers will have little basis for evaluating how reasonable those assumptions are. When these initiatives don't get funded, guess what happens? Surprise! A periodic need to do transformational or modernization projects.

Once the project has been funded, IT leadership must *oversee* it to ensure its success. Hunter and Westerman explain:

> This is the role of a well-structured software development life cycle (SDLC) methodology, which specifies, for an initiative of a given type, what must be done, by whom, in what order, and with what expected outcomes and deliverables.[4]

> As the project reaches each gate in a series, the project is reviewed with sponsors, the project team, and the project management office for progress against goals and key risks. Each gate calls for a go-no go decision for the next stage of activity and funding.[5]

The output of the governance process is a scope and a plan; the project then proceeds through a well-defined series of execution steps that can be measured against that plan. Governance is separate from oversight (though, confusingly, the term "governance" is often used for both)—the former makes the strategic investment decision and the latter ensures that the decision is adhered to. It fits nicely into the contractor-control model, since the IT organization can now be held responsible for delivering on the approved investment decision and must oversee the project based on the plan it has committed to.

The project follows a well-defined, templated process (the SDLC), which is arranged as a series of phases, each of which ends with a "gate"—that is, a decision on whether the project is to be allowed to continue to the next phase. The rigorously enforced structure of the SDLC and the chance for the program to be halted at the gates appear to establish control over the delivery process, and as I've said, *control* has been the central concern of IT for a long time. The phase milestones also offer a simple way to gauge the project's progress. The project's status can be "green" (successfully hitting milestones), "yellow" (at risk of missing a milestone), or "red" (missing milestones). If the status is yellow, overseers ask the project manager to explain how he or she will get the project back on track. If the project becomes "red," then they demand corrective action—a remediation plan.

Now, the project team has to propose a plan that "gets them back to green," and the overseers feel satisfied that they've done their difficult duty. In some cases, the project team can take action that will get them back on schedule—but only by increasing risk. They can rush through development, increasing the likelihood that defects will be discovered later. They can add to the size of the team, increasing the risk that untrained people unfamiliar with the project will actually slow them down.[†] They might take shortcuts, reduce documentation, or try a riskier architectural approach. They might incur technical debt.

The project team has to produce a plan—after all, it is *accountable* for keeping the project on schedule. Accountability in this context is another way of saying blameability—overseers control the project by threatening blame. But if a project is behind schedule, is it clear that the project team is at fault? In our highly interconnected enterprise, there are many other possible explanations for delays. The estimates might have been too low. The team might have encountered obstacles outside its control. The users might have added scope.

Remember that these are the same project executors that we chose to execute the project—presumably because we believed we could trust them to make good decisions. They were probably trained, or at least hired, by the enterprise to make sure they had

---

[†] In *The Mythical Man-Month*, Fred Brooks argues that adding people to a project that is already behind schedule makes it slip even further behind schedule. This principle has become known as Brooks' Law. There is some evidence that with a well-executed DevOps process, Brooks' Law no longer holds.

the right skills. So when the project is off schedule, is it natural to first suspect those project executors?

These Waterfall governance and oversight practices are not only inconsistent with Agile principles, but also fail to take advantage of the power of the Agile way of working. By proceeding with agility, we can reduce the risk of our governance decisions—once we admit that there is substantial risk in making decisions in an uncertain world, the subject of the next chapter—by quickly deploying functionality, learning, and adjusting plans. We can conduct experiments that test the assumptions in our business cases. We can reduce the overhead of our governance processes and make smaller, incremental decisions with correspondingly lower risk. Lastly and critically, we can encourage the teams that create value for the company rather than standing in judgment of them.

Before we dive into an Agile governance and oversight model, let's think about what characteristics such a model should have in order to both take advantage of the Agile mindset and remain consistent with it.

First, the investment decision and the oversight process would form a seamless continuum wherein the execution of the initiative would yield valuable information by which the governance decision could be adjusted. We would manage risk by only committing resources to the smallest piece of work that would give us such useful learning.

Second, we would gauge progress by seeing operational results. Agile and Lean approaches allow teams to quickly put product in the hands of users. This not only delivers value immediately, but also lets us validate the features that have been deployed.

Third, we would carefully set boundaries for planning. A detailed plan is a less effective basis for governance than validated learning based on actual delivery. The more advance planning we do, the longer it takes to get a product to market; the longer it takes to get a product to market, the more risk we assume.

Fourth, our governance decisions would not be based on a set of required requirements, but instead on high-level objectives. Instead of telling the project team how to do its job, we might begin the project with a hypothesis of what will best accomplish the objectives, but then allow requirements to change. Based on what we learned, we would re-validate these hypotheses.

Fifth, we would have a transparent, trusted process for turning business objectives into product parameters. In place of a fixed set of requirements, we would review the team's process by which they will make requirement decisions and decide whether we trust the people who will manage that process.

Sixth, we would focus on optimizing *the whole*—that is, the whole of our IT capability. Are the assets we are building—the EA asset, people asset, and data asset—as valuable as they can be? Is the architecture flexible in the ways that we care about? Is it scalable, resilient, performant, secure? Will it help reduce the cost of developing capabilities likely to be needed in the future?

Needless to say, the Waterfall governance process described by Hunter and Westerman does not match up well with these characteristics. It sacrifices feedback cycles for pre-defined requirements, staged investments for upfront "go or no-go" decisions, learning for pre-planning, and fast delivery of value for detailed analysis and "first time right" delivery.

In a Waterfall model, it was logical to make investment decisions at the project level, since that was the granularity at which we implemented those decisions. We funded a pre-defined scope of work, then delivered that scope at the end of the project as an FOC. Once the go-ahead was given, the project would continue until it accomplished its full scope or was canceled.

But there are economic costs to governing at the project level. For one thing, by the time we bring the project into the governance process, we have already spent considerable effort trying to plan it—eliciting, accumulating, and organizing requirements. Grouping our requirements into large projects conflicts with the Lean practice of reducing batch size. The larger the batch of requirements—that is, the larger the scope of our project—the more waste we will have in our delivery process and the lower our throughput will be.

Everything changes when we move to a DevOps model. We can—in theory—work at the level of individual features, achieving the Lean ideal of "single-piece flow." We can include or exclude individual features from the investment and deploy each feature individually as soon as it is ready. Our unit of practice becomes, rather than the *project*, the *capability* or the *feature* (I won't distinguish), which a full-stack engineering team can quickly drive from concept to production. But our governance model has remained the same, based as it is on projects and coarse granularity investments.

> We cannot govern at the granularity of the individual capability if governance means convening a Star Chamber and asking for a show of hands.

Of course, we cannot govern at the granularity of the individual capability if governance means convening a Star Chamber and asking for a show of hands or a nod of hooded heads.

However, governance decisions are already being made at a granular level, whether explicitly or not—a product owner, perhaps, is making the feature-prioritization decisions; a tech lead might be making the architectural decisions. Can we—somehow—explicitly push some of the decisions we used to think of as Star Chamber decisions down to the teams themselves? Can we find a way to make high-level investment funding decisions at high levels and lower-level funding decisions at lower levels, and keep the two consistent?

I believe that we can, and in the process, satisfy the criteria I have listed above.

Over the last few years, I have been experimenting with different ways to provide an Agile environment in which my teams can work, and at the same time satisfy the heavy demands of US federal government oversight. In speaking to the government officials responsible for overseeing our IT programs—our very own Star Chamber—I frequently heard them say things like, "I want you to tell me what you are going to do and when you are going to finish, then I want you to tell me your status and what is left to do. I want to know exactly what I will get for my money and when." My team would respond by producing its Agile interpretation of what the overseers were asking for. That might include lists of user stories, burndowns, definitions of done, product roadmaps, and, well, in the government, about 100 different piles of paper. Now, I believe that this was a dead end: it was a Waterfall solution to the problem.

Yet in a sense, the overseers were right to demand what they did—they were effectively the customers of our Agile governance process, and we had to find a way to satisfy them as customers. In turn, they needed to turn around and satisfy their stakeholders—

generally Congress, inspectors general, the media, and the public. So we decided to develop an Agile oversight process incrementally, "piloting" an oversight rubric, getting feedback from the overseers, and refining it. We wound up with a formal process that seems to satisfy their needs and yet also lays claim to being Agile. Since we did this in the most challenging of environments, I believe the ideas are quite sound and widely applicable.

What we realized is that the key requirement—that we tell the overseers exactly what we were planning to do and what we'd accomplished so far—could be satisfied in several different ways. We had responded by giving the overseers plans and requirements, but the overseers never really read all of the requirements and planning documents because that was more detail than they really needed. Their decisions were not really based on the planning documents—they wanted to see those details only so that they could have confidence that the team knew what it was doing and was putting appropriate thought into the project. For that purpose, the more documentation the better—it was a demonstration of how much thought was going into the project.

But when it came to making the governance decision, what the Star Chamber really cared about was whether they believed the money would be well spent, and spent on an initiative that was important to the agency. Business case is not really decided by requirements—it is decided by the project's intended outcomes and intended spending, and by whether they believe the team is capable. Nothing else seemed relevant. What we really had to show the Star Chamber was (1) that the desired outcome represented a critical goal for the agency, (2) that the outcome justified the spending that was proposed, (3) that the team was capable, and (4) that the Star Chamber would frequently be consulted and would be able to influence the team's actions, including changing or eliminating the budget.

None of those four things involves requirements, demands documents, or grants Gantt charts any special importance.

Just as in any Agile initiative, we would try to create the best solution to meet the actual business objective—in this case, the objectives of the Star Chamber.

The governance and oversight process we created continues from where I left off in chapter 5, in the discussion of requirements. In that chapter, I showed how teams could begin from a set of desired outcomes and use techniques such as impact mapping to generate activities that would produce those outcomes in a way that accommodates learning. Impact mapping encourages us to visualize a change that we desire—a future state of the company in which our outcome has been realized—and then brainstorm ways to get there, each of which can be explored as a hypothesis, validated and pursued.

We began one of our IT programs[††] with a set of four objectives, all related to a demand from one of our customers who is always right—Congress—that we dramatically increase the number of customers we could serve. One of the four objectives was that our case processors be able to process many more cases per day than the 70 they could currently do on average. Another was that customers signing up for our service be less likely to abandon their applications partway through, a metric that was hovering disturbingly in the 40 percents. A third was that a larger percentage of our cases be processed by our automated system so that the human-case processing was less necessary. And a final goal—please note this—was that the system used for processing

---

[††] I apologize for this, but I am going to have to keep this description vague and change some of the details, because it is internal government business.

cases be able to scale to meet a much higher volume of cases. In other words, there was a technical goal that was given equal weight to the functional goals; the consequence of a CIO seated at the table.

Those four outcomes—or impacts, or behavior changes, or "to be" capabilities—supported by our EA were the core of what we continued to call a "program." I would have preferred the term "investment theme," perhaps, which suggests a group of related investment initiatives, but our customer was also particular about this. Based on a judgment of the value of the initiative and the funds available, we (leadership) decided that a tentative budget of about $20 million per year for three years was about right for this effort.

A few quick things to point out. For each of the four outcomes, we did not know how much we would be able to move the metric. At this point, there was no concrete evidence that would let us estimate it. Any targets we put into the business plan would have been fictions, and we were willing to admit to our uncertainty. However, compensating for this uncertainty was the fact that the budget was set at "approximately" $20 million dollars per year. The budget would be adjusted based on what we learned about the achievable outcomes.

Now, the first governance and oversight step. We presented to Our Very Own Star Chamber the proposed outcomes and budget, some justifications of why we believed it was plausible, and just enough description of the execution team and its process to convince the Star Chamber that the team was capable. Then, we did something unprecedented in formal government oversight—we had a discussion. The Star Chamber had the chance to give feedback, steer the program in different directions, and ask that the budget be changed. It was a full participant, not just a passive judge of proposals. We agreed to give Our Very Own Star Chamber a monthly one-page summary of the program's status (more on that later) and appear quarterly for a more detailed discussion. At any time, they could call us in if they saw something alarming in the monthly update. With that, the program was approved to begin.

Now the focus shifted to oversight at my level, and, as with many of our Agile programs, we set up a regular cadence for reviews. Every two weeks, we would have a quick meeting between the program team, me, and the business unit leader who was my peer. The main purpose of these meetings was to laugh a lot, make fun of the Star Chamber's serious facial expressions, and enjoy the successes we were having—in other words, an opportunity for, um, "vigorous discussion." Every quarter, I would do something I called a release cycle review, and then we would go back to the Star Chamber for an update discussion.

Perhaps you are not impressed by how agile this was, but it was replacing a governance process that involved 100 documents and 13 gate reviews. No matter; give me a few more paragraphs to explain how each of these steps worked.

For the second piece of magic, we passed the program objectives and budgets to the teams that would be responsible for them. The teams were not given sets of requirements, or plans with milestones, or magic potions. Rather, it was up to each team to figure out the appropriate set of requirements. The teams were simply handed a business problem.

We handed one of the objectives to a product owner, Bill, and two Scrum teams. This is a verbatim account of our discussion. "Bill," we said with an appropriately stern expression on our collective face, "you are a very experienced case processor. Can you find a way to get the number of cases per day to be significantly higher than 70?" He said it would be no problem. So we made this deal with him:

- Bill, here are some Agile development teams you can work with.

- Work with them to increase the number of cases per day from 70 to a much higher number.
- We trust you and the teams to figure out the best ways to increase that number. You can make up whatever requirements you want. Communicate them among yourselves however you want—through discussion, in writing, or with smoke signals.
- For every additional case per day you can achieve beyond 70, you will get a gold star. (Hey Bill, we are the government, you know. We can't just give you bonuses or buy you rounds of drinks.)
- We suggest that you prioritize your work based on whatever will have the greatest impact on that number, because at some point we will take the teams away, and then you won't be able to earn any more gold stars.
- Bill, if you waste any time on things that won't increase the number of cases per day, then we will take you outside and shoot you (mean-looking facial expression).
- You will have our support; let us know what impediments we can remove.
- Every two weeks, you can come back and see us to brag about what you've accomplished. You tell us how high you've gotten the number and more or less what you are thinking of doing over the next two weeks. We'll present you your gold stars and any further direction we have.

Then we went back to doing our senior leadership things and Bill took a deep breath and cleared a space on his wall for gold stars.

As we usually do, we began Bill's initiative with an impact mapping exercise. We assembled Bill and his teams, a few subject matter experts, the executive sponsor, and me to brainstorm ideas that might help increase the number of cases per day—our desired impact. As part of the exercise, for each branch of the impact map, we asked the participants to take a wild guess at the number of additional cases per day they thought we would gain by pursuing that branch. With a bit of discussion, the group arrived at a consensus wild guess for each branch. That consensus guess was our hypothesis: we think that if we build this capability, it will produce that outcome. By conducting this exercise together, we were able to get a shared understanding of the problem space and the proposed solution space.

We repeated the exercise with the other impact owners and teams, and then, with these impact maps in hand, including the impact guesses, we created a roadmap for the entire initiative, prioritizing the capabilities with the highest projected impacts and juggling to fit within the budget. Bill then started to turn the first few capabilities of the impact map into user stories. But we agreed that the roadmap and the stories were only tentative. Bill had the authority to change the roadmap and make whatever user stories he wanted at any time, as long as he made sure he was earning gold stars.

Because Bill's teams were using a Continuous Delivery technique, they began to show results right away. As the first features were released to production, we began to see the number of cases per day increase. If it had not increased—well, that simply would have told us that the hypothesis we were starting with might not have been correct, and we would have stopped working on that branch of the map and moved on to the next one. This was Bill's job to manage.

Every two weeks, we had our brief review with Bill, where Bill told us what the team had been doing. It was not a big surprise, because I sometimes stop in on sprint reviews to see what is going on. We congratulated Bill on his success and talked about what the team had learned and about what it was thinking of doing in the next couple of weeks. We asked if there were any impediments we could remove.

If results were not good, we would ask Bill how he was planning to change direction, but this has yet to happen. I know it feels like we are missing something—perhaps we should be a little harsher and exercise our oversight responsibilities better by finding something to berate Bill for. But the truth is that, if something was going wrong, we would all be implicated in it—after all, Bill has done exactly what we asked, given us full transparency, and incorporated our feedback.

I still have my quarterly formal release cycle reviews of this and other initiatives, followed by my quarterly check-in with Our Very Own Star Chamber. I will just describe my review here, since I have convinced the Star Chamber to use my method for conducting their review, as well.

In my review, I want to gauge two things: how successful the initiative has been, and how good its plans for the future are. There is nothing else that matters to me. Based on my review of these two things, I can make or suggest adjustments.

To gauge the success of the project to date, I need to know only two things from Bill. The first is what the initiative has delivered so far. Delivery refers only to finished, deployed capabilities that are being used by the business, and I am especially interested in any measures of the delivered value of those capabilities. To show me what the initiative has delivered so far, the team prepares a *Value Delivery Register*—a high-level summary of the value that has been delivered.

The second thing I want to know is how much we have spent so far. Spending in this case is measured in dollars, or in time, or in whatever other metric is most appropriate (what we are typically looking for is opportunity cost). For Bill's initiative, the costs are simply the amount of time the Agile teams have spent so far. We use a simple, one-page document we call the *Financial Summary* for this purpose.

By comparing these two things—value delivered versus opportunity cost—*Value Delivery Register* versus *Financial Summary*—I know how successful the initiative has been or how healthy a project is.

To gauge the plans for the future, I again need to know two things. I need to know, as of now, to the best of the team's knowledge, what value it thinks it will deliver in the future—its *roadmap*—more detailed for the near future and more coarse-grained and tentative for the long term. Then I need to know what its high-level *budget* is for that future work. By comparing these two things—*roadmap* and *budget*—I can decide whether the business case for the investment is still attractive. Often, the plan for the future is to continue exploring the ideas originally brainstormed in the impact map. That makes it easy.

I referred to budget rather than planned spending or estimated cost—a deliberate choice of wording. With an Agile approach, I expect to hold the budget fixed, and allow the scope to vary in order to stay within that budget. The projection of future costs is based on a budget we have agreed upon, not on an estimate of the cost of the remaining scope.

I add one small extra. It is important not just how much value the team has delivered, but also whether that value relates to the original charter of the team or the initial outcomes they were charged with delivering. So when the team is reporting on the value delivered, I ask that they frame it in terms of the outcomes we agreed on, and when they are describing the roadmap, I ask that they explain it in terms of outcomes planned.

What decisions can I make at these reviews? I can decide that the initiative has already generated enough value and its resources are best re-deployed elsewhere. I can decide that I need to make changes in the team, perhaps adding skills that are missing. I can take Bill outside and shoot him to set an example. I can remove impediments the team is facing or coach them on how to remove the impediments themselves. I can adjust the budget. I can ask the team hard questions. I can dispute the roadmap. Really, I can make whatever adjustments I need to as a leader.

If the initiative is delivering frequently, if the team is learning, and if the team is testing whether the features are delivering the expected outcomes and making adjustments accordingly, then the initiative is on track and will be successful. If the team is doing all of this and the outcomes do not follow, that simply means that the work was successful in testing the hypothesis and finding that it was not valid—so investment may be stopped and no money wasted. You probably expected me to say "no *further* money is wasted," but that would be falling into the trap of thinking that learning has no value.

The review gives me, and then Our Very Own Star Chamber, the chance to cancel the initiative if necessary. But failing projects should never be terminated; only successful ones. A failing initiative implies that there is an important business goal that is as yet unfulfilled; the decision to cancel the initiative is a decision to leave the goal unmet. Instead of canceling it, my responsibility is to improve it in order to make sure it does achieve the business's goals.

> Failing projects should never be terminated; only successful ones.

On the other hand, a successful project is a good candidate for termination. A successful project, in the world of Continuous Delivery, is one that has been delivering new capabilities frequently, starting with the most valuable and moving to less and less valuable capabilities. If that is the situation, then the business case for each incremental capability is becoming less and less compelling, and at some point, other initiatives are likely to become more valuable. I can save the business the rest of its intended investment and instead direct it toward the next important objective.

In a review of Bill's case processing initiative, the team showed me a graph of how the number of cases per day had been increasing over time. I could see that it was still on a steep upslope—a convincing reason to continue investing. For another outcome we were monitoring, the abandonment rate of applications, we saw that the team had made a sharp 25% difference with its first set of changes, but since then had tried a few other ideas with little change in the metric. We redirected the teams working on that objective to another.

This oversight approach is simple and powerful. Requiring only four short documents, it nevertheless gives all stakeholders good insight into the status of the initiative. It serves as an extension of the governance process to reduce risk and maximize the return of the investment. It allows me to have control—or at least influence—over the direction of the initiative. It is based on a positive, supportive approach—what I most want to hear about are successes to date and good ideas for the future. It encourages conversation about impediments and lets the team coordinate with other teams and with enterprise initiatives.

It is also a logical extension of the continuous feedback and learning principles that underlie all Lean and Agile practices. Automated tests give developers fast feedback on whether their code works. Static code analysis gives developers fast feedback on whether it conforms to standards. Continuous integration quickly lets the developer know if he or she has created merge conflicts with another developer's changes. Daily standups and burndown charts give the team rapid feedback on whether it will finish the work of the sprint on time. Sprint reviews provide frequent feedback from stakeholders. And my two-week and quarterly reviews give the team feedback from management. There is magic here: all of these types of feedback increase the velocity of development without anyone working any faster!

An IT leader coming from a Waterfall environment will undoubtedly have worries about the approach I have described. Here are a few questions I have received when presenting these ideas at conferences:

1. How can we manage to a budget if we are constantly changing our requirements and priorities?
2. How can we hold people accountable? Clearly, no matter what the development model, sometimes people don't perform well. How can we know when this is happening and take action on it?
3. What is to stop the project teams from constantly de-scoping and only delivering a fraction of what they were supposed to deliver?
4. How can we maintain a sense of urgency with no deadlines and therefore no schedule pressure?

Let's address each of these concerns.

## Budgets

How can we control spending in an Agile initiative if we admit from the outset that we don't really know how long things take, and if we plan to constantly make changes as we proceed?

If budget adherence is important to you, then the only option available to you is the Agile approach. When a Waterfall project reaches the end of its planned timeframe and budget and is running behind schedule, its only choice is to continue and go over budget. The business need is still there, funds have already been sunk, and there is no useful product yet. Of course, we can abandon the sunk costs and just cancel the project, but if the business need is real, then we will still have to start a new project.

Because an Agile project begins delivering valuable capabilities long before the budget is exhausted and delivers them in prioritized order, we can stop work when the budget runs out and know that the money was well spent. In addition, because we are always transparent about schedule, we know all along how the project is really doing, and we can make adjustments as we go in order to make the most of the remaining budget. You could even say that the Agile approach simply is the disciplined approach of working within a budget. A department of a company, when it is given a budget lower than it requests, must make difficult decisions about what not to do. Similarly, an Agile team working within a timebox must make hard decisions about which features not to implement.

## Accountability

In the Waterfall, we could at least hold teams accountable for delivering on time; without our schedule milestones, it seems like the team is free to slack off, right? What if I suspect that the team could be delivering better value for the money? How can I distinguish between unavoidable delays and slowness that results from an unproductive team? What if the team is at an impasse, or if for some reason I don't believe that they will be able to accomplish what they are trying to accomplish?

The critical question that I must ask as an overseer is this: "What do I need to do to help the team get me better value for my money?" When the team cannot accomplish objectives, I am forced to conclude that they cannot do it *within the given constraints*. The team might need members with different skills. It might need permission to try an experiment. It might need the help of another part of the organization. It might need a policy to be waived. But if the task is possible and the team cannot achieve it, then there is a constraining factor. My job is to remove it.

What if someone on the team is really just not performing? Perhaps not putting in his or her share of effort, or being careless, or uncooperative? Well, then, dealing with the problem is simply another example of removing an impediment for the team. All of the tools of the manager come into play here as usual—counseling, training, or removing the problem employee. But note that I can't judge employee performance by whether or not the team hits pre-planned milestones. I have to use other sources of information to determine that there is a problem.

That is to say that an Agile manager is a servant-leader. Once he or she has set the vision, the people who know best how to make it successful are the project team—they are closest to the action. His or her job is to find out what is holding them back and remove the obstacles. Think of it this way: the people who add value to the business are the creators; the people delivering the IT capabilities. The developers, testers, designers, infrastructure engineers. Everyone else is waste. Management is waste. Leadership is waste. Only the project team accomplishes the project's goals. Everyone else is administrative overhead.

> Your job as a leader is to find out what you can do to help, and do it.

You can stop being waste by contributing to the development effort. Your job as a leader is to find out what you can do to help, and do it.

# De-Scoping

The principles of Agile and Lean thinking require that we *not* do things. "Maximize the amount of work not done," says the Agile gnome.[§] "Don't build faster, build less," Jeff Patton says.[6] This sounds lazy, like the team is getting away with something. "Yes, they hit their schedule milestones, but they did it by not doing the work!" In practice, it is actually a very good way to adjust the project so that it finishes on time. The idea, of course, is to eliminate requirements that aren't really needed or that aren't badly needed.

There's a great irony in the fact that this makes people uncomfortable. The same people probably fight hard against scope creep. But scope reduction is the opposite of scope creep—for the same reason that scope creep is considered undesirable, scope reduction should be considered desirable. Very desirable, because it leads to a lower maintenance burden later on, and because it reduces the likelihood of defects.

I think the reason we don't like the idea is because it seems like the program team is cheating by giving us less for our money. This seems wrong because we still have the contractor-control model in our minds. But the team is actually giving us *better* value for our money—what's the problem? When IT is viewed as a contractor, it seems like they are violating their agreement and, well, ripping us off.

As in many other instances in this book, our insistence on *control* is actually destroying business value. If you don't believe me, ask the Agile gnome.

---

[§] Another interesting side note. Did you know that another word for maxim is gnome? Not the "ageless and often deformed dwarf of folklore," as Webster's says (and which is based on the Latin *gnomus*), but a different word based on a Greek root. But it is hard to resist the idea of a Yoda-like gnomus giving us advice on how to be agile.

# Urgency

One seeming advantage of the plan-driven approach is that it creates urgency. If a team is slipping behind schedule, then it will put in extra effort, work long hours, and become creative in finding ways to get back on schedule. How can Agile teams feel urgency when they have no deadline pressure? In Scrum, for example, the team is only required to make "best efforts" to complete the work it commits to for an iteration, but if it is unable to do so, some work can be carried forward into later iterations. Doesn't that remove all urgency?

The assumption seems to be that urgency—which is really a question of motivation—comes from eagerness to follow a plan. But it seems to me that urgency and motivation are more a product of leadership than of pen and paper. My eyes glaze over when I see a Gantt chart and I can't even read and process it, let alone be motivated by it. Urgency isn't about the plan; it is about the context management creates about how the plan should be interpreted. Let's be honest: if urgency is what we are looking for, then adherence to a plan isn't really what we want anyway. The plan may be leisurely, or unachievable in a way that is demotivating.

It would be more accurate to compare milestone-based urgency to the urgency introduced by the impending end of an iteration. In a Scrum practice, each user story is either done or not done—there is no "partial credit." At the end of an iteration, the team will be praised only for work that is completely finished according to its "definition of done." As a result, when the end of an iteration looms, the team tends to scramble to finish tasks in progress. On the other hand, in the plan-driven approach, the current milestone is only a stage on the way to a later release, and the team knows it can "make up" any delays later in the schedule. How can that create as much urgency as the immediate Agile deadline, which affects what goes into production immediately?

Perhaps this urgency thing is also a remnant of the contractor-control model. Why does the IT team need any more sense of urgency than anyone else in the company? Many employees do their day-to-day jobs on a sustainable basis, putting in an appropriate amount of effort every day. Are we just worried that the geeky IT folks are apt to do a bunch of non-value-adding geeky stuff if there is no pressure on them to finish off the business functionality?

I'd like to talk a bit more about this deadline-urgency thing. There are two kinds of deadlines: those imposed by incontrovertible business needs and fictional ones. A real deadline might involve automating a conference that will take place on a particular date; if the work is not done by that date, then it will have no business value. In that case, all trade-offs should be made to get the work done. Scope should be reduced if necessary. Resources should be added liberally.

Every other deadline is fictitious. The stereotypical pointy-haired manager who says "This *must* be on my desk by tomorrow morning" may feel like he is in control, but he is actually making trade-offs. The depth of the work may be reduced, the quality may suffer, and the employee might get burned-out. Is that worth it? It *might* be. What is the manager willing to sacrifice by having the work done by tomorrow morning, and why?

Deadlines are an old-school way of creating a sense of urgency. Lean thinking gives us an alternative. I'm going to use a way of speaking that is liable to make the Agile community uncomfortable now, but here it is: what we really want is not for things to be delivered according to plan—what we want is for things to be delivered as *soon as possible*. Every task should be done ASAP.

Yes, I said every task. This idea is uncomfortable because requiring something ASAP was a device that managers historically used to control their employees. It is shorthand for saying "I'm not even going to give you a deadline for this because that might give you enough time to relax." It was also shorthand for "This is top priority and urgent."

When I say that every task should be done ASAP, it sounds like I am saying that everything is top priority. I get that. But ASAP is just a way of stating the obvious: the goal of a Lean process is to shorten cycle times. "Shorten cycle time as much as possible" is equivalent to saying "Deliver as soon as possible." What more urgency could there be? And yet—really—how much more humane could a manager be? For the manager is saying "as soon as possible." Not sooner than possible; not later than possible. Of course, it is possible that the manager thinks "possible" includes having the employee work all weekend. I am not advocating that, except in special cases. Every task should be done ASAP—given normal, humane, sustainable working conditions.

> ASAP is just a way of stating the obvious: the goal of a Lean process is to shorten cycle times.

The manager—if this is done correctly—is aligned with the employee in trying to improve "what is possible." For example, the manager must reduce the employee's need to switch between tasks, because Lean theory teaches us that task-switching is a source of waste. So the manager is saying, "Please work on this task until it is finished, then do something else, and I will organize your responsibilities that way." If the employee needs a sign-off or approval from someone and is likely to have to wait—a classic source of waste in the Lean sense—the manager should help.

I have asked employees to do something and had them respond with, "When do you need it by?" If I give them a deadline on this task and also give them a deadline on another task, I might be creating a situation where it is impossible to meet both deadlines. The only humane answer I can give is "as soon as possible, of course." By saying ASAP, I am empowering them to find ways to shorten cycle time and to solicit my help in doing so. Deadlines, on the other hand, are just like milestones in the stage-gate approach.

> Working with deadlines, in a sense, is the opposite of working with a true sense of urgency.

If you are worried that the lack of deadlines reduces urgency, you shouldn't be. Scrum provides urgency in terms of sprint boundaries; Lean provides urgency by specifying that everything be done ASAP—that is, by requiring continuous improvement toward short cycle times. Working with deadlines, in a sense, is the *opposite* of working with a true sense of urgency.

The governance and oversight process I have presented here has a serious deficiency: it is based on the idea of a discrete initiative that needs to be governed. But I have argued elsewhere in this book that companies should be in a state of continuous transformation, grooming the EA through small, incremental investments. A formal governance process seemed necessary when we thought that IT was in danger of becoming misaligned with the business and the projects were large enough to be risky. But now, if IT is simply part of the business—if, as I say, IT folks generally *are* trying to help the business maximize business value and if we finally bury the contractor-control model—then do we really even need a governance process anymore?

How are other parts of the company—marketing, for example—governed? Not by a steering committee. The CMO and other professionals in the marketing department have a deep understanding of the company's products, the market, and the tools of marketing. They make decisions about how to spend their budget in line with their marketing strategy and what they learn from the market. They test marketing campaigns and then decide where to invest. They look at the value of their brands and decide how to build it over the long term. They have strategic objectives and learn from experience how best to achieve them.

This is not to say that marketing operates independently of the rest of the organization. Marketing agrees on goals with senior leadership, then executes against those goals. They help define the products the rest of the company will produce; they work with other senior leaders; they report to the CEO and are held accountable by him or her. They receive feedback both from the market (revenues) and from the rest of the enterprise.

What if IT simply had a budget, like marketing, and a plan, a vision, and objectives consistent with the enterprise's strategy? What if it spent that budget to support the strategy, whether on new projects, projects already underway, or O&M? In fact, why don't we get rid of those terms entirely? IT spends its money, consistent with its strategy, to advance the company's objectives.

In other words, what if we fund a capacity—at budget time, let's say—and then simply let IT leaders make decisions about how to best apply that capacity? Periodically, we could adjust the capacity—hiring more IT experts, reducing the number of IT experts—based on an assessment of the company's needs. Just like any other part of the company, IT leadership would make good decisions about how to deploy its capacity to support the company's strategy and operations, and the CIO would receive feedback from the CEO on whether or not he or she was doing a good job of investing the IT resources.

This would mean that IT would have to be trusted to do the right things. It wouldn't be possible to measure IT against project milestones, and it couldn't be forced into alignment through a formal Star Chamber process. Scary? Or is it just that the contractor-control model is again in our way?

Perhaps we should all be less frightened of this model. If IT is continuously transforming the company through small, incremental investments that immediately deliver corporate outcomes, then IT can be evaluated on the same basis as the rest of the company. It was harder to do this in the past, where IT projects might involve large investments and take a number of years to show results. But with small investments comes smaller risk and earlier opportunities to evaluate performance. IT becomes more like the rest of the enterprise. Do we really need to put smaller investments through the heavyweight governance and oversight process of a large initiative? Maybe all we need to do is get the budgeting process right and then make sure IT manages its budget well, just like any other part of the company.

> With small investments comes smaller risk and earlier opportunities to evaluate performance.

In effect, the budgeting process then becomes a hypothesis-testing process just as we said the governance process should be. The budget formulators are effectively saying, "My hypothesis is that if we invest the following amounts of money in the following categories, that will maximize the outcomes as framed by the leaders of the company." The resources available for investment get passed down through the layers of management, with incremental decisions being made on how to distribute the investment. Those investments are overseen more or less in the way I described above: a periodic check-in to see what is being accomplished with the investment and then adjustments to spending and the distribution of funds based on what has been learned.

This could eliminate the troublesome distinction between "keeping the lights on," or O&M spending, and IT project investments. We might stop committing the sunk-cost fallacy and assuming our base budget is fixed, and we might find that our O&M spending can be used productively to accomplish the change needed to support continuous transformation. We could continuously invest in grooming the EA asset, in polishing the hairball, in increasing its value, through small, everyday investments. Funds could be allocated where they are most useful across the entire portfolio of IT spend categories.

Yes, I know there is a problem with this. Run the business spending is typically *expensed* while investment initiatives are *capitalized*. I am not sure that that still makes sense in an Agile world, but I do not propose to change generally accepted accounting principles. I will just note that financial accounting is about how we report our activities, not necessarily how we make managerial decisions. And those accounting standards may be more flexible than they seem.||

---

|| I am not an accountant, so please ignore everything I am about to say. But this may be worth a conversation with your CFO. The FASB guidance, ASC 350–40, in section 25–7, does imply that upgrades and enhancements that "result in additional functionality" should also be capitalized. To the extent that we are continuously improving the system and making sure it continues to serve the changing company, perhaps there is room to continue capitalizing. Of course, then you still have to figure out when and how to depreciate it. With features constantly being deployed to production and being transformed and changed—potentially surviving forever like Theseus's boat—well, there's a reason I didn't go into accounting or become a CFO.

Whether or not we can go to the extreme of treating all IT spend as something budgeted and under the control of IT leaders, we must acknowledge that the classical approach to governance is deeply connected with the contractor-control model; it is one where the business must ensure that IT stays aligned with its goals and priorities. Oddly, this has the effect of taking the responsibility of strategic IT decisions out of the hands of the CIO. On the other hand, an Agile approach is one that engages all participants in a value-discovery-and-creation process, using feedback cycles to align IT work with desired outcomes. It is the invitation to a seat at the table.

Governance has traditionally been viewed as a filter; a way of allocating scarce IT resources among many competing projects. But in a world where IT is integral to strategy, it makes more sense to begin from strategic objectives and produce investment themes that accomplish those objectives. When combined with Agile and Lean practices, this approach can focus IT planning, reduce risk, eliminate waste, and provide a supportive environment for teams engaged in creating value.

# 10

# RISK

For tragedy and comedy come to be out of the same letters.

—**Aristotle,** *On Generation and Corruption* (paraphrasing Democritus)

The new always happens against the overwhelming odds of statistical laws and their probability, which for all practical, everyday purposes amounts to certainty; the new therefore always appears in the guise of a miracle.

—**Hannah Arendt,** *The Human Condition*

Certainty about what the future holds is the missing element in the CIO's toolkit. It is the only thing that stands between many CIOs and their seat at the table.

IT leaders are a very intelligent bunch. If they could only know exactly what will happen tomorrow, next week, and next year, I am certain they could make excellent decisions and win praise from all corners of the business. Think about how smoothly projects would run and how under control IT would be—plans could be made to correspond with what will happen as the project is later executed. Equipment could be replaced just before it fails. Instead of testing for defects, we could just foretell how systems would later fail in production and correct those problems now.

Of course, if we cannot know the future, then we have to think a bit differently. We cannot expect to demonstrate control by showing that our plan exactly matches reality. Given an uncertain future, control is more about our ability to make changes as circumstances develop. In a way, it is the opposite of making a good plan, since a good plan can turn out to be bad, and if so, effective control means changing the plan.

But control in an uncertain world has another dimension—it also means making good decisions based on an assessment of probabilities. Such decisions cannot always be judged based on their results. If there is an 80% chance that Event A will happen, there is still a 20% chance that it will not. A good decision that depends on Event A happening still stands a chance of being wrong. All decisions made under uncertainty are decisions made "in fear and trembling," to borrow outrageously from Kierkegaard—they are still decisions that can lead to bad results.

As the future slips into the past, uncertainty disappears. There is now a 100% chance that it rained yesterday. We can now celebrate the brilliance of my decision to carry an umbrella, despite the fact that the weather forecasters said that there was only a 20% chance of rain. What was perhaps a stupid decision yesterday morning has now revealed my insight and executive decision-making acumen. While the other executives in my company got drenched, I alone made the right call. Or did I?

Of all parts of the company, IT is one that faces a spectacular amount of uncertainty. A large part of our jobs as IT leaders is to make decisions in the face of the unknown. Does gaining that seat at the table just depend on randomness, on outcomes that are outside of our control?

It turns out that people are not very good at dealing with uncertainty. Even very simple problems of probability can be mind-bending—our intuitions are just plain wrong. Here's a game:

Let's say that I am going to turn over a series of cards whose faces are blue or red. You have to guess what color each card is before I turn it over. Over time, you notice that the cards seem to turn up blue about 60% of the time, so you are pretty sure that 60% of the cards are blue. What's your best strategy?

Obviously, guess blue 60% of the time and red 40%, right? No. You will do better if you guess blue 100% of the time. Never guess red, even though you know that some of the cards are red! If you use this strategy, you will win 60% of the time. With the other strategy, you will be right 52% of the time (.6 × .6 + .4 × .4).[1] Winning this game requires the courage to accept that you will definitely be wrong 40% of the time. It is hard to shake the idea that you are being stupid—you know that some cards are red, yet you never guess red!

For another famous example, remember the show *Let's Make a Deal*, in which the contestant is asked to choose one of three doors, behind one of which there is a car that the contestant will win if he or she guesses right? After the contestant guesses, the host throws open one of the other doors and shows that there is no car behind it. The host then points out that there are two closed doors left, the one the contestant chose and another one, and asks if the contestant wants to switch doors. Since there are now two doors, the odds seem to be 50% that the car is behind each one, so it doesn't matter, right? But the correct strategy is *always* for the contestant to switch doors—in fact, doing so will double his or her chances of winning.* Our intuitions hesitate to accept that, even when it is explained carefully.[2]

A final example: Let's say that you are tested for a rare disease that occurs in one out of every thousand people. The doctor informs you

---

* The chance that the contestant guessed right originally was 1/3. That is the only way he or she could win if he or she sticks with the original door. In the case he or she guessed wrong—a 2/3 chance—he or she will win if he or she switches doors.

that the test is 99% accurate—that is, if you have the disease, the test will be positive 99% of the time, and if you don't have the disease, the test will be negative 99% of the time. Unfortunately, the test comes back positive. How worried should you be? Not very, it turns out. With these parameters, the chance that you actually have the disease turns out to be only about 9%.[3][†]

We reward executives for successful results. But as an IT leader making decisions under conditions of tremendous uncertainty, your choices will often turn out to be wrong. Do you have the courage to guess "blue" every time because it is the best strategy for your company? Are you worried that others will think you indecisive when you switch your choice from door #2 to door #3—and, in fact, you change doors every time the question is asked? Once you have reduced the chances of a fatal disease in your systems enough, will you deploy them boldly even when others are preparing them for hospice care?

> As an IT leader making decisions under conditions of tremendous uncertainty, your choices will often turn out to be wrong.

Let's say that an executive must choose between two courses of action: Course A with a 40% likelihood of being successful and a payoff of $5 million, and Course B with a 60% likelihood and a payoff of $4 million. The success of Course A versus Course B, let's say, depends

---

† You must calculate the conditional probability that you have the disease, given that you have tested positive. Because so many people don't have the disease, the 99% false positive rate results in a large number of false positives. There is a good chance that you are among them.

on the direction that the stock market takes, which is uncertain. The executive decides on Course B.

Well, it turns out that the market goes in the direction favoring Course A, and the executive's decision results in no payoff for the company. If he or she had chosen A, the company would have gained $5 million. The executive clearly made the wrong decision. In another company, the president made the opposite decision after the same analysis, and gained $5 million for his or her company. He or she clearly made the right decision, and as a result he or she is more successful—and more employable.

Did the first executive really make the wrong decision? Didn't the second executive make an unwarranted gamble? Would you rather hire the first executive or the second? To say that the second executive made the "right" decision is to say that he or she somehow foretold the future. But that didn't happen: That executive made a mistake in his or her evaluation—but even mistakes sometimes turn out well. The first executive is the CIO we want to be.

Agile and plan-driven models have very different ways of dealing with uncertainty. Of course, plan driven approaches, even Waterfall, have always acknowledged that the future is uncertain. But this uncertainty was treated as a potential aberrance—a *risk* or eventuality whose impact required mitigation. The basic plan would remain valid, and the risk of the unexpected could be managed *within* the plan by itemizing potential risks, actively working to prevent them, and, if necessary, building slack into the plan to manage the potential impact of the risk on schedule.

Such an approach assumes that the risks are bounded and can be itemized, that we can know the risks in advance, and that we have a way to (try to) control them. But the relationship between uncertainty, risk, and change is far too complicated for such control when delivering IT systems, where complexity is overwhelming and the number of potential failure modes is high. The business changes: new employees come and go, suppliers change their prices, strategies are developed, world events impact markets, and competitors change their strategies. The ideas and vision that generated the IT project might turn out to have unexpected side effects. In weighing the things known for certain against the uncertainties of the future, we are sure to find that the uncertainties dwarf the certainties, and that the uncertainties are not small potential deviations from the initial plan—they are the very substance of the project.

The Agile way to deal with uncertainty is to create options and then "buy" information to more accurately assess probabilities. As Jim Highsmith puts it, "traditional teams attempt to drive out uncertainty by planning and analysis. Agile teams tend to drive out uncertainty by developing working software in small increments and then adjusting."[4] Waterfall plans are made at the moment of greatest uncertainty— the beginning of the initiative. But as the initiative proceeds, we learn more and more to reduce uncertainty. By working in an Agile way, we can leave options open and be prepared to accommodate a range of scenarios as the future unfolds.

> The Agile way to deal with uncertainty is to create options and then "buy" information to more accurately assess probabilities.

Jez Humble and his co-authors suggest that instead of using detailed planning to manage risk, we instead use experiments.[5] When we encounter a risk, we should think of something we can do that will help us gain information to mitigate it. We build something, measure results, and thereby learn enough to cope with the uncertainty. "The purpose of measurement," they remind us, "is not to gain certainty but to reduce uncertainty."[6] Uncertainty is still a given, but we want to drive out as much as we can until it stops being cost-effective to do so. We can take this as yet another definition of what it means to be Agile.

Risk is the chance of a negative impact resulting from uncertainty. We can reduce risk—often at a cost—but there is generally no way to eliminate it. Almost all of our decisions have potential negative consequences, if only the opportunity costs of not having chosen a path that would have turned out to be more profitable.

The decisions of IT leaders are especially risky because they affect large areas of cost and potential revenue. In a sense, IT leaders take on all of the risks of the enterprise, since IT's unknowns include all of the other business unknowns—in other words, the result we get from an IT investment not only depends on the IT-specific risks, but on all of the other business risks, as well. If we build a new IT system to support a line of business and that line of business declines, then the return from our IT system declines, as well. The Chief Information Officer is also the company's Chief Uncertainty Accommodator.

Let's say that the CEO tells the CIO that he or she wants the company's IT systems to stop crashing so often. Fine, says, the CIO—I can spend $1 million, and I think that will get our systems to four nines of availability—that is, 99.99% uptime. The CEO mutters something in his or her native language but agrees to spend the money. A few months later—crash! The business is reeling after their system is down for two hours. Boy, is the CEO mad! He or she has just spent $1 million to avoid downtime, and the CIO promised that there would be only a .01% chance of outages!

Of course, that .01% chance of outages is equivalent to 8.7 hours of downtime a year. That is not much, but it is something. There is no question that the downtime is painful—it always is. But is it out of line with the expected 99.99% availability? Hard to tell until more time passes, but it may not be. Is the CIO accountable (blamable)? You know there will be frantic, urgent attempts to get the system working again, and fingers will be pointing at IT the whole time. But the CIO—as far as we know—did his or her job just right.

To make the example more vivid, suppose that (given diminishing returns) the CIO could have spent an additional $10 million to get the system to five nines of availability (99.999%). The CIO judged—correctly, let's assume—that the additional spending would not have been worthwhile from a business value standpoint. But had he or she spent the money, the CIO would have been praised for reducing the company's downtime. He or she would not have received threatening phone calls, but would have handled uncertainty poorly.

> The presence of uncertainty does not fit well with the contractor-control model of IT.

Come to think of it, if the target was four nines of availability, then the CIO should be rewarded when those 8.7 hours of downtime actually occur, since if there are fewer hours of downtime, then he or she might have overspent!

I'm joking—uncertainty means that, even with perfect execution, there will sometimes be more than 8.7 hours, sometimes less. But there is a very serious point to be made here: the presence of uncertainty does not fit well with the contractor-control model of IT. One expects successful outcomes from a contractor—that is what you pay them for. We don't want to hear from the contractor that the system's failures are, well, just bad luck.

If we accept uncertainty—*embrace* uncertainty—then we have to get used to the idea that, over the short term, this downtime is essentially statistical *noise*. Even if the average downtime works out to be just 8.7 hours a year over time, that means there *will* be downtime, and when it happens, its significance is...nil. There is no one to blame for it. But IT leaders are always available for blame. That is why I say that good IT leadership requires courage. The decision to achieve four nines of availability is a decision to sometimes look incompetent and accept the blame.

Information security, as we know, is also about managing risks.

Hackers break into our network. Fire the CISO? Maybe not. The CISO probably knew of ways to increase security, but also knew what they would have cost—both in dollars and in lost opportunities. He or she probably realized that the more he or she tightened security, the more it would restrict company employees from doing their jobs—particularly from innovating and experimenting. The CISO might have balanced costs and risks and made the best decisions possible—the fact that only one hacker managed to break in might indicate success, for all we know.

Again, in an environment of uncertainty, decisions cannot be assessed just based on their consequences unless we study the consequences over a long period of time or over a large number of discrete trials. And when it comes to security, it is hard to know what a trial is. Were there lots of hacking attempts that were foiled by the measures the CISO did put in place? Were hackers discouraged from even trying because of the CISO's efforts? What would the costs have been of putting more measures in place? Would those measures have increased the cost of everything else the company does? Would they have prevented the business from seizing business opportunities that presented themselves?

Testing is a way of reducing the risk of a software release, but no amount of testing can guarantee that the release will not have defects or unexpected side effects. In fact, there are diminishing returns to testing. At some point, we will release the software knowing that there are still defects, even though we don't yet know what they are.

The decision to release the code is made under uncertainty—another decision made in fear and trembling.[tt] When someone discovers a defect in production, they will still say, "This system was not tested well enough!" The defect might even have severe consequences—there is no way to know in advance, because this is one of the defects we did not find in testing. If so, then the cry from users will be, "Look how terrible the testing was! Even this horribly severe defect did not get caught! Our testing needs to be at least good enough to catch things like this that can do terrible harm to the company!" Only they don't usually say it in exactly those words.

It is hard to know how to respond to this sort of criticism. The critical defect was missed in testing, but the risk-based decision to move to production might still have been the right one, despite the consequences.

---

[tt] I know, I'm repeating the Kierkegaard reference. It's a double inside joke. Kierkegaard also has a book called *Repetition*.

When we organize our work around projects that deliver product only at the end, we are primarily concerned with two categories of risks: cost risk and schedule risk. Schedule risk is the risk that the deployment is delayed relative to the original schedule. How big is this risk? And how severe are the consequences?

I'd advise caution here. We are not talking about the cost of delay of the system—that is a measure of divergence from "as soon as possible," not of divergence from schedule. If capabilities are not released as soon as possible, then there is a cost to the company. But if they are not released according to a pre-planned schedule, the only true cost to the company is the cost of having the wrong expectations. In that case, the real risk is that we will believe the schedule!

Why do people feel like there is risk in an Agile approach? I think the answer is that they are worried about the schedule for delivering what they think of as FOC. The perceived risk is that the project will be "finished" late. But this, as we know, is based on the outdated idea that we define the scope of the system ahead of time and keep working until we deliver it. That is precisely what we do not do in an Agile approach.

Instead, we focus on reducing the risk of deploying functionality later than "as soon as possible." We deploy small value-adding chunks, continuously. In the Waterfall, we were worried about getting FOC delivered soon; with an Agile approach, we go this one better—we make sure that we deliver each individual piece of functionality soon. And if it becomes truly necessary to hit a schedule milestone, then we can adjust our scope to be sure that we do so.

The importance that we have attached to the timing of FOC is just another example of the misconception that IT delivery is about delivering discrete, finished *products*. We want our FOC because we think that is the point at which we are finished investing and just need to "maintain." But unless we want functional and technical debt, a lumpy EA, and a need to do an expensive and risky transformation effort, FOC is in no sense a "final" operating capability.

With that out of the way, we can talk about real risk.

The main risk we should be worrying about is the cost of not meeting our *business objectives* on the designated schedule and at the designated cost. That is a very different thing. The best way to manage this risk is to keep discovering things that don't need to be done in order to meet the business objectives. By building a minimal viable product and then only adding to it what is still needed—based on evidence from actual usage—we can reduce the risk of cost and schedule overruns by trying to do less work.

> The main risk we should be worrying about is the cost of not meeting our *business objectives* on the designated schedule and at the designated cost.

In fact, as we saw in the last chapter, we can easily constrain our project to operate within budget. Because we deploy units of value throughout the process, and because we work in priority order, we can simply say that when we exhaust our budget, we will stop. Sure, there is risk that we might not get as much scope accomplished as we would like to. But we have options. Ultimately, that is what we want, since we cannot make uncertainty go away.

Then there is the risk that we are overbuilding features—that is, the risk that the requirements include features that will never be used, or when they are used, will not add that much value. If such an outcome is rare, then we shouldn't worry too much. But studies show that in most pre-planned systems, two thirds of the features are rarely or never used.[||] Again, the Agile approach mitigates this risk.

There is the risk that business needs may change over the course of a project. There is the risk that technology might advance and give us better and less expensive ways to create the capabilities we need. There is the risk that the way we build the features might not be optimal for their users—a very large risk, since our instincts and assumptions are usually wrong when it comes to usability. These very real risks are precisely the ones we manage through an Agile approach.

Surprisingly, one of the most powerful risk-management techniques introduced in the Agile world is the idea of testing *in production*. We used to consider this extremely bad practice, as code was supposed to be tested *before* it went into production—as well it should, but it should be tested in production, as well. Think of testing as a kind of learning about how our code behaves, or as a kind of proving that our code behaves in a good way. Why should we stop learning when we hit the "deploy" button?

In a way, testing in production has always been our ideal in the sense that production is where we actually want our features to work, and test environments can never perfectly mimic what stresses the features will face when they are actually used. Testing in production always seemed wrong because the consequences of a failure were high. But what if there were a way to limit the danger?

There is. Teams practicing Continuous Delivery deploy small changes to production frequently. Since each change is small and

---

[||] The reference is to a presentation made by Jim Johnson, the Chairman of the Standish Group, at the XP 2002 conference. He is referring to the Chaos studies done by the Standish group that reported a startlingly high percentage of failing IT projects. According to Johnson, 64% of features are "rarely" or "never" used. But this was based on a survey of four companies, so it must be taken with a grain or a large pinch of salt.

has been tested through a rigorous automated test suite, the risk of deploying bad code to production is low. The risk is further mitigated by having an easy and fast way to roll back the change, and monitoring and alerting in place so that problems are discovered quickly. As a result, the team can balance the amount and type of testing done before release (and its cost) with the risk and cost of discovering a problem in production.

There are many things we can't learn about our code until we put it into production—in particular, we can't learn how it behaves in production until we put it into production. This is the inspiration behind Netflix's Chaos Monkey. Chaos Monkey is an open source script that randomly kills off virtual machines in production. If the system is robust, then it should self-heal. The cluster scheduler should notice that a VM is dead, set up a new one, and deploy it to replace the dead one. In the meantime, the load balancer should re-balance the load among the working VMs. It would seem to take guts to run this in production, but really it takes guts not to have a Chaos Monkey. Otherwise, how do you know that your system is resilient in production?

Continuous Delivery teams can also use canary deployments, as in the "canary in the coal mine" that communicates that there is poison in the air by dying before the miners do. Let's say that we have fully tested a new version of one of our microservices. Fully tested means that there is still some risk. But not to worry—we can deploy it to just a few of our clustered servers. We watch for problems—that is, we test in production—and if we find any, we quietly roll back the changes to those servers.

We might also test in production to learn better how our users interact with our software. In A/B testing, we deploy two versions of our user interface—some users receive Version A and some receive Version B. We then collect data on which version better accomplishes our goals, whatever they might be. For example, a goal might be to maximize the time users spend on our site (if we are showing them ads). Or it might be minimizing the time it takes them to complete a transaction. Once we collect the data, we decide whether to proceed with A or B.

Do these techniques sound risky? Are our intuitions about risk sound?

Continuous Delivery itself seems full of risks to many people when they first hear about it. Deploying hundreds of times a day? Allowing developers to make changes directly to production environments? But again, a calm assessment shows that we are actually lowering risk.

Our automated regression test suite, as we have said, makes sure that the new, small set of changes does not break anything that was working before. Security? Our automated security tests also run with every change, and security engineers have been involved throughout the development process. Code quality? Automated static code analysis tools take care of it. Manual end-user testing? Well, users have been working with the developers to create the new functionality, and the product owner approved it.

We can do even better in our Continuous Delivery environment. We "charter" exploratory tests to focus on new functionality that we judge to be risky. We design each of our features with the help of user-experience experts to avoid usability issues. And, if necessary, we deploy new features with toggles—that is, the features will be deployed but not yet available to users until we have managed down any identifiable risks.

What of the risk from not having separation of duties? In our old model, where development was a different skill from operations, it was easy to draw a line between the two and call it separation of duties. But why is that the appropriate line for a control? In those days, system administrators were supposed to serve as a check on the developers. But did they actually review the code to know if there was funny business going on? If they did, were they competent to do that review? Worse, there was no check on the administrators. They could log into the production environment and make changes to running systems, possibly even without detection.

In a Continuous Delivery environment, *no one* has direct access to production servers. The system is immutable once deployed, and can only be changed by tearing down the old servers and replacing them with new ones. The development teams can only deploy their code via deployment scripts held in the version-control system. Everything is transparent and auditable—the version-control system will preserve a history of the changes made, who made them, and when they were made. Bad behavior can be traced. We can set up our processes so that no code can be deployed to production without a peer code review by another developer.

Because we can deploy with no downtime, we can deploy during normal daytime hours, which means we can watch the production system, notice immediately if there is a problem, and roll back the changes right away. Best of all, being able to deploy so quickly reduces our "time to repair" if there are any issues in production—including the discovery of security vulnerabilities.

All of this is to say that our intuitions are terrible when it comes to assessing risk.

When we build a building, we engineer it to be sturdy. We don't want it falling on people. There are risks—earthquakes, wind, meteors, termites, Horsemen of the Apocalypse, whatever; we take these into consideration when we plan the structure. There is a long history of structural engineering practices that are known to be effective. The architects and designers of the buildings consider these things when they are designing, and the builders while they are building. They don't build the building and then bring in another crew to make it sturdy when they are finished, and they don't make it sturdy by building a wall around it so that it is shielded from the wind and the meteors.[§]

When we engineer a software system, we need to engineer it in a secure way. I don't mean that we have someone add the security later. I don't mean that we build a perimeter around our network so that threats can't get near our system. I mean that security is just part of our job. It is about how we build our system; it is a matter of everyday hygiene. In the old days, when threats were not so real, we could leave security to the experts and just call them when we needed them. Now, we know that our systems are under attack at all times by sophisticated and determined adversaries, some of whom might be inside our doors already (both figuratively inside the doors of our network or literally insiders within the company's offices). Security is a how, not a what. It is how we build.

> Security is just part of our job. It is about how we build our system; it is a matter of everyday hygiene.

Many diseases can be prevented by washing our hands. It is simple, routine, and powerful. Add a few other good habits—using

---

[§] At least, that's how I've always imagined it. I might be wrong—I know very little about building buildings, but I plan to stay ignorant as long as it makes for a useful analogy.

condoms and occasionally stepping away from the computer screen to breathe fresh air—and our chances of making it through another day go up considerably. The Open Web Application Security Project (OWASP)[7] has given us a list of the top ten web application vulnerabilities—just one of which, SQL injection, has accounted for 83% of breaches.[8] We need to make avoiding SQL injection and these other nine vulnerabilities an everyday matter of hygiene.

I am not saying that simple hygiene will absolutely keep us safe. Even if you wash your hands and use a condom, you might still get bitten by a malaria-carrying mosquito. But good hygiene should be expected of everyone. A software engineer can wear yesterday's clothes and forget to shower, but he or she'd better remember not to pass queries to the database blindly lest he or she come down with a severe case of SQL injection.

Our instinct is to focus on the fancy protections against the extremely subtle attacks, but the basics of security are not complex, and it is the basics that we mess up on consistently. Security is not the guys in the dark glasses with impenetrable network diagrams on their huge computer screens. It is your grandmother telling you that you'd better brush your teeth.

The Rugged DevOps movement promotes a hygiene-based approach to security.[9] "Rugged" organizations are organizations that have developed a culture of creating software that is "available, survivable, defensible, secure, and resilient."[10] Rugged organizations build rugged software because ruggedness is one of their values—they treat it as a matter of quality like any other matter of quality. A piece of code that has a preventable security flaw is like a piece of code that has any other kind of flaw—broken.

Writing our software in a rugged way is often cheap or free. It costs nothing extra to write a program in a way that makes SQL injections impossible. Buffer overflow attacks are easily preventable. Adding these controls after the fact would cost money, but writing the programs using good practices is free.

We can automate much of our security compliance regime. There are two ways to do this: automate testing for potential weaknesses and automate processes for building rugged systems. It's funny that organizations often already use automated security tests, but then limit them to security experts who come in to test *after* the system is built. Security is treated as a "gotcha"—we don't want to tell the development teams what exactly we are testing for, because then they might just build so that they pass those tests. Hmm...Why not make the tests robust enough that they actually test for the things we're worried about, so that if the code passes the tests, it is secure by definition?

We can also pre-build rugged components. A good place to start is with authentication, authorization, and identity management. If the company can develop a single sign-on login system that meets its needs and is rugged and well tested, then it can confidently use that component in every system it develops in the future. If the company combines this with a good set of business processes and policies regarding access controls, it will have taken care of one of the most vulnerable areas of any system.

Similarly, the company can standardize its audit logging, reporting, and monitoring, and its processes for using these tools. Every new system can plug into APIs and take advantage of these features with little effort, and every company can guard against social engineering attacks, which are the usual vector for malicious activity. Two-factor authentication can help against the tendency of users to give away their passwords or leave them written down and lying around. Protection against phishing emails is available, or at least users can be taught how to avoid such attacks. Processes can be set up to destroy pieces of paper to reduce the risk of dumpster-diving.

These types of hygiene practices do not interfere with Agile Continuous Delivery processes—in fact, they make it easier to be Agile. They provide the latent value that keeps our EA smooth and polished.

The contractor-control model destroys business value by encouraging behaviors that do not tolerate risk. IT's incentive is to spend liberally on testing, even though it is actually the business's money that is being spent. Or the business may insist that IT keep testing and testing—regardless of the cost—because the business does not want to accept any risk.

> The executive's job is to take risks, not to avoid them.

A senior executive's job is to manage risk. We often interpret this as reducing or mitigating risk. But really the executive's job is to *take* risks, not to avoid them. Since all action directed toward the future is risky, the executive must decide which risky actions to take and how best to take them. Investing in the stock market is risky, but if you want to earn a return, you have to do it. You balance risks and returns, and choose investments.

The simple reason that the contractor-control model of IT breaks down is the presence of uncertainty. Plans are made with an eye toward the future, but the future is largely unknown. Thus, rigid adherence to a plan cannot be effective—at best, the plan is valid only as long as the assumptions it makes are valid. The seated CIO is the one who tries new foods—well, if they look edible.

The presence of uncertainty is the simple reason why Agile approaches work better than plan-driven approaches—it is also the reason why a good IT leader will often have to make "wrong" decisions. An IT leader adds business value by adopting an intelligent attitude toward risk.

# 11

# QUALITY

But one should not be too right if one wants to have those who laugh on one's own side; a grain of wrong actually belongs to good taste.

—**Friedrich Nietzsche**, *Beyond Good and Evil*

Whatever deeds arise in accord with the virtues are not done justly or moderately if they are merely in a certain state, but only if he who does those deeds is in a certain state as well: first, if he acts knowingly; second, if he acts by choosing and by choosing the actions in question for their own sake; and, third, if he acts while being in a steady and unwavering state.

—**Aristotle**, *Nichomachean Ethics*

The IT world has a strange relationship with quality. Think about it. Virtually everything we do is based on the assumption of failure. To quote Hunter and Westerman: "Nothing is perfect (especially something as complex as IT)."[1] This attitude is built deeply into our psyches, our way of communicating with the business, and our emphasis on problem-solving skills. We are the people who can get away with failing frequently, while the rest of the enterprise gets punished for even one failure. It is a point of pride—*we* understand that failure is normal in IT, and the rest of the organization doesn't get it. The art of IT has always been an art of failure. It is a little strange.

We would like our systems to be available 100% of the time, but we know this is unachievable. We are willing to live with four nines of availability, say, when we really want a one and two zeroes. I can't tell you now what will fail next month, but I am pretty sure that something will. So, my strategy for achieving high availability is to assume failure and try to protect against its effect by adding redundancy. But this costs money—more and more the more nines we want. Thus, we agree on failure as a solution.

When we are developing code, it is a given that it will have defects, so we must find ways to minimize their impacts. We do plenty of testing, hoping that our tests will expose most of the bugs and that they will be corrected. We understand that these defects may need to be triaged; we might not fix all of them before we go to production—after all, there are business trade-offs. So we deploy systems with known defects. Of course, more defects will be discovered in production, and they will then be fed back into the triage pipeline. It would be unreasonable to expect to launch a complex software system without bugs!

We know that schedules and costs will be overrun. We can admit it—everyone knows that delivery is never on time and on budget; if it were to happen by accident, we would be pretty sure that it was because the costs were overestimated in the first place. Non-IT managers have gotten used to doubling or tripling the estimates given to them by the IT folks. When the system is finally deployed, it requires people camping out in the office overnight, pizza, Red Bull, heroism—and somehow the developers expect the business to reward them for it! Furthermore, we know that, soon after the system is deployed, it will turn out that the hardware is no longer adequate and must be upgraded; that the software is outdated and must be replaced.

We know that there are security flaws lurking in our systems. Even if we have worked out all the known kinks, there are still zero-day exploits that will bring us down. There are also insider threats and social engineering. We cannot really protect against those things, so we have to settle for rapid response to security breaches.

The assumption of flaws is deeply embedded in our approach to IT. It is part of our culture, our way of thinking. Defects, failures, and IT go together in our minds.

One of the hardest things to explain about IT to outsiders is why all this failure is considered acceptable. Why aren't IT people judged against the usual standards? Anyone else in the company who caused outages and expensive mistakes would be fired. IT folks develop thick skins, or at least good rationalization skills. But why would you trust your company strategy to the guys who can't even make customer invoices add up right? How can IT deserve a seat at the table if it is always failing?

> One of the hardest things to explain about IT to outsiders is why all this failure is considered acceptable.

The way we talk about failure contributes to the business-versus-IT divide: it is yet another reason why, to the business, IT is a *them* that must be controlled. *They* will bring our business to a grinding halt by messing things up if we don't control them. *They* get away with murder.

We know from the preceding chapter that IT folks are making decisions to balance risks with costs of mitigating those risks, and—we hope—making good decisions. The decision to allow systems to fail is actually a good business decision, although it might be difficult for other parts of the business to credit. A more appropriate conversation, we in IT think, would not be about the negative nature of failure but about successfully choosing the amount of failure that we allow.

This is a hard conversation to have as long as IT is in a contractor relationship with the rest of the business. When the business folks hand off a requirement to IT and agree to pay for a product, they expect it to work: every defect or failure in production is essentially a breach in contract. Some IT organizations have overcome this problem by explicitly agreeing on service level agreements. I'm not sure I really like this approach—it further relegates IT to the status of a contractor and service provider rather than a part of the business. I'd prefer an approach where IT proactively delivers to the business the level of service that it, in its understanding of the trade-offs, believes is best, and accepts the consequences boldly.

It's possible that we are mixing two issues here. There are "failures" that are calculated and there are failures that are, well, bad. We freely mix the two concepts, sometimes using the need for calculated failures as a way to justify the other failures. Quality in our world should not be about whether things fail—it is about something better described as "impeccability." It is about making the right decisions under the face of uncertainty; it is about doing things the right way; it is about holding ourselves to high standards. As Aristotle says, "Whatever deeds arise in accord with the virtues are not done justly or moderately if they are merely in a certain state, but only if *he who does those deeds is in a certain state as well*."[2] It is not just about success or failure, but about acting in an impeccable way, as well.

Let me come right out and say it: we have to raise the bar on impeccability. Just because we accept failure doesn't mean that all failures are acceptable. We owe it to the enterprise to approach closer and closer to impeccability, and we have room to do so.

What if we were to adopt a zero-defect approach to software development? Sort of like the *andon cord* in the Toyota manufacturing process—the cord that any employee can pull if they notice an error, thereby stopping the entire production line. Is this plausible? If not, how close can we come? We can break this into two questions. First, can we fix every defect we find in testing? And second, can we test for everything we would consider to be a defect?

Let's start with the first question: Can we have zero *known* defects? Traditionally, we have not really tried—instead, we have recorded defects in a defect-tracking system, intending to fix them later. The amount of waste we have built into our defect-tracking process is immense. When a defect is encountered, someone collects information on what exactly was observed and what actions are required to replicate it. He or she enters it into the bug-tracking system with enough detail and context for someone to understand it later, and attaches a severity level of critical, high, or low to it. The severity level is then used in "triaging" the defects and deciding which ones to fix. This triaging takes time and is repeated periodically.

When the defect is finally selected for remediation, an engineer—who has been working on other things and therefore must come up to speed on the issue—replicates the problem. The engineer marks in the defect-tracking system that he or she now "owns" the defect then makes the fix and updates the system, complete with instructions on how to test the fix. Someone else then reads the defect record, tests the fix, and finally updates the system to show that it has been tested.

This is an expensive process. What if we tried to eliminate it? We could automate most of the tests and have them available before the developer begins or by the time he or she finishes developing the feature. The developer could run the tests him or herself or have them run automatically as he or she finishes the code. Any defects found can be immediately fixed. The automated tests would have to pass before the code was accepted into the build, so absolutely no known defects would be allowed. We would have avoided the overhead of the defect-tracking system and insisted on 100% elimination of known defects. So far so good.

One small problem: I have learned the hard way that another strategy developers can use for eliminating failing tests is to ... eliminate failing tests. Developers have been known to comment out or delete tests that are not passing, figuring that they will come back to them later to make them work, but in the meantime, the code is passing. This sounds pretty sneaky and terrible, doesn't it? Well, then, it bears some thought that this clever technique is really equivalent to the technique of triaging defects that have been entered into the bug-tracking system: the developer is making a conscious decision not to fix something right away. There is a kind of dishonesty in the idea of triaging known defects.

> There is a kind of dishonesty in the idea of triaging known defects.

Not all testing can be done immediately by the developer. Some defects might be discovered further downstream as users get their hands on the feature, or as other developers integrate their code with this developer's code. Now we need our defect-tracking system, right? Maybe, but there are some other strategies we can try first. We want to move all downstream testing as far to the left as possible—that is, we want it to happen as soon after the developer finishes his or her code as possible. This is facilitated by Continuous Delivery, since the feature will be making its way through all the remaining steps quickly before deployment.

If someone does discover a defect downstream, one strategy he or she can employ, rather than entering the issue into a defect-tracking system, is to use "wideband communication"—a fancy term for *talking*. That is to say, he or she can simply show the defect to the developer and have a conversation around it. The developer can ask questions and gather more information from the discoverer. The advantages are a more effective process and faster communication; the disadvantage is that the tester might have to interrupt the developer, who by now is working on the next feature. But if we commit to the idea of fixing defects as soon as possible, then we might need to accept that trade-off.

Finally, we might have to accept that some defects will get entered into the defect-tracking system; at the very least the ones discovered in production. Here, I offer my final suggestion on the matter: defects should never be prioritized or triaged. There are only two types of defects: those that will be fixed immediately, and those that will never be fixed and should not be entered into the defect-tracking system. There is no "later" when it comes to defects.

The second question I raised was whether our testing can be good enough to catch all defects. The answer is—of course not. But I think we can come pretty close.

Studies have shown that the most time-effective way to catch defects is through peer code reviews rather than through the usual "black box" testing. A study by IBM, for example, found that each hour of code inspection saved 20 hours of testing time and 82 hours of rework that would have been necessary if the defects found in that hour had made it to production.[3] Many teams now require that each piece of new code be peer reviewed before being promoted through the delivery pipeline. Or they use pair programming, where programmers work together in pairs, with one at the keyboard and another literally or figuratively looking over his or her shoulder. It is a powerful method for eliminating defects.

Automated performance tests can also be included in the delivery pipeline. One way to do this is to create simple performance tests that give a performance baseline. Then, as each feature is added, the same performance test is run as a regression test and the performance with the new feature is compared to the performance baseline. If there is a material difference, then it can be reported immediately to the developer for attention. This can draw the developer's attention to many different types of underlying defects.

With behavior driven development (BDD) and acceptance test driven development (ATDD), users can write tests themselves. When we add human exploratory testing, frequent feedback from users, demonstrations at sprint reviews, static code analysis, and the rest of the Agile toolkit, we can be pretty good—though not perfect—at catching defects early in their lifecycles. This is what we are looking for: impeccability, not perfection in results.

We can extend this zero-defect principle beyond software development to include operations. If we architect our applications to be cloud-friendly, twelve-factor applications,[4] then we can manage them in clusters of containers. If a particular service is deployed in a container to, let's say, a cluster of four servers and one of those servers crashes, the other three servers can carry the load for the very short time it takes the system to provision a new virtual machine, load the container into it, and add it back to the cluster. Autoscaling of virtual machines can be used to keep the system performing well when it experiences sudden increases in usage. As the system becomes more stressed, it can automatically add new nodes to the cluster. And with serverless computing services like Amazon Lambda, we don't need to be concerned about servers anymore, let alone worry about their reliability.

I'm not sure how many nines of availability we can get just by following these good design practices, but does it matter? Good practices should be our baseline. Higher availability than that is a business decision. If we strive for impeccability, then we do not need to be the part of the enterprise that is all about failure, though failures will occur.

If we cannot eliminate all failure modes, then what *do* we mean by quality? Products in stores are understood to have differing levels of quality—an expensive suit may be said to be of higher quality than a cheap one. Consumers are offered different levels of quality at different prices; companies align their brands to convey a promise of a particular level of quality. A company can choose its market positioning, perhaps offering low prices with the sacrifice of quality, or maybe choosing to serve the high end of the market with high-quality merchandise and high prices. Toyota has been said to care so much about quality that employees are free to stop the production line if they see any defects, but, of course, they don't pull the stop cord when they realize that a Toyota is not as high quality as a Bentley—quality, in this case, means that the car is produced as intended.

I wonder what the equivalent is for software that is intended to be used *within* the enterprise. I have heard managers instruct their teams not to "gold plate" features, but I believe they are really asking the teams not to add features unnecessarily; they are probably not referring to the quality level of individual features. Decisions are being made somewhere in our process about how nice the suspension feels or how fresh the fish is, but I'm not sure that we have an explicit process for making these decisions. Instead, we talk just about whether features as a whole should be included or not, and whether or not the feature "works."

In the plan-driven model, quality was easier to understand. We specified what the system should do, and then measured quality as adherence to that specification. The opposite of a defect was "working as designed," even if the design was poor. In the Agile world, though, it is a more complicated matter. Clearly, we do not mean adherence to specification, but do we mean spare-no-expense-best-in-class? Probably not that, either. Yet we are constantly making quality decisions, especially in a Continuous Delivery model, as we decide whether the quality of each individual feature is adequate for the feature to be deployed. It is easy enough to say that the feature is ready for deployment when it passes all of its tests. But is quality a simple yes-or-no attribute? If it passes its tests, is it high quality? And how can we assess the quality of something that is unfinished—that will later be added to, incrementally?

Perhaps we should separate the concepts of *deployability* and *quality*. A feature is simply *deployable* when it passes its tests; that is a yes-or-no question independent of quality. Once the feature is in production, we can assess its quality based on its fit to need, or perhaps its actual success in accomplishing the business outcome for which it was intended.

But this still seems to leave something out—a feature might accomplish its desired outcome but still be unpleasant to use, inelegant in design, or just plain sloppy. Imagine a screen for use within the company that has a typo—it doesn't necessarily affect outcomes, but it still reflects bad quality. I guess you could say that it affects outcomes in that the sloppiness will affect how employees feel about their jobs, and that will have an indirect effect on the company's performance, but this seems a stretch.

There is also the internal quality of the code. Is it maintainable? Is it accumulating technical debt? Is the architecture flexible and extensible? Some of these attributes might cost more to obtain, and some might not. Does it cost more to do good design work? Sometimes? Our notion of quality must certainly encompass the effectiveness of our EA asset. How effective will that asset be in meeting our future needs? Is it designed in a way that will give us options for the future, prepare us for different scenarios, reduce the cost of future work, and have a lower risk of bugs arising and a higher chance of spotting and diagnosing those bugs if they do occur?

These questions of quality are difficult, and perhaps beyond what I can cover in this book. Let me take refuge in the old trick of listing things that we can probably agree on and thus avoiding the hard questions:

- The meaning of quality must include much more than whether the feature has bugs; it must extend to its nonfunctional characteristics and the feature's effect on the overall EA asset.
- We can't stop assessing the quality of a feature when we deploy it—in fact, that is when we can *start* assessing its quality. Testing, in essence, is our way of deciding that the experiment of launching the feature in production is ready to begin.
- As with many other things Agile, quality is a continuum. In the Waterfall, a feature is either "working as designed" or not; in the Agile world, there is no such basis for judging quality.
- There is still room for a notion of impeccability, here: we always want to increase quality attributes if we can without increasing cost, and we always want to make good decisions trading off quality and costs. The typo on that screen should not be there—it costs the same to spell the word correctly.

When introducing Agile practices into my organizations, I have tried to give greater transparency to business stakeholders and involve them throughout the delivery process. As a result, the business stakeholders can see a lot more of the "sausage making," so to speak. They are often shocked and scared. The developers run tests and they fail. Performance tests show slowness and cast doubt on the system's ability to scale. Problems arise and no one immediately knows how to fix them. Arguments break out between technical people about the best architectures and the best solutions to problems. The team suddenly realizes that two pieces of the system don't interface well, and now they have to do some rebuilding (why didn't they just do it right in the first place?) Aren't *all* of these people supposed to be experts?

The non-IT folks are astounded at how calm we all are while this is going on—to them, everything sounds like a cause for panic. To IT people, however, all of this is the normal course of things: failures simply tell us where we need to focus our attention next. Technical disagreements are often signs of a healthy team and a healthy process, and we know that some issues cannot be solved right away: often even just diagnosing the cause of an issue takes time and thought.

Ultimately, none of this relates to quality—it is just process. Our production process, that is, involves course corrections, experimentation, and developing things in broad brush strokes, and then coming back later to tidy up. Only the characteristics of the code that gets deployed matter when we talk about quality.

It is no wonder that a CIO trying to gain a seat at the table by showing how well he or she ensures quality is having trouble getting seated. The CIO's table manners are terrible—he or she is constantly dropping food into his or her lap, then picking it up again and putting it carefully back on the plate. IT is a mess!

Part of our Agile approach, then, is to turn what would otherwise be quality issues into process: defects cease to be defects if they are just a normal part of how the sausage gets made (someone please assure me this is not how real sausage making works!). Quality is in the attributes of the deployed features and their effect on business outcomes. Since quality is in the attributes of the deployed product, feedback from users and monitoring in production are critical. The faster we can turn information about how the capabilities are performing in production into improvements, the more value we are adding.

Perfection is not necessary when we first release a capability, but impeccability is. The delivery teams still have a responsibility to achieve the best quality possible through everyday good practices—in other words, the quality that costs approximately nothing. Agile approaches place greater responsibility on the developers for avoiding defects: they write their own tests and ensure that their code works before they commit it to the main pipeline. Surprisingly, this syncs up with the intuitions of our business stakeholders! Why *should* we tolerate developers' mistakes? We all know that the sooner we catch defects the less it costs to fix them.

One of the mistakes of the Waterfall process was that it left testing to the very end and put it in the hands of a separate group of testers rather than the developers themselves. It was viewed as a control or a check on the developers—part of an "acceptance" process that was necessary in a contractor-control paradigm—but its effect was to remove some of the responsibility for quality from the developers.

One way to "move quality to the left" is through training. In my organization, we have actually taken the step of making our QA department responsible for training the developers. A small number of error categories are responsible for most defects: race conditions, null pointers, unvalidated parameters, unsafe threads, for example. The more aware developers are of these sources of defects—the more top of mind—the more the developers can avoid them. The more versed they are in good design patterns, the more fluidly and consistently they will apply them.

Let's go back briefly to the concept of hygiene. We can think of quality in general—not just security—as a matter of keeping one's hands clean. Illnesses happen, true, but that is hardly an excuse for not washing your hands when leaving the restroom. An interesting read related to this topic is Atul Gawande's *The Checklist Manifesto: How to Get Things Right*. Gawande, a surgeon, shows that simple checklists have proven very effective in medicine and many other disciplines for reducing mistakes. The value of a checklist is twofold: it forces the participants to pay attention to each critical step in the process, and it forces them—if it is a well-written process—to have conversations at the appropriate moments.[5] A checklist approach can be useful in IT, for example, in deciding when to turn on a feature that has been toggled off. Security compliance regimes like FISMA are essentially checklists, though admittedly they do not meet many of Gawande's criteria for an effective one.

Agile methods have introduced a few other important practices for reducing the number of defects. By trying to avoid task switching—for example, by having a Scrum Master "protect" the team from interruptions—Scrum has eliminated one of the biggest causes of defects. With pair programming, Developer B watching over Developer A's shoulder is able to spot potential defects and remember the side effects that Developer A is about to forget.

Why in the Agile world do we talk about the need to fail and to fail often? This is a linguistic ambiguity—we are talking about a different kind of failure—in fact, a kind of failure that is the opposite of defects and outages. Trying things out is a way of *learning* in the Agile world; it is a kind of feedback cycle that lets us make good decisions in the normal course of work. Let's say that we are deciding between two different open source products for building a piece of the system and do not know enough of their impacts to make the choice. In the old-school way of making the decision, we would do research, debate the choice, maybe do a proof of concept. In our new world, we can simply implement one of the approaches and see how it works for us. We could even try the other approach as well and compare. We are comfortable with the idea that we will break things in testing, because the end result of doing so is that we can make a decision more quickly and with more good information available. "Failing" in this sense is simply an efficient process we use to select among alternatives.

> Fail often, fail fast—but fail well.

Experimentation—which also implies the willingness to fail—can be used effectively to manage risks and stimulate innovation in user-experience design and in requirements definition. Failure, in this case, is a sign that we are trying things, innovating, testing our hypotheses—all good things. A good amount of failure is an indication that we are making good risk/value trade-offs. The risk of small failures caught quickly in testing is so low that we should be encouraging plenty of that kind of failure to increase innovation and informed decision-making.

While the old way of thinking valued "getting things right the first time," Agile approaches value trying the right thing—that is, finding the right experiment to reduce uncertainty or confirm or refute a hypothesis. Would it be better to make a good decision in advance so that we don't waste time and effort on failing solutions? Not really—trying things out, given today's velocity of software delivery, is a very effective and cheap way of doing research.

But not all failures are good. Good failures are the ones that deliver information cost-effectively for making decisions. Good failures encourage innovation. Good failures are the ones that stem from a good understanding of uncertainty and how to manage it.

Fail often, fail fast—but fail well.

A system suddenly fails!

It turns out that this is the most mission-critical system there is! Without it, all the pandas will die and all the bacon in the world will begin to taste like kale! World peace is at stake!

This is a disaster. Whose *fault* is it? The CEO calls the CIO in a panic and tells him or her that this is very serious. The CEO describes the negative impact that the outage is having on the company; and this after the company has invested money in new servers that were supposed to be more reliable!

The CIO responds with appropriate seriousness—he or she understands how this outage is hurting the business. He or she turns around to the IT staff and tries to find out what and who are to blame. The CIO demands an after-action report, or a post mortem. He or she pushes the staff to see that the problem is fixed right away and to provide frequent updates so that the CIO can answer to the CEO. The CIO's reputation and seat at the table are at stake (not to mention the poor pandas).

This CIO is a wimp. He or she knows—or should know—whether the product is being produced impeccably and if the code is being deployed after the appropriate amount of risk-mitigating testing. Although we are uncomfortable admitting this, the failure in production does not really call for blame. In a world of uncertainty, we cannot judge performance just by results. IT leaders must be able to determine whether the delivery process is impeccable and appropriately risk-mitigating *outside* of whether or not there is a production failure. Furthermore, the good IT leader may have deliberately decided to accept a certain amount of failure. If, as an IT leader, you have verified impeccability and good risk management, then the production incident just demonstrates the success of the laws of probability. It verifies that the universe is operating as expected. Buy the team a round of beers.

It is true that, while single failures are not necessarily a sign of a problem, results do matter—if the system fails repeatedly in production, then there is clearly a quality problem. But the problem is not the failure in production, per se; the problem is the lack of impeccability and risk management. IT leadership's ability to assess these aspects of its delivery process is broken.

This is one reason that IT leadership is, to me, a technical discipline. Assessing impeccability is a matter of assessing the performance of an employee—all managers, not just those in IT, need to have a sense of how their employees are performing. The difference in IT is that the performance is in a technical domain and requires technical skills to assess. Appropriate risk management is also the responsibility of IT employees, so their leaders must be able to assess risks in a technical setting. The CIO is responsible for the enterprise's technical risk posture, which is something that cannot be known just by observing results. It is hard to believe that a non-technical CIO would be able to make good strategic decisions under uncertainty.

Over the long term, an impeccable IT organization making good risk-based decisions will achieve the best results possible. But the contractor-control paradigm encouraged the organization to assess IT's performance by the immediate consequences of its work, which made it possible to think of the CIO's role as fundamentally non-technical—a role that could be played by executives with non-technical backgrounds. On the other hand, in a model where IT is a central part of the business—contributing technical expertise the way the CFO contributes financial expertise and the CMO contributes marketing expertise—IT leaders add value by being technical. They must be experts at assessing quality in technical practice: impeccability in construction, value contributed to the EA, avoidance of technical debt, architectural simplification, and good risk decisions based on technical experience.

For an IT leader to rely on his or her honest assessment of quality—independent of what those who are less tech-savvy believe and with a CEO screaming over the phone that the pandas are dying—requires courage.

---

It is difficult for IT to gain a seat at the table when IT is always failing, but on the other hand, an IT leader who is reacting to statistical noise—failures that he or she has already chosen to accept—is destroying business value. An IT leader must have the necessary technical skills, make impeccable decisions under uncertainty, and then have the courage to face the consequences.

---

# SHADOW IT

Inscrutably involved, we live in the currents of universal reciprocity.

—**Martin Buber**, *I and Thou*

It is of the first importance to men to establish close relationships and to bind themselves together with such ties as may most effectively unite them into one body.

—**Baruch Spinoza**, *Ethics*

Shadow IT—rogue IT, IT that is out of the control of the IT organization—is what has saved IT up to this point. It is a powerful phenomenon that we have not yet learned to take advantage of, caught up as we are in the contractor-control model of IT. Shadow IT is what happens when the IT organization is unable to meet the needs of a part of the company, perhaps due to capacity constraints or to the governance process's limitations. When shadow IT arises, it means that someone is helping fill that gap—that is, doing what IT is unable to do. That person is performing IT's work—they just don't happen to report to IT.

Is it a given that someone who doesn't report to IT is not as capable as someone who does? Why should IT leaders care about who gives the enterprise its IT capabilities? Or, to put it more bluntly, shouldn't IT care more about whether the company's needs are met than about who does the work of meeting them? In fact, if the CIO had a seat at the table—a true enterprise perspective—his or her concern would be making sure the company had the technology it needs to carry out its strategy, even if the IT department was unable to provide it.

Perhaps the reason we think it is important that the people creating IT report to the IT organization is that we think it is important for them to be "managed" by IT. But, as I've touched on previously, the command-and-control paradigm for management—especially IT management—is fading and being replaced by a team-based, complex adaptive system model. And is it really a matter of skills? Take another look—plenty of people are becoming IT savvy, and for certain functions, less and less deep IT knowledge is necessary.

Admit it: this is about control. IT has been given heavy accountabilities and believes it needs control over all IT activities in order to deliver on them. IT is outraged by shadow IT because it is supposed to control IT on behalf of the enterprise. And, of course, IT deserves to claim credit for IT successes.

> Can we *encourage* shadow IT so that we can take advantage of all of the skills and enthusiasm that exist across the enterprise?

I know—there are lots of reasons why we hate shadow IT, and I am missing the point. Shadow IT can cause security vulnerabilities. It can result in unmaintainable systems. It can violate IT standards (but remember those from the chapter on EA?). It can commit the company to ongoing maintenance expenses (but remember the discussion on sunk costs?). Yes, I know all of this.

This argument is backwards. Instead of looking for ways to eliminate or reduce shadow IT, we should instead ask ourselves what we can do to make sure that shadow IT does not come with those negative consequences. Can we *encourage* shadow IT so that we can take advantage of all of the skills and enthusiasm that exist across the enterprise? Can't we empower people throughout the enterprise to help move the company forward, using the tools of technology?

You—IT—*j'accuse!* You are playing the contractor-control game, driving a wedge between yourselves and the business!

Accompanying our transition to an Agile IT world and subtler in its implications has been the rise of *community* as a way of practicing IT. This change is due in large part to the rise of open source, but can also be traced to the demographics and inclinations of today's emerging workforce, as well as to the interdependence of participants in a DevOps model.

GitHub, the current center of the open source world, hosts some 38 million open source projects,[1] acting as both a source code repository and an environment in which project teams can collaborate. Developers working on an open source project share their code in a GitHub repository, document it, and exchange ideas, feature lists, and status information there. Someone who wants to work on the open source project can "clone" the repository onto their computer, make changes or additions to the code, test them, and then contribute them back to the open source project by making a "pull request"; that is, asking the leaders of the project to review the code and accept it into the project.

It also helps to think of GitHub as a social community—a gathering place of the geek world. Developers can set up personal profile pages and link them to the projects they participate in. By following links, one can find the code that the developer contributed to for each project, how active the developer is, and what sorts of projects the developer is interested in. Developers gain a reputation as leaders in their specialties by participating in projects. They gain the respect of other developers. They network and share ideas. They discover others with similar interests. And they do all of this in the context of producing something of value and of contributing to a community. This community is social and socially responsible; it is a celebration of intelligence, commitment, and coding skills.

An employer who is considering hiring a developer can research the developer's profile on GitHub. There, the employer can see what projects the developer has contributed to and can look at the code that the developer wrote. It is an ideal way to assess a candidate's software-engineering and collaboration skills.

Of course, the candidate can also look for the employer's contributions to the open source community. Are people who work for the company participating in open source projects? Is the company "giving back" to the community? If the company is represented on GitHub, are they doing interesting things? Are their employees good coders? Do they look like they would be fun to work with? Participating in the open source community is an inexpensive way for a company to build a brand as an employer of technical talent.

Working in the open can have tremendous advantages. It can give us the benefit of crowdsourcing, for one. It can hone our skills and get us feedback. If we make changes to an open source product and contribute them back to the community, then those changes may become part of future releases of the product, thereby relieving us of the sole burden of maintaining the code. This is a powerful model.

In the chapter on build versus buy, we already saw how open source changes the economics of custom development, but the implications go much deeper. Many open source projects are well known to the developer community. If you decide to use Spring for your Java projects, there will be a huge base of developers who are already familiar with it. In fact, you could say that at any given moment, there is a set of open source products that are so well known that being familiar with them is a kind of literacy for the developer community.

Even the proprietary products we buy are often built out of open source components. The existence of a vibrant open source community is an incentive for vendors of proprietary software to make their products conform to open standards, making it more likely that open source products will interoperate with their products.

Much of the work of the IT community is done in public now rather than in walled-off, ID-card-protected corporate campuses. The CIO, when he or she sits, sits before the public eye.

The great theorist of the open source community is Eric Raymond, whom I referred to in the chapter on build versus buy. His book, *The Cathedral and the Bazaar*, lays out the economic arguments for open source and explores the dynamics of the open source community.

At first glance, open source can seem to defy the economics of common sense, but Raymond presents several models that help make sense of the open source economy. Much has been written on the so-called "wisdom of crowds"; the idea that the more diverse inputs one has into a decision process, the better the decision will be. Citing Linus Torvald's comment that all bugs are shallow if they are exposed to enough eyeballs, Raymond argues that, "given a large enough beta-tester and co-developer base, almost every problem will be characterized quickly and the fix obvious to someone."[2]

He contrasts the open source economy with our everyday economy. "Our society is predominantly an exchange economy. This is a sophisticated adaptation to scarcity that, unlike the command model, scales quite well. Allocation of scarce goods is done in a decentralized way through trade and voluntary cooperation."[3] But code is not scarce. We can create more of it any time we want, and we do not need to compete for a limited supply of it. As a result, the economics of the open source community more resemble those of a gift culture or economy. "Gift cultures are adaptations not to scarcity but to abundance…in gift cultures, social status is determined not by what you control but by what you give away."[4] In an economy of abundance, the measure of success is one's reputation among one's peers. The open source community is not a strange exception to economic logic, but a place where people follow the rules of abundance rather than scarcity.

Open source has advantages when it comes to productivity. Not only does it harness the wisdom of crowds, but it also allows participants to do the things they are passionate about. No one tells open source participants what they must work on or how they must do their work. Instead, the open source model harnesses their enthusiasm and creativity.

This is consistent with what we have learned about motivation through works such as Daniel Pink's *Drive*. What is motivating, Pink says, is intrinsic incentives rather than those imposed from outside.[5] The strongest motivations, according to Pink, are autonomy, mastery, and purpose.[6] In the open source community, contributors have considerable autonomy; they can learn and master their craft and gain recognition for their mastery, and they can select the project that they are most passionate about or that best offers the type of purpose that motivates them. No wonder the open source community is so productive!

Raymond believes that the open source movement has a lot to teach us about managing IT. He contrasts the openness of the hacker culture to the closed, control-oriented nature of other software-development environments. "Hackers are naturally anti-authoritarian. Anyone who can give you orders can stop you from solving whatever problem you're being fascinated by ... authoritarians thrive on censorship and secrecy. And they distrust voluntary cooperation and information-sharing."[7]

On the one hand, we have open source hacker culture: transparent, cooperative, and driven by passion. On the other hand, we have proprietary software culture: command-and-control based, secretive, and liable to interfere with passionate activity. Of the two, open source culture has been phenomenally successful, while proprietary culture has suffered from suboptimal economics, dampened motivation, and questionable outcomes. "Joy is an asset," Raymond says.[8] He goes on:

> Indeed, it seems the prescription for highest software productivity is almost a Zen paradox; if you want the most efficient production, you must give up trying to make programmers produce. Handle their subsistence, give them their heads, and forget about deadlines.[9]

As are Agile approaches in general, the open source model is not based on control, but rather on empowerment and direction-setting. It is based on a shared vision rather than a set of requirements delivered from the outside world (the business) to the developers. And the open source model depends on releasing code and then improving it based on contributors' experience with the code in operational settings. There is more to these similarities than meets the eye. The open source model is aligned with theories that view businesses as a type of Complex Adaptive System.

The theory of Complex Adaptive Systems draws upon evolutionary biology and complexity theory. When an environment—a business, for example—is sufficiently complex, it is no longer subject to straightforward control mechanisms. In fact, "the behavior of such complex things is typically neither deterministic nor linear; rather, living systems continuously reorganize themselves in unexpected ways."[10] A CAS hovers on the edge of chaos;[11] it is a network of complex interactions that pursues "multidimensional objectives";[12] an evolutionary system that magnifies small changes into large effects.

John Henry Clippinger III's book *The Biology of Business* includes essays by a number of contributors, all painting today's businesses as Complex Adaptive Systems and discussing what it means for a manager to manage in such an environment. The contributors see the role of management as guiding the evolution of the enterprise indirectly through its influence, setting incentives and communicating visions that will help the enterprise self-select the right set of survival behaviors. But the limitation of the manager's power lies in the proposition that "control cannot be imposed—that instead, control emerges if managers create the right conditions and incentives for it to do so."[13] Management's role "cannot be extricated from, or elevated above, the fray of selection and emergence";[14] its challenge "is to create the conditions and contexts that select for a range of desired outcomes as in the process of natural selection."[15]

This is increasingly the view of organizations taken by Agile and Lean theorists, and it is remarkably similar to the worldview of open source. Consider Raymond's description:

> Yes, the success of open source does call into some question the utility of command-and-control systems, of secrecy, of centralization, and of certain kinds of intellectual property. It would be almost disingenuous not to admit that it suggests (or

at least harmonizes well with) a broadly libertarian view of the proper relationship between individuals and institutions.[16]

The CAS that the company's IT function represents can be thought of as a community—a community that embodies many of the values of the open source community.

I had a revelation when I was talking to some former Google engineers recently. They had been telling me about how their development teams sometimes ran into deep performance issues that required the expertise of someone on a different team, say a site reliability engineer (SRE). I asked them how they then were able to get the attention of the other team—in other words, how they were able to involve a team that was busy working on something else. Their answer was that they—get ready for this—ask. The expert on the other team tries to be helpful.

The conclusion I drew from this, using my CIO powers of extreme over-generalization, is that people are naturally willing to help, especially if they are being paid for it and they are motivated by achieving outcomes for the enterprise. Raymond is all over this one. "Hackers solve problems and build things, and they believe in freedom and voluntary mutual help."[17] That I had rarely seen such behavior in the enterprise led me to think that, perhaps, we are putting obstacles in the way of what would otherwise be natural behavior. For example, if we insist that people work through a management chain of command when trying to get help from a different organizational silo, or that if we evaluate someone based on their "productivity" toward a particular goal, we are disincentivizing them to cooperate on a different goal? Or that if we build a culture of loyalty to a silo, then we make it easy for an employee to turn their back on an employee from a different silo?

But somehow, companies like Google can make this sort of interaction work. People enjoy working as part of a community. There is a natural, human aspect to it—we enjoy people—but we also know that good technical people like to win the respect of other technical people. They like to show off. Asking for legitimate help brings out the best in them. I say "legitimate" fully conscious of the "flames" that are ignited in online communities when someone asks a stupid question that they should know the answer to—you know, the comments of the RTFM ("read the fucking manual") variety. There are community norms that have developed in the public spaces where engineers share ideas.

> A successful business can harness the community aspect of today's IT work environment.

A successful business can harness this community aspect of today's IT work environment, nurture it in their own organizations, and use it as a principle for building the capabilities of what I have called the people asset. Many of the challenges I have described in this book—challenges of governance, oversight, requirements, quality, Enterprise Architecture—can be addressed by borrowing ideas from the community model.

These community-oriented trends are consistent with changes in the IT workforce and the expectations of today's employees. These expectations are largely set by the "unicorns"—the leading technology companies and prominent startups. While the unusual perks that these companies offer are striking and attention-grabbing, it is more the work style and pattern of interactions that are the important point.

I am going to take the risk of over-generalizing again to paint a picture of today's emerging workforce. These characteristics reinforce the changes I have been describing, making them almost inevitable. As new people enter your organization, your way of working *is* going to change—and it will change to be more of a community-based, adaptive organism, a gift economy where individuals are respected and honored for their contributions to the community.

**Respect for skill:** Your new IT workforce will respect co-workers who have impressive technical skills, and will have little respect for people who don't. Skill is demonstrated through hands-on "shipping" of product. Management for the sake of management is *not* respected. On the other hand, a manager who can make solid technical decisions, contribute to technical discussions, or even sit down and code is likely to command admiration. Leaders emerge informally based on who has the best technical skills, and great technical performers are motivated by the chance to work with other great performers.

**Get things done:** The IT workforce wants to ship code. They expect to make an impact. They will be frustrated by obstacles placed in their way. Some companies that use a DevOps approach make it a practice that new employees deploy code to production on their first day of work. This both helps the employee overcome the fear of deployment and gets the employee used to the idea that they can ship code without barriers. As in the open source economy, success and motivation are based on outcomes.

The hierarchy must be flattened. Layers of management get in the way of goals. The employee wants the shortest possible path to shipping code without needing layers of approval. Management should be close enough to the action that they can demonstrate understanding—witnessing employees' contributions and removing impediments. Employees expect to be able to argue and have their voices heard, even in a meeting with more senior managers.

**Cross-functional and team-based:** It used to be natural for ops specialists to do ops, developers to do development, and testers to do testing. Now, crossover skills are increasingly important. On a delivery team, employees will help each other across roles in the interest of shipping code. If there is a backlog in exploratory testing, people who normally do development will help test. Software engineers will oversee their code in production and help make changes to the infrastructure if necessary to improve performance. Security skills are *de rigeur*. We speak of T-shaped people, people who have broad skill sets, with depth in a particular area. In the open source world, one is not funneled into a particular specialty—if you can contribute in one area, then it doesn't matter that your "job description" is in a different area.

Learning and experimentation are taken for granted. In the old days, COBOL programming was one specialty and FORTRAN programming was a different specialty. Today, it is assumed that a software engineer can learn new platforms and will be given the opportunity to do so. Someone who programs in Ruby should be able to learn Python quickly. They should also be able to switch between different continuous integration tools, different build tools, different deployment tools, and different types of deployment containers. In the open source world, you can join more than one project, and the projects can be of very different types.

**Fairness and social responsibility:** The workplace must be fair. Arbitrariness provokes negative reactions. If someone needs to be on-call to solve problems ("wear a pager"), then everyone should share in that responsibility. Moral outrage is easy to provoke. Teams are expected to help each other, so incentive structures that encourage teams to focus only on their own deliveries will be frowned upon. Companies should be transparent. In the open source world, norms are enforced by the community.

**Focus of roles is changing:** The software engineer role is increasing in importance. Tests and infrastructure are now both represented in code; with SDN, soon even the network will be. Infrastructure can now be tested, like code; it can be placed in version control. Newly important roles include those of the data scientist: the expert in working with data, with a mastery of statistical inference techniques, machine learning algorithms, and data obtaining and cleaning; the site reliability engineer (SREs), with expertise in maximizing performance in a web-centric environment, and the user experience (UX) researcher and designer.

**Technology matters:** Finally, as Martha Heller says, "most IT people are technologists; they need to work with technology, to touch technology, to walk and talk technology—at least some of the time."[18] They are in your IT organization because they enjoy technology; they are proud to be technologists. It is time to shake off the last traces of the attitude that this is something to be ashamed of or that they need to be controlled, learn to speak the language of the business, or start wearing jackets and ties.

> A CIO who sits at the table will have created a community in which smart, motivated employees can be creative.

It is not just that our model of the enterprise is moving in this direction, that our environment is moving in this direction, and that the workforce is moving in this direction; it is not just that we need to adapt. No, the amazing thing is that we can actually use this community-oriented model to overcome some of the problems IT has faced and to achieve positive outcomes for the company. I will give a few examples to show how we can use community principles to change our legacy IT model.

First, think about the silos we typically create between different applications. Often, each application has its own codebase; sometimes, these codebases are even hosted in different repositories. Sometimes, developers on one application do not have access to code from other applications. In light of this, let's start by making sure that we have a single repository for all of our code and that it is open to all of the developers. Starts to look like the open source community, doesn't it?

> We can actually use this community-oriented model to overcome some of the problems IT has faced and to achieve positive outcomes for the company.

Now developers can begin to reuse code from other projects. But more than that, they don't need to "fork" the code and make another copy. Instead, as in the open source community, they can contribute improvements back to the original project and continue to share the same codebase. One project team can help another project team.

The organization can create communities around reusable pieces of code, track suggestions on how to improve them, and let different teams contribute whenever it becomes practical for them to do so in the course of their work. In fact, the EA function can now be about shepherding or *stewarding* these reusable architectures. Instead of being standards enforcers, the EA folks can be hands-on developers who improve the architectural components in a way that benefits all of the systems and projects; they can inspire development teams to participate in their component improvements. They can get teams to make their components more reusable, or they can help teams to do so. An EA function that is hands-on will be respected by the development teams rather than shunned as an obstacle.

A community-based approach can also help us allocate IT resources better. Have you seen this problem? Team A depends on Team B for some changes, but Team B does not have the time and the resources, so Team A is delayed in its work. Cycle times are shot. Frustration abounds. But what if Team A could help by doing some of Team B's work for them? In an internal open source community model, Team A can just modify B's code, commit it back with a pull request for the experts in Team B to review and approve it, and—bam!—the work is done. We've achieved a Lean goal—to work each item all the way through to completion rather than letting it sit in inventory, and thereby decrease cycle times. Resources have been efficiently reallocated to where they are needed, and neither team needs to feel frustrated.

In some DevOps organizations, a platform team sets up an infrastructure that can then be used by the delivery teams. The delivery teams can manage the full stack—they can develop, test, deploy, and operate their code—on the platform that has been engineered by the platform team. This is another way to design a community and encourage community behavior—teams devoted to helping other teams. And if one of the delivery teams needs changes to the platform and the platform team is too busy, well, the delivery team can help the platform team.

Community thinking can apply to organizational structures, as well. What is a flattened hierarchy—preferred in Agile organizations—other than a community environment? The community environment abhors deep silos; it favors open communication between different teams and between teams and management.

Why haven't we always done things this way? Well, remember that a CAS leadership sets up the incentives that help determine how the system will evolve. Have we set up incentives for teams to help one another, or have we set up incentives that measure each team based on its assigned output, discouraging it from spending time on things that might help other teams? Have we made heavy-handed declarations of "accountability" (blame), thereby incentivizing teams not to allow other teams to touch their code? Have we facilitated the kind of code sharing and collaboration that this model calls for? Or have we been obsessed with a control-oriented paradigm and the incentives it brings, and in the process gotten in the way of what seems like a natural way of working—a humane, helpful, collaborative environment?

Throughout this book, I've spoken a lot about delivery teams and about IT leaders. But what about those in between—the so-called "middle management" folks? If senior leaders are setting visions and incentives, nudging delivery teams toward an effective Enterprise Architecture, then what are the folks in the middle doing? What role do they play in the IT community?

The question is especially urgent, because we have thoroughly linked middle management's role to a contractor-control paradigm. Think about what determines how many middle managers you need. Traditionally, it is "span of control." A given middle manager can "control" a certain number of direct reports; as the company scales, it therefore needs to be organized into a hierarchy with more layers and more middle managers. Accountability-blame gets passed down from layer to layer, so a middle manager's job is to get maximum production out of his or her corner of the enterprise.

In a Lean sense, it would seem that the less middle management the better—what we care about is production, not control, and the middle managers aren't the ones who produce. That makes middle management waste—sorry, guys. A flattened hierarchy plus team empowerment should allow us to eliminate middle management, right? But it doesn't feel right—we know that middle management is contributing something very important, and that, in fact, the model falls apart if they are not there. But how?

For an interesting take on this question, I recommend Paul Kennedy's *Engineers of Victory*, an exploration of how the Allies won World War II.[19] While other books focus on the role of the leaders—Churchill, Roosevelt, and maybe their larger-than-life generals such as Patton and MacArthur—Kennedy, a Yale history professor, looks instead at the middle managers—the little-known officers who solved the tactical engineering questions that needed solving in order arrive at the eventual victory. He discusses five particular problems the Allies faced as of March 1943, and what it took to solve those problems: how to control shipping in the Atlantic Ocean, how to stop the momentum of a blitzkrieg, how to use bombing strategically, how to land troops on a hostile beach, and how to deal with the immense distances across the Pacific Ocean. Each of these how-to's was solved through the efforts of creative problem-solvers in the middle ranks. Ultimately, their ideas empowered the lower ranks to succeed.

Kennedy talks about planes that could fly higher than enemy fighters, quirky equipment that could help tanks clear away obstacles, plans of battle that took away the advantage of fast-moving enemy armies, and many other ideas that ultimately helped the Allies to achieve those five strategic goals. His point is that these developments were "under the radar," so to speak, of the famous generals, but at the same time above the everyday concerns of the soldiers in the field.

The critical role of middle management, it would seem, is to give delivery teams the tools they need to do their jobs, to participate in problem-solving where the problems to be solved cross the boundaries of delivery teams, to support the delivery teams by making critical tactical decisions that the team is not empowered to make, and to help remove impediments on a day-to-day basis. The critical insight here, I think, is that middle management is a creative role, not a span-of-control role. Middle managers add value by contributing their creativity, skills, and authority to the community effort of delivering IT value.

We are moving toward a world in which IT empowers—a world in which instead of passively waiting for requests from the business, IT reaches out and creates platforms that can be used to move the business forward. One way IT can accomplish this is by putting flexible tools in the hands of business users—business intelligence tools, data analysis tools, collaboration tools, and support for mobility and remote work, for example. To go a step further, IT can just as well put development toolkits and platforms, support for self-provisioned cloud environments, test tools and automated test suites—tools that were formerly reserved for people reporting into the IT department—into the hands of the broader community outside of IT.

IT can open its code within the IT department, across the company, and ultimately across the open source community. The non-IT folks can contribute too. If they know how to program, great—they can contribute to the codebase, especially in areas that affect them or that they are passionate about. If they know how to do graphic design, then they can contribute design work. They can contribute documentation, do testing, or suggest solutions. Just as in the open source community, people can make suggestions to improve the code, and others can respond to those suggestions. IT can act as the shepherd, the community organizer, and the main contributor to this community.

> IT can act as the shepherd, the community organizer, and the main contributor to this community.

It is in this context that I say this: support shadow IT! It is a way to overcome the business-IT-contractor relationship. It is a way to motivate employees and to stimulate innovation. Finally, it is a way for IT leaders to break out of the contractor-control model, bring in the best ideas from the IT world, and contribute to the company's framework for execution rather than trying to own it.

---

Agile ways of working support a community approach to IT, where IT leaders achieve their objectives by mobilizing the skills and passions of a broad community and encourage the members of that community to work together across organizational silos in a way that values skills and contributions.

---

# Part III

## *Sitting at the Table*

# THE CIO'S PLACE
# AT THE TABLE

Genuine philosophers, however, are commanders and legislators: they say, "thus it shall be!"

—**Nietzsche**, *Beyond Good and Evil*

Use what language you will, you can never say anything but what you are.

—**Ralph Waldo Emerson**, *The Conduct of Life*

So, where does all of this leave us? I have tried to give hints in each chapter of how I would think about—or rethink—each of the traditional concerns of senior IT leadership. Let's review.

The role of senior IT leadership has always been framed in terms of control—the underlying theme of interactions between IT leaders and the rest of the business has been to "keep your people under control, provide good customer service, deliver what you say you will deliver, and you will be rewarded with a seat at the table." This way of thinking has become less and less tenable as we ask IT to step up and play a more central role in the company by driving its digital agenda. It is also unsustainable because IT initiatives involve considerable risk and uncertainty. It is entirely possible that senior IT leadership is doing all the right things, and even achieving good outcomes for the company, but is not delivering as planned, expected, wished, or fantasized. Good IT leadership must mean something other than demonstrating control.

Agile approaches hold the promise of changing this paradigm, but IT organizations have not thoroughly absorbed this message. Traditional Agile methodologies—if anything can be called traditional after only two decades—still distinguish between the role of the business (provide a product owner, decide on priorities, flesh out acceptance criteria, make business value decisions, and implement the new system and harvest the value from it) and the IT team (find solutions, craft a product, worry about security and standards, save money on technology, and establish control over delivery). Agile literature, ever suspicious of command-and-control management, does not really investigate the role of senior IT leadership, except in connection with transitioning to Agile processes.

> IT is now a critical part of every business's strategy, even if only to automate back-office functions—which in itself is a strategy.

IT is now a critical part of every business's strategy, even if only to automate back-office functions—which in itself is a strategy. Because IT is now central to competitive strategies, product strategies, and all parts of the value stream, it must support change at the speed of business change. But, unfortunately, we have set up IT around a control paradigm rather than a creative and enabling paradigm. This has caused business stakeholders to perceive IT as a limiter, a constraint, an impediment in achieving business objectives. As a result, businesses have found it necessary to set up new organizations—"digital services" organizations, "chief data officer" organizations, so-called bi-modal IT—that essentially have the same skills that the IT organization *should* have had in the first place. The consequence is a predictably uncomfortable overlap of functions, and IT organizations that increasingly have the dying skill sets of earlier decades.

But the concepts of Agile and Lean development already suggest a solution to this dilemma, if we are willing to change some of the fundamental assumptions and if senior IT leaders are willing to lead in the way that is demanded by the new mode of thinking. And the new thinking is fundamentally different—it is not a matter of new development techniques or even new project-management techniques—it is a different way of thinking about what is valuable, and what role IT should play in the organization at large.

The critical change is that of moving from a plan-driven approach to an Agile approach, based on learning and adapting. This is deeply opposed—let me say that again—*deeply opposed* to the control paradigm. If the main goal of IT leadership is to demonstrate that they can control projects and make them deliver according to plan—in other words, that they can eliminate uncertainty from the real world—then they cannot be Agile. You cannot strictly adhere to plans and also be Agile, which is to say that you cannot strictly adhere to a plan and also facilitate change and organizational responsiveness. It is not a conflict in execution—it is a conflict of *values*.

The essence of the plan-driven style is to begin with a set of requirements, or a scope. This scope is tossed over the wall from the business to the delivery teams—the business figures out what its "business need" is, and then IT delivers it. Because the requirements are known in advance, a plan can be made for fulfilling those requirements. But working in this paradigm reduces agility: a fixed set of requirements by definition doesn't change. It is also wasteful: if the delivery teams deliver all of the requirements, then they have probably delivered a lot of features that will not actually be used. But we have discouraged teams from eliminating this waste by complaining that they have "de-scoped," implying that they are being lazy for not finishing all the work.

The assumption behind fixed scope is that the business knows what it needs. The lesson of *The Lean Startup*, Eric Ries's book about new product development in both startups and enterprises, is that it doesn't—that the requirements are really only hypotheses about what will create the hoped-for outcomes and what will please customers and users.[1] The business and the delivery team should be engaged in a joint voyage of discovery, testing hypotheses. There can be no "tossing over the wall" of requirements—it is too risky.

The idea that we do "projects"—fixed sets of requirements with fixed schedules—leads us to think that there is an end to product delivery; that at some point we will have "finished" producing that product and will only need to maintain it. This is exactly what Agility argues against—our needs are fluid and will always be. The result of thinking in terms of products is that, over time, after the system is "finished," it begins to diverge more and more from the business's actual needs. Value is left on the table—at least in terms of opportunity costs—and eventually the company must do a large-scale transformation or rip-and-replace of an old system, which is risky and distracting.

The alternative to the project-oriented view might seem to be a product-centered view, where products have a roadmap and continue to develop over their lifecycle. But even this view is questionable. Users internal to a company do not really care about products the way that the buyers of an off-the-shelf product care about it. Users only care about capabilities. We mislead ourselves by grouping those capabilities into products and managing them at this coarser level. It is a metaphor gone bad. In fact, architecturally, we hardly deliver products anymore—with the move to microservices, we are just delivering REST and JMS endpoints independently. A better alternative is to think in terms of the overall IT asset—the collection of all capabilities and the technology that supports them—and look to optimize the whole. I refer to this asset as the Enterprise Architecture, using the term a bit differently from the usual.

Focusing on the EA suggests a different approach to build-versus-buy decisions. Senior IT leadership needs to groom the EA asset so that it is lean, tailored to the business's operations and strategies, and supportive of Agility through simplicity and technical excellence. Along with changes in the economics of software development, this can make custom development much more attractive relative to buying off the shelf than it has been considered in the past. With a Lean, Agile process, new capabilities can be delivered in rapid iterations and made to fit the company's needs quite exactly. On the other hand, the "buy off the shelf" approach is another way of assuming that we know our requirements in advance, and can find products that deliver that pre-defined set of requirements.

The old way of designing projects around fixed scopes of requirements, or buying a system off the shelf, lent itself to a certain type of governance process, an approach that analyzed "investments" in large batches of requirements, created a business case for each investment, and then had some group of senior stakeholders prioritize and "green light" selected investments. But in an Agile environment, this process is not a good fit. For one thing, its granularity is too coarse. We make a decision to move forward with a large batch of requirements, but in truth, some of those requirements have less of a business case than others, and the business case will change as the project moves along.

Another problem is that the business case is necessarily based on assumptions, but the governance decision—necessarily made at a single point in time—must treat those assumptions as valid. Instead, we need a governance process that validates those assumptions as the project progresses and that accommodates changes to requirements based on what is learned. In an uncertain environment, we have to stop pretending that we can know at a point in time what we should do over the entire course of the project.

Our focus should instead be on oversight—that is, in my definition, the senior decision-making that happens during the execution of the initiative. We need to set up fast feedback cycles—very consistent with Agile and Lean practices—between the executors and the executives. The executive stakeholders can give feedback and make course corrections—the most important of which are the removal of impediments—in order to maximize the value of the investments and re-allocate investment resources in an agile way. Rather than testing the progress of the initiative against fixed milestones and deliverables, we measure it in terms of what it has delivered, how cost-effectively it has done so, and what it plans to deliver. Instead of trying to deliver on a schedule, the project team tries to deliver *as soon as possible*—in other words, to become Lean, thereby reducing costs and increasing responsiveness.

The real driver of this approach to governance and oversight—and of the new way of thinking about IT and its role in the enterprise—is uncertainty and risk. We are simply not good at understanding uncertainty—a business case that pretends to have precision and that has fancy graphics can easily persuade us that we know the future and can thus make decisions based on that knowledge. We can misperceive the relative risks of exceeding cost and schedule milestones versus building a product that does not achieve its desired outcomes. We can make bad decisions about security out of fear or complacency, lacking good intuitions of risk. But an IT leader is a manager of uncertainty, and making good risk decisions is critical to the job. Agile approaches to oversight and governance are the best route to managing the real risks effectively. The old control-based paradigm not only creates unrealistic goals—ignoring uncertainty—but also adds to risk.

Quality is closely related to risk. When we test a system, we are mitigating the risk of defects appearing in production. As with other risk-based areas, we will not be able to achieve certainty, nor will we be able to evaluate success just through what we observe as the future becomes the past. There are almost certainly diminishing returns to incremental testing, and setting the appropriate bar for quality is part of a risk-management strategy. In the past, this has led us to an attitude that views defects and failures as unavoidable. IT employees are known to be the folks who constantly create failures and don't suffer any consequences from them.

Despite this, we can distinguish between good execution—impeccability—and poor hygiene. As with many things in DevOps, we want to move quality "to the left"; that is, achieve higher levels of quality earlier in our process. With good training on typical defects and on how to avoid them and high managerial standards, developers can produce "rugged" code in the first place, and then fast-feedback testing and peer code reviews (or pair programming) can find many of the remaining defects.

Feedback is a natural consequence of community. The old control-based paradigm led naturally to organizational siloing, where "accountability"—blame—is passed down a structured man-agement chain. This disincentivizes many community behaviors that have proven to be extremely powerful, particularly in the open source community. While the control paradigm pushed standards and policies down from up above, a better model for Agile leader-ship is encouraging behaviors and practices, and especially designs, to emerge evolutionarily from the ground up. This increases agil-ity—the velocity of change—and takes advantage of the wisdom of crowds. Leaders can act as stewards, facilitating good interac-tions between teams and managing in a way consistent with the theory of Complex Adaptive Systems. Community-centric models can be rolled out in IT organizations and across enterprises and ecosystems to improve our ability to deliver value responsively and in accordance with Lean principles.

In the Agile world, senior IT leadership, and the CIO in particular, must look at their jobs in a new way if they want to secure that seat at the table. Here are a few of the critical characteristics of the new IT leadership role.

**Driver of Outcomes:** Business organizations achieve their desired outcomes through technology. When technology was only used to help the organization derive its outcomes, the role of IT leaders was simply...well, to help the organization derive its outcomes by providing whatever IT capabilities the organization said it needed. IT was responsible for delivery of capabilities—the rest of the organization for determining what capabilities were needed and for harvesting business value from them.

> In the Agile world, senior IT leadership must look at their jobs in a new way if they want to secure that seat at the table.

But now that technology is so central to the business—now that we are living in a digital world—that handoff between a business and an IT department no longer makes sense. Instead, IT leaders must take responsibility not for delivery, but for outcomes, in the same sense that marketing and sales are not just responsible for delivering TV commercials and sales calls, but for delivering revenues, as well. IT must drive outcomes in terms of revenue, cost reduction, sustained competitive advantage, employee happiness, and innovation.

It doesn't matter whether all of these outcomes are directly created by people who work in the IT department—in fact, that will likely never happen. The magic is in how people use technology, not in the technology itself. Install a spreadsheet program or a business intelligence tool on the desktops of business users and it does nothing. These tools must be used creatively in order to drive value creation. IT value is not created by IT people alone, and that is precisely what IT leaders must care about—the value generated through the use of the technology.

IT cannot have an arms-length, contractor-control relationship with the rest of the business. In an Agile and Lean world, IT is engaged in a voyage of discovery with the rest of the business, bringing its particular skills to bear as the enterprise works as a single unit to discover and implement ways of creating value. The business does not know what it needs, it does not know what the outcomes of its actions will be, and it faces risk and uncertainty. IT plays an important part in driving the enterprise forward in the face of uncertainty.

There are good reasons to think that IT leaders might be very good at driving business outcomes. Martha Heller points out that "CIOs have a bias for action. They respect deadlines and they want results. Their teams do too."[2] She also points out that the CIO is the only executive who sees business processes from beginning to end.[3] With this end-to-end understanding of the business, a discipline and mindset of accomplishing goals, and an inclination toward innovation and change, IT leaders bring a lot to the table when it comes to working together as a company to achieve business outcomes.

The new enterprise is a community in which IT plays an important part by enabling, guiding, and providing skills. Shadow IT is a manifestation of this community aspect of IT. That is fine; all that matters for IT leadership is IT outcomes.

**Manager of Uncertainty:** One reason, I would argue, that IT leaders have the skills to drive outcomes is because of their ability to deal sanely—that is, rationally and intuitively—with risk and uncertainty. While other executives might over-perceive risk in an initiative, IT can make sure that risk is managed down appropriately, and then make good decisions about when it is time to "launch." Companies face the uncertainties of the future—and IT leaders are experts at dealing with uncertainty.

Making good decisions under uncertainty has always been an important part of IT leadership. Should we build our systems in Java or .Net? Or perhaps in Node.js? This decision involves assessing the future of these platforms, their likely roadmaps, and whether or not there are likely to be programmers with the required skills in a few years. Senior IT leaders have to assess the risk of deploying new systems and the extent to which these risks have been mitigated through testing. They must gauge the security risks of a system given the unknown activities of potential attackers. Risk and uncertainty are simply the day-to-day reality for IT leaders.

Agile and Lean thinking give IT powerful ways to manage uncertainty. By establishing short, robust feedback cycles and flexible decision-making processes, by creating options and grooming enterprise capabilities so that they will be responsive to change, and by demonstrating the value of information, IT can lead the organization in learning and in deriving business value from good risk management and from making the most of opportunities that present themselves.

That is good, because enterprises need not only to change quickly, but to anticipate the future and prepare themselves to participate in it, as well. Strategic planning requires skill in managing uncertainty, and IT manages the assets—EA, people, and data—that will determine how adept the company is at facing the future.

**Steward of Assets:** I have argued that senior IT leadership has the responsibility for stewarding three critical assets: the Enterprise Architecture asset, the IT people asset, and the data asset. These three assets represent the capabilities of the company and its ability to address the future. EA is the collection of capabilities that lets the business do what it does; it is a map of the organization written in IT systems. The health of the EA asset determines the company's agility and costs in the future. Because the EA is grounded in technology, only IT leadership can truly steward it; polishing and grooming this asset requires an understanding of technical debt, security risks, and architectures that will be enabling or constraining in the future. Both the IT skills asset and the data asset are future-directed bearers of latent value that are critical to the company's ability to earn future profits. Overseeing them falls naturally to IT leadership.

I have read that product owners or other "business folks" are capable of making decisions on things like security and technical debt—that they can prioritize stories to address these things—as long as the technical team explains them in terms of business value. As I argued in *The Art of Business Value*, I do not believe that this is so; implicitly, it depends on the idea that there is a common currency of business value such that the product owner can compare the business value of the security story against the business value of a functional story and prioritize them rationally. But that common currency does not really exist, especially on the level where it can be used to compare individual features. Business value is a more nuanced topic than it first appears.

So, senior IT leaders guide the technical capabilities of the firm by overseeing the development and fine tuning of its EA, people, and data assets. Senior IT leaders must be stakeholders in generating and prioritizing investments; they should be the quickest to find the delta between the EA as it is now and the EA as it must be in the future. That delta, by definition, is the IT initiative that must be pursued.

**Contributor:** For decades, CIOs have been told to stop acting like technology geeks and begin acting more like business people. They have been told to speak the language of the business, to focus on profits and cost reduction. I submit that this view is very closely tied to the idea that the CIO must control the technical geeks, and is an attitude primarily rooted in fear. Not that CIOs shouldn't speak the language of the business—it is more that IT language has become a dialect of business language. The non-IT parts of the business have been forced to learn about technology, about digital strategy, about the internet and its peculiarities. They are learning to speak the language of IT— which happens to be very expressive when talking about IT. I have had no problem teaching my non-technical peers and managers to "speak geek." They can sound convincing when relaying information about the cloud, email, servers, regression testing, automated deployments—and can ask good questions around these subjects.

So, what's the problem? I'm not sure there is one. The senior leadership team includes someone called the CFO, who helps lead the company from the point of view of someone who is an expert in finance; the CMO is someone who contributes expertise in marketing to running the company; the COO contributes expertise in operations as one of a group of leaders of the company. It follows that the CIO is the member of the senior leadership team—the team that oversees the entire enterprise—who contributes deep expertise in information technology.

I do mean to say *deep* expertise. Increasingly, everyone in the enterprise knows a lot about technology; the CIO, then, is the person who knows *more* than everyone else. The CIO should be more technical, not less—that is how he or she contributes to enterprise value creation; otherwise, the role would not be needed. According to one of Heller's CIOs, "IT is like a teenager living with his grandparents. He is changing every day, and they don't understand him."[4] The CIO's job is to bring this understanding to the organization.

Jim Highsmith makes an interesting prediction in *Adaptive Leadership*: "Product owners are the customers of today," he says, "while technical and quality leaders are the customers of tomorrow."[5] I wonder if he is thinking along the same lines as me. If IT strategy is really about stewarding the EA asset so that it is flexible, high-quality, and a good fit to business goals, then the stewards of that asset should be the "customers" for any work that advances the asset. The more that we see the business as digital, the more we must acknowledge that it is technical to its core and the more the technical stewards of capability need to drive investment and capability definition.

Heller's CIOs seem to be coming around to this position, as well. "Lately, I am finding that CIOs are flexing their technologist muscles again,"[6] she says. If we drop the idea that the CIO's job is to protect the organization from technology and technologists, we can instead rely on the CIO to administer doses of technology when needed, to change the business's discourse to discussions informed by technology, and to sharpen the business's ability to use technology to create competitive advantage.

**Influencer and Salesperson:** The CIO's job is not just to manage the IT department—it is to be one of a team of senior leaders managing the entire business. True, the CFO manages the finance department, but the CFO's primary job is to steer the entire business with his skills in finance. The CMO manages the marketing organization, yes, but the C in CMO means that the CMO is really leading the entire enterprise in a way that is consistent with good marketing principles and his or her own marketing strategy. So, too, for the CIO.

The critical skill for someone who is leading an enterprise, only a portion of which is under his or her control, is the ability to manage through influence. The CIO needs to sell his or her ideas to the rest of the organization—to influence the use of technology in areas he or she does not directly control. To do so, the CIO must build relationships with peers; understand the outcomes they desire; demonstrate how his or her ideas can help them achieve their outcomes; and explain, convince, and follow through.

This is very different from the treatment in most books about IT leadership, which often speak about how the CIO must communicate to other executive leaders how much value IT is contributing. This, to me, is a horrible way of thinking—defensive and wasteful. The time, resources, and dollars the CIO is spending on that communication would be better spent on influencing the activities of the company. What executive leadership wants is not fancy brochureware explaining all the good things IT is doing. What they want is for IT to be *doing* the good things. The CIO looks at business dynamics from the point of view of technology and contributes ideas based on this focus, negotiating, convincing, and compromising his or her way into making an impact.

> The CIO looks at business dynamics from the point of view of technology.

Daniel Pink, whose book *Drive* has been very influential in the Agile community's thought about motivating employees, has also written a book on selling called *To Sell is Human*. "People are now spending about 40 percent of their time at work engaged in non-sales selling—persuading, influencing, and convincing others in ways that don't involve anyone making a purchase,"[7] he says. This makes sense, he says, because "a world of flat organizations and tumultuous business conditions—and that's our world—punishes fixed skills and prizes elastic ones."[8] Flat organizations do not lend themselves to command-and-control, but rather to indirect influence through softer skills. Sales skills, though often unacknowledged in the technology world, are the key to managing in the community environment that has been the legacy of open source.

**Orchestrator of Chaos:** We have spoken of the business as a Complex Adaptive System. In a CAS, leaders lead through creating the conditions that help evolution select for the desired behaviors and outcomes. Senior IT leaders are important influencers of evolution in this sense. The CIO has a number of tools at his or her disposal for encouraging evolution to proceed in a way consistent with the company's desired outcomes. The CIO hires employees and trains them; organizes them into teams; and facilitates communication between those teams. The CIO issues policies and standards where appropriate, makes governance decisions, distributes budget resources among teams, and delivers feedback. He or she provides tools and sets up the environments in which teams work. All of these elements create a context for the teams—add the CIO's articulation of a vision and adjustments of behavior through feedback, and we have a powerful set of mechanisms to guide the business's evolution.

In his book *Implementing Beyond Budgeting*, Bjarte Bogsnes is not just concerned with the mechanics of a budgeting process, but also with the assumptions behind our approach to budgeting and its impact on the people in our organizations. The real problem Bogsnes sees in our budgeting approach is that it is used as a way of controlling people's behavior.[9] But the sort of control provided by budgets is neither appropriate nor effective in the complex environment of a business organization. Instead, according to Bogsnes, "what we can do is to create the conditions needed for good performance to take place.... good leaders should create clarity, capability, and commitment."[10]

"With consumerization and cloud services, the role of IT moves from integrator to orchestrator, and orchestration is different because you no longer have direct control of all of the pieces,"[11] says Ralph Lara, CIO of Clorox, as cited in Heller, and he might as well have been talking about management in a CAS.

I began this book posing the question of how senior IT leadership can play a role in an environment of autonomous teams working directly with product owners from the business. The answer, I think, lies in this kind of leadership by influence. Takeuchi and Nonaka, the authors of the Harvard Business Review article that was an inspiration for the Agile community, say that "subtle control is also consistent with the self-organizing character of project teams."[12]

Craig Larman and Bas Vodde, in their book *Scaling Lean and Agile Development*, have this to say:

> Self-organizing teams do not just happen, they need the right environment. The organization is responsible for supporting the team development by creating the conditions needed for teams to succeed. Switching to self-organizing teams means the job of the traditional project manager changes from directing the team to creating these conditions.[13]

Not just the project manager, the authors might have said, but leadership in general.

The answer to my question is simply that IT leaders do not need direct "control" of the teams' activities, because they lead indirectly—as do all of the executives with seats at the table.

**Enabler:** The control metaphor has extended to the way that IT systems interact with other human beings; or perhaps it is a reaction to the control dynamic imposed on IT. Systems are built to compel behavior, and users are trained on how to use systems as directed. IT personnel channel users into particular ways of doing things; saying "no" is normal. Our systems give error messages when the users misbehave. Of course, this makes a lot of work for IT folks—every time there is a new special case, we have to change the rules to allow it. Every time there is an exception to standards, there is paperwork involved in granting the exception.

Perhaps it is time for a new way of thinking about this reverse-control dynamic. What if the job of IT is to enable activities rather than to discourage them? If users are becoming more sophisticated consumers of IT, perhaps we should be putting the burden on them to do what is right with the tools we give them. Business intelligence systems have been created on the basis of trying to enforce a single version of the truth—one set of reports that everyone can agree on. But today, that approach is fraying at the edges: in the days of data science and big data, it is important to let the people with real data skills explore freely; constraining them is value-destroying.

Yes, I know that we have constrained the use of our systems in order to preserve data integrity—we don't want users to make mistakes that puts our data into a non-logical state. And so what? Is that really what matters most to us? Perhaps, in many cases, we can allow more freedom because the price of non-logical data is low; or perhaps, in other cases, we can automatically correct errors. Remember that data is used mostly for analysis—transactions that create or update data are a smaller and smaller fraction of our database use. Freedom is powerful and motivating.

We have been afraid of "rogue" application development, or shadow IT. There has been good reason for that. Rogue applications are often unreliable and insecure; IT winds up having to fix them when they become mission critical. But are they always insecure and unreliable? Do they have to be? If everyone is really becoming more tech savvy, might it not be a better idea to support and encourage rogue development? I have tried giving sophisticated folks outside of IT programming environments with controls built in, and shared source code repositories. We have held hackathons where anyone can participate using those tools. If a user wants to check out a piece of code, make changes to it, and then contribute those changes back to the IT team, who am I to tell them they can't? Or, to put it another way, why would I accept that behavior if they report to me and not accept that behavior if they do not report to me?

If we treat IT and the business as a whole as a community, we can focus on enablement; it is the control paradigm that puts boundaries around what people can do. Those boundaries are wasteful, and we must drop them wherever they are not necessary. Risk there may be, but big is the benefit, as well.

**Impediment Remover:** The leadership model that seems to work best with Agile approaches is servant-leadership. The Agile team is committed and hands-on; they will tend to know best how to accomplish the objectives they are given. The best thing that a manager can do is to help the team do what it knows how to do by removing impediments. Tell the team what you need, let them do their work, and ask them how you can help. There are many things that a senior manager can do more efficiently than the Agile team because of his or her organizational power; those things should quickly be brought to the manager's attention, and the manager should deal with them immediately.

Autonomous teams need to interact, and senior leadership sets the context in which that interaction takes place. Is it encouraged? Do teams feel comfortable asking one another for help? Are direct interactions allowed, or must communication go through a Scrum Master or a bug-tracking system? Senior leadership can reduce the friction that causes wasted energy and that slows the release train.

Commitment to reducing cycle time means that everyone—teams and leaders alike—are engaged in reducing it by doing whatever is necessary. Leaders have powers that the teams lack—often the impediments slowing cycle time can only be removed by those in power. Leadership influence, you might say, is an important asset the team has in doing its job. The leader's contribution to the IT community is his or her use of power for the common good.

**Manager of Managers:** Previously, we've explored the role of IT leadership in creating community and the role of IT middle managers in acting as problem solvers, linking together strategy and execution by making rapid decisions and developing tactical solutions. The old span-of-control model for middle management makes less sense in an Agile world of empowered teams. But what of command and control? Does it disappear entirely in the Agile world?

I'm not sure, to be honest.

While the Agile community speaks of the need for cultural change across the enterprise, I'm not sure that it recognizes its own cultural biases and the impact they have on the success of Agile transformations. Even just the words "command and control" bring on a strong negative reaction in many. In my experience, this dislike lasts right up until the moment that the team faces a tough impediment—then they would like management to order the impediment to go away—or until some of the developers are not following good technical practices. Perhaps they are breaking the build and not fixing it immediately, or perhaps they aren't writing enough unit tests. At some point, the team relies on management to fix the problem.

Of course, coercive behavior by management feels wrong on many levels, and is not a good *cultural* fit with Agile processes, which bring their own value system. Orthodox Agile practice, I think, would advocate working with those who are "disobeying" the "rules" of good technical practice; perhaps helping them to conduct experiments that will show them why writing more unit tests is a better idea, and maybe incentivizing the impediment-inserters to stop inserting those impediments. These approaches have value, but they also might work against the effort to be Lean. On one hand, we want to encourage self-organization and self-governance; on the other, we want to forcefully and quickly remove impediments.

Perhaps removal of impediments is so important—really, it is a key to the empowerment of the team—that the faster it happens the better, and the fastest way is often through a touch of command and control. In a sense, it doesn't matter whether impediments are removed through management's coercive authority—its ability to compel behaviors—or through gentler means. What matters, arguably, in an Agile process is that the team is not commanded and controlled in its *ability to find a solution to the business problem at hand*.

Underlying the Agile way of thinking is a vision of what it looks like when a development project is running perfectly. You have a small team of high-energy, smart software engineers who respect each other and enjoy each other's company. They bounce ideas around and help each other find solutions. Each comes up with great ideas that make the others think of more great ideas. Before someone can finish stating a challenge they are having, someone else has already come up with—and coded—a solution to it. Stuff keeps getting done, and users keep smiling and telling the developers how brilliant they are.

Then come the template zombies. Progress halts while somebody fills out the paperwork that will allow the system to go to production. Management has brilliant ideas based on what a salesman told them and wants the team to explain why it hasn't created the shmurf feature and why they haven't dealt with the scary security issue that the security company told them about. Let's face it: management is waste. They don't code.

> Let's face it: management is waste. They don't code.

When a team is really working, all management can do is get in the way and reduce business value. Agile concepts were created by working developers who know what real productivity looks like, and they rightly want to set up a way of working that leads to that state. Agile approaches are a brilliant way to work toward what the developers know actually works. But when things aren't working so perfectly, management needs to use its powers to clear away all of the impediments that prevent the team from getting into that productive flow.

As long as a team has boundaries, there will be decisions that need to be made from outside its boundaries, and people who need to be—er, um, "influenced"—on the outside. The team should have the primary responsibility for exercising that influence and for framing those decisions. And the team requires empowerment—that is, freedom from command and control—within its solutioning boundaries, but the effort of coordinating the activities of different teams, other actors, and other parts of the business still requires some sort of management.

In an Agile world, IT leaders are not leading a customer service organization or a contractor that delivers product in response to requirements. Rather, IT leaders are driving outcomes for the business through the enterprise's digital way of being in the world.* That way of being is based on harnessing the power of bits—their infinite flexibility, their ability to create options and to drive and encapsulate learning, the fact that changing some ones to zeros can make a Google out of an AltaVista. Software is thought recorded in ones and zeros, and thought is as flexible as human creativity. IT leadership is about participating in the decision of what sequence of ones and zeros is the business's strategy, and then arranging the ones and zeros in that order. Hunter and Westerman say: "We can sum up this paradigm change as rule number 1: it's not about IT. It's all about business."[14] Indeed it is—and the business is all about IT now.

> Software is thought recorded in ones and zeros, and thought is as flexible as human creativity.

---

* A nod to Heidegger.

IT leadership runs the business along with the others who run the business. The seat at the table is earned by being at the table.

# EXHORTATION AND
# TABLE MANNERS

How much personal timidity and vulnerability this masquerade of a sick hermit
betrays!

—**Friedrich Nietzsche**, *Beyond Good and Evil*

Against truth said in laughing, is there a law?

—**Horace**, *Satires*

It's the last chapter and I already did a summary in the previous chapter. There's nothing left to do but end on a message of hope. And that's what this book is meant to be, really. We have been laboring under a mistaken view of IT for a number of decades—perhaps not surprising when you have a brand-new discipline created *ex nihilo* by a bunch of playful, passionate, socially inept geniuses. But we've learned stuff, and if we can break out of the old model, the learnings promise a new generation for IT leaders.

Pity the poor old-time CIO, the prospect of a seat at the table dangled just ahead if only he or she could prove control over those pocket-protector geeks and—oh, yeah—provide good customer service too. Control what is uncontrollable, violate the laws of probability, be creative and conjure up business value—as long as you do exactly what you are told. Deliver service with a smile while standardizing, constraining, and saying no. Martha Heller calls these "paradoxes"[1]; I call these impossibilities. There is only one thing to do: refuse the mission and perform a better one in its place, in full confidence that it will turn out right.* Instead of trying to control the uncontrollable, show the company how to harness uncertainty for competitive advantage. Act, simply, with courage.

Courage has always been a core value of the Agile community; Extreme Programming named it as one of the four values (along with communication, feedback, and simplicity) that drive the Agile principles. Kent Beck explicitly charges executives with providing "courage, confidence, and accountability."[2] Courage, I say, is the value most needed by Agile IT leaders. Consider the following points that I have raised.

> Courage, I say, is the value most needed by Agile IT leaders.

IT decisions, we have seen, are made under extreme uncertainty, and I have suggested that IT play a larger role in the business's management of uncertainty and risk. The Agile way to manage risk is not to overanalyze, not to become mired in analysis paralysis, not to hedge and document as a way of covering one's posterior in case things go wrong. No, the Agile way is to—boldly and with commitment—try what seems right and see if it works. The risk is carefully controlled by fast feedback and a "fail quickly" mentality, but the initial move is a bold yet calculated leap of faith that fully exposes IT leaders to criticism. Fail proudly! Have courage!

We have discussed how risk-based decisions may be correct and yet still lead to failure. More than that, we have seen cases where good risk-based decisions necessarily lead to failures—the decision to have three nines of availability means that .1% of the time, IT will

---

* Another nod to Kierkegaard.

have failed to provide good service. When the system is down, IT leaders are villains and goof-ups, and the other 99.9% of the time is suddenly irrelevant. To be an excellent IT leader, one must make the decision to expose one's lack of performance to the world. Good luck! Have courage!

Similarly, we will create business value for the enterprise by testing software until diminishing returns from testing suggest that we do the rest of our testing in production. We will have defects, we will have roll-backs, and we will make people wonder how we could be so dumb. And then, we will humbly fix the problem. We will do this because it is best for the company. We are brave!

As IT leaders, we will be called on to make governance decisions even though we don't have perfect information. We will be called on to oversee projects without even the crutch of a Gantt chart. Will we insist on more and more information, or will we accept the uncertainty, experiment freely, and allow the experiments to fail?

Or will we step back timidly and shoot down new ideas by saying that they are too risky—as if doing nothing and letting competitors move forward were not riskier. If we don't take risks, then the company's decline will be blamed on the market, while if we take risks, then only we will be blamed. Courage is how we turn uncertainty into profit.

We will trust our teams and empower them, and we will serve them as servant-leaders. Yes, we will make ourselves vulnerable by doing so. We will not be able to both "control" them and empower them; we will have to trust. Not "trust but verify"—trust but influence and motivate. The teams that create value for us create value for us; we do not. We are overhead. We must allow them to create value, help them to create value, and trust them to create value. They will do so if we have chosen our teams wisely and infused them with the right vision, and if we sweep aside their impediments. Courage, my fellow IT leaders!

What of plans? The nail-biters among us want detailed plans before they are willing to launch into an initiative. They ask their people, "Have you thought of this? Have you thought of that?" and nod sagely. I say that the sage is the sick hermit to whom Nietzsche alludes. The CIO thinks and does, thinks and does, thinks and does, never letting an opportunity to do fade away as he or she thinks and thinks and thinks. Taking action in the face of uncertainty requires courage, and it is what IT is all about.

DevOps is not for the faint of heart. Developers push a button to deploy their own code into production. We follow the principle that when something is difficult, we do it more often. When something is frightening, we do it more often. When something is broken, we keep doing it until we fix it. Then we unleash a Chaos Monkey in production—we deliberately break our live system over and over again to make sure it is resilient. What if it is not? We will take the consequences and fix it.

Will we sell IT's value to the enterprise? I am telling you that this is pure waste. Do not sell your accomplishments to the business. Your accomplishments are the business's accomplishments. The shrill noise of an IT leader trying to speak the language of cost obfuscation—I mean cost avoidance—is like the frequent boastings of someone with an inferiority complex. Do what is right—produce outcomes—and your contribution will be appreciated, or you will find a better job. Do it with the courage and confidence of someone who knows how important he or she is.

> Do what is right—produce outcomes—and your contribution will be appreciated, or you will find a better job.

The business wants functionality. Now. After we finish creating the necessary functionality, they want more. After that, they want even more. After all, they need and require it. But you know—don't you—that if the functionality is not built to foster agility later, if the Enterprise Architecture will not stay lean, up-to-date, and flexible, that the business will suffer for it in the future. Needs are now; requirements are now; but agility is about how we face the future, in all its uncertainty. Do you have the courage to make the case for investment in those things you know are important, even if the business value involves uncertainty and the future? Are you brave enough?

We know how to renegotiate supplier contracts and save money. We know how to consolidate, standardize, and browbeat to save money. We can show "results" and beg for our seat at the table. But that seat isn't coming, because those things are not strategy. Strategy is about envisioning outcomes and driving toward them. To drive outcomes, we need to step outside the comfort zone, to work in uncertainty and difficult-to-measure areas. We have to broaden our perspective to include the harvesting of value, not just the production of systems and the deployment of capabilities. That means we must take accountability for things we don't control. We have to take accountability for influencing others. That's right—if we don't influence others, we fail at producing outcomes. Yet, we can do it. We are the people who have mastered technology and cut away at the cutting edge!

"Adaptive leaders," says Jim Highsmith, "are those who have vision and foresight; who can articulate clear direction; who can persist in the face of ambiguity, uncertainty, and doubt; who can adapt before their focus becomes obsession."[3] Yes, we can adapt and change—but what happens when the CEO calls us into his office and says, "Yesterday you told me we should do yada yada, and now you are telling me we should do so-and-so. Make up your mind!" Will we, with backs straight and expression confident, say, "Yes, Sir CEO, we should do so-and-so, because things have changed since yesterday."

No one else can make the electrons that run the business leaner or more agile the way we can. No one else understands uncertainty the way we do. We don't just understand the tools and the principles—we get how to achieve outcomes with them. We are magicians, possessors of the potions and scrolls, motivators of the armies of geeks, and seers of the future.

And we care—boy, do we care. That's how we got our skills. Curiosity, motivation, intellectual prowess. We want to apply these skills to solving the enterprise's problems in a world where the tools are the tools we know. The lesson of the "unicorns"—the Silicon Valley startups that are setting the pace for the technology community—is that when you combine passion with technical excellence, amazing things follow. The job of the IT leader is to inspire passion and inspire technical excellence in service of the enterprise's objectives.

And that, my friends, is what this book has been all about. We do not get that seat at the table by meekly doing the things we are comfortable with. We get that seat at the table by embracing uncertainty—by negotiating it with agility and leanness and doing what's best for the enterprise, not by pretending to have control over what is by its nature uncontrollable. We get the seat by not worrying about getting the seat, and instead by courageously embracing the new and the beyond-the-plan.

Take a seat.

Wretched, wholly wretched! Keep your hands off beans!

—**Empedocles of Acragas**, *On Nature*

# REFERENCES

## A

Adzic, Gojko. *Impact Mapping: Making a Big Impact With Software Products and Projects.* Surrey, UK: Provoking Thoughts, 2012.

Ancona, Deborah and Henrik Bresman. *X-Teams: How to Build Teams that Lead, Innovate, and Succeed.* Boston: Harvard Business School Press, 2007.

Anderson, David. *Kanban: Successful Evolutionary Change for Your Technology Business.* Sequin, WA: Blue Hole Press, 2010.

Avery, Christopher M. "Responsible Change." *Cutter Consortium Agile Project Management Executive Report*, no. 6, 10 (2005): 1–28.

## B

Beck, Kent, with Cynthia Andres. *Extreme Programming Explained: Embrace Change* 2nd ed. Boston: Addison-Wesley, 2005.

Bogsnes, Bjarte. *Implementing Beyond Budgeting: Unlocking the Performance Potential.* Hoboken, NJ: John Wiley and Sons, 2009.

Brooks Jr., Frederick P. *The Mythical Man-Month: Essays on Software Engineering, Anniversary Edition.* Boston: Addison-Wesley, 1995.

Brown, Carol. "The Successful CIO: Integrating Organizational and Individual Perspectives." Graduate School of Business, Indiana University. 1993. Other reference: SIGCPR Proceedings of the 1993 Conference on Computer Personnel Research. New York: ACM, 1993. 400–407.

# C

*CIO Magazine*, January 2016.

Clippinger III, John Henry, ed. *The Biology of Business: Decoding the Natural Laws of Enterprise*. San Francisco: Jossey-Bass Publishers, 1999.

Cohn, Mike. *Succeeding with Agile: Software Development Using Scrum*. Boston: Addison-Wesley, 2010.

# D

DeMarco, Tom. *Why Does Software Cost So Much?: And Other Puzzles of the Information Age*. New York: Dorset House Publishing Company, 1995.

DeMarco, Tom, Peter Hruschka, Tim Lister, Steve McMenamin, James Robertson, and Suzanne Robertson. *Adrenaline Junkies and Template Zombies: Understanding Patterns of Project Behavior*. New York: Dorset House Publishing, 2008.

Drnevitch, Paul and David Croson. "Information Technology and Business-Level Strategy: Toward an Integrated Theoretical Perspective." *MIS Quarterly* 37, no. 2 (June 2013): 483–509.

Dyche, Jill. *The New IT: How Technology Leaders are Enabling Business Strategy in the Digital Age*. New York: McGraw-Hill Education, 2015.

# E

# F

Feathers, Michael. *Working Effectively with Legacy Code*. Upper Saddle River, NJ: Prentice Hall PTR, 2005.

Financial Accounting Standards Board (FASB). Publication 350. Available through Public.Resource.org at https://law.resource.org/pub/us/code/bean/fasb.html/fasb.350 .2011.html.

Fowler, Martin. "Strangler Application." June 29, 2004. http://www.martinfowler.com /bliki/StranglerApplication.html.

# G

Gawande, Atul. *The Checklist Manifesto: How to Get Things Right*. New York: Picador, 2009.

Greening, Dan R. "Why Should Agilists Care About Capitalization?" *InfoQ* blog, January 29, 2013. https://www.infoq.com/articles/agile-capitalization.

# H

Hackman, J. Richard. *Leading Teams: Setting the Stage for Great Performances*. Boston: Harvard Business School Press, 2002.

Heller, Martha. *The CIO Paradox: Battling the Contradictions of IT Leadership*. Brookline, MA: Bibliomotion, 2013.

Highsmith, Jim. *Adaptive Leadership: Accelerating Enterprise Agility*. Upper Saddle River, NJ: Addison-Wesley, 2014.

Highsmith, Jim. *Agile Project Management: Creating Innovative Projects*. Upper Saddle River, NJ: Addison-Wesley, 2009.

Hobbes, Thomas. "De Corpore." In *The English Works of Thomas Hobbes of Malmesbury, Vol. 1*, edited by Sir William Molesworth, Charleston, SC: Nabu Press, 2012.

Hope, Jeremy and Robin Fraser. "Who Needs Budgets?" *Harvard Business Review*. February 2003. https://hbr.org/2003/02/who-needs-budgets.

Hubbard, Douglas W. *How to Measure Anything: Finding the Value of Intangibles in Business*, 3rd ed. Hoboken: Wiley, 2014.

Humble, Jez, Joanne Molesky, and Barry O'Reilly. *Lean Enterprise: How High Performance Organizations Innovate at Scale*. Sebastopol, CA: O'Reilly Media, 2015.

Hunter, Richard and George Westerman. *The Real Business of IT: How CIOs Create and Communicate Business Value*. Boston: Harvard Business Press, 2009.

# I

# J

# K

Kennedy, Paul. *Engineers of Victory: The Problem Solvers Who Turned the Tide in the Second World War*. New York: Random House, 2013.

Kim, Gene, Kevin Behr, and George Stafford, *The Phoenix Project: A Novel About IT, DevOps, and Helping Your Business Win*. Portland, OR: IT Revolution, 2013.

# L

Lane, Dean. *CIO Wisdom: Best Practices from Silicon Valley's Leading IT Experts*. Upper Saddle River, NJ: Prentice Hall, 2003.

Larman, Craig and Bas Vodde. *Scaling Lean and Agile Development: Thinking and Organizational Tools for Large-Scale Scrum*. Upper Saddle River, NJ: Addison-Wesley, 2009.

# M

"Manifesto for Agile Development." February 11–13, 2001. http://agilemanifesto.org.

McChrystal, Gen. Stanley. *Team of Teams: New Rules of Engagement for a Complex World*. New York: Portfolio Penguin, 2015.

McGowan, Brendan. "IT Communication in Crisis: Results from the CEC's 2015 Power of Effective IT Communication Benchmark Survey." Boston: CIO Executive Council, 2016.

Mlodinow, Leonard. *The Drunkard's Walk: How Randomness Rules Our Lives*. New York: Vintage Books, 2008.

# N

Narayan, Sriram. *Agile IT Organization Design: For Digital Transformation and Continuous Delivery*. Upper Saddle River, NJ: Pearson Education, 2015.

# O

# P

Patton, Jeff. *User Story Mapping: Discover the Whole Story, Build the Right Product*. Sebastopol, CA: O'Reilly, 2014.

Paulos, John Allen. *A Mathematician Reads the Newspaper*. New York: Anchor Books Doubleday, 1995.

Pink, Daniel H. *Drive: The Surprising Truth About What Motivates Us*. New York: Riverbed Books, 2011.

Pink, Daniel H. *To Sell is Human: The Surprising Truth About Moving Others*. New York: Riverhead Books, 2012.

Plato. "Republic." In *Plato: The Collected Dialogues*, edited by Edith Hamilton and Huntington Cairns. Princeton: Princeton University Press, 1961.

Plutarch. *Life of Theseus*. Retrieved July 4, 2016. http://classics.mit.edu/Plutarch /theseus.html.

Poppendieck, Mary and Tom Poppendieck. *Lean Software Development: An Agile Toolkit*. Upper Saddle River, NJ: Addison-Wesley, 2003.

# Q

# R

Raymond, Eric S. *The Cathedral & the Bazaar: Musings on Linux and Open Source by an Accidental Revolutionary*. Sebastopol, CA: O'Reilly Media, 2008.

Reinertsen, Donald G. *The Principles of Product Development Flow: Second Generation Lean Product Development*. Redondo Beach, CA: Celeritous Publishing, 2009.

Ries, Eric. *The Lean Startup: How Today's Entrepreneurs Use Continuous Innovation to Create Radically Successful Businesses*. New York: Crown Business, 2011.

Ross, Jeanne W., Peter Weill, and David C. Robertson. *Enterprise Architecture as Strategy: Creating a Foundation for Business Execution*. Boston: Harvard Business School Press, 2006.

Ray, C. Claiborne. "The Weight of Memory." *The New York Times* Science Q&A, October 24, 2011. Retrieved July 9, 2016. http://www.nytimes.com/2011/10/25/science/25qna .html?_r=0.

*Rugged Handbook: Strawman Edition*, August 2012. Retrieved July 10, 2016. https:// www.ruggedsoftware.org/wp-content/uploads/2013/11/Rugged-Handbook-v7.pdf.

# S

Schwaber, Ken and Jeff Sutherland. "The Scrum Guide: The Definitive Guide to Scrum: The Rules of the Game." Scrum.org. October 2011.

Schwartz, Mark. *The Art of Business Value*. Portland, OR: IT Revolution, 2016.

Surowiecki, James. *The Wisdom of Crowds*. New York: Anchor Books, 2004.

# T

Takeuchi, Hirotaka and Ikujiro Nonaka. "The New New Product Development Game." *Harvard Business Review* (January 1986).

Trethewey, Kevin and Danie Roux. "The Spine Model: Making Sense of Human Work Systems." Retrieved June 25, 2016. http://needs.values.principles.practices.tools.

# U

# V

# W

Weill, Peter and Jeanne W. Ross. *IT Governance: How Top Performers Manage IT Decision Rights for Superior Results*. Boston: Harvard Business School Press, 2004.

Weill, Peter and Jeanne W. Ross. *IT Savvy: What Top Executives Must Know to Go from Pain to Gain*. Boston: Harvard Business School Publishing, 2009.

Westerman, George, Didier Bonnet, and Andrew McAfee. *Leading Digital: Turning Technology Into Business Transformation*. Boston: Harvard Business Review Press. 2014.

Wiegers, Karl E. "Seven Truths About Peer Reviews." Originally published in *Cutter IT Journal*, July 2002. Available at http://www.processimpact.com/articles/seven_truths .html. Retrieved July 13, 2016.

# X/Y/Z

# OTHER

In the chapter on Agile and Lean Thinking, I reference the many studies on project failure and feature bloat. Some of the sources I drew on heavily with references to the many studies were:

- Faeth Consulting. "IT Project Failure Rates: Facts and Reasons." http://faethcoaching .com/it-project-failure-rates-facts-and-reasons/.
- International Project Leadership Academy. "Facts and Figures." http://calleam.com /WTPF/?page_id=1445.
- *This is What Good Looks Like* blog. https://thisiswhatgoodlookslike.com/2012 /06/10/gartner-survey-shows-why-projects-fail/.
- ZDNet. "Study: 68 Percent of IT Projects Fail." http://www.zdnet.com/article/study -68-percent-of-it-projects-fail/.

For the little philosophy references in each chapter, I reviewed the entries from the following sources to inform my summaries:

- Wikipedia (http://en.wikipedia.org).
- The Stanford Encyclopedia of Philosophy (http://plato.stanford.edu).
- Internet Encyclopedia of Philosophy (http://www.iep.utm.edu).
- McKirahan, Richard D. *Philosophy Before Socrates: An Introduction With Texts and Comments*, 2nd ed. Indianapolis: Hackett Publishing, 2010.

# NOTES

## Introduction

1. Christopher Avery, "Responsible Change," *Cutter Consortium Agile Project Management Executive Report* 6, no. 10 (2005): 1–28.

2. Martha Heller, *The CIO Paradox: Battling the Contradictions of IT Leadership* (Brookline, MA: Bibliomotion, Inc., 2013), Kindle loc. 203.

## Chapter 1

1. Puppet Labs and DORA, *2016 State of DevOps Report*, https://puppet.com/resources/whitepaper/2016-state-of-devops-report.

2. Gene Kim, "Why Everyone Needs DevOps Now: My 15 Year Journey Studying High Performing Organizations," Slideshare.net, posted by Gene Kim, January 21, 2013, slide 28, https://www.slideshare.net/realgenekim/why-everyone-needs-devops-now?qid=8be1b584-f5c9-4ab1-90ea-8942791e1154&v=&b=&from_search=1.

3. Richard Hunter and George Westerman, *The Real Business of IT: How CIOs Create and Communicate Value* (Boston: Harvard Business School Press, 2009), Kindle Locs. 1502–1503.

4. Heller, *CIO Paradox*, 63.

5. "Manifesto for Agile Development," February 11–13, 2001, http://agilemanifesto.org.

6. Heller, *CIO Paradox*, 212.

7. Hunter and Westerman, *Real Business of IT*, Kindle loc. 148.

8. Hunter and Westerman, *Real Business of IT*, Kindle locs. 593–595.

9. George Westerman, Didier Bonnet, and Andrew McAfee, *Leading Digital: Turning Technology Into Business Transformation* (Boston: Harvard Business Review Press, 2014), 11–13.

10. Peter Weill and Jeanne W. Ross, *IT Savvy: What Top Executives Must Know to Go From Pain to Gain* (Boston: Harvard Business Review, 2009), Kindle locs. 281–282.

11. EY, *The DNA of the CIO: Opening the Door to the C-Suite*, http://www.ey.com/Publication/vwLUAssets/ey-the-dna-of-the-cio/$FILE/ey-the-dna-of-the-cio.pdf.

12. Galen Gruman, "CIOs may finally get a seat at the grown-ups' table," *InfoWorld*, November 15, 2016, http://www.infoworld.com/article/3139041/cio-role/cios-may-finally-get-a-seat-at-the-grown-ups-table.html.

13. Hunter and Westerman, *Real Business of IT*, Kindle loc. 494.

14. Hunter and Westerman, *Real Business of IT*, Kindle loc. 594.

15. Brendan McGowan, *IT Communication in Crisis: Results from the CEC's 2015 Power of Effective IT Communication Benchmark Survey* (Boston: CIO Executive Council, 2016), 7.

16. George Lin, "The Tao Perspective" in *CIO Wisdom: Best Practices from Silicon Valley's Leading IT Experts* (Upper Saddle River, NJ: Prentice Hall, 2004), 54.

17. Peter Weill and Jeanne W. Ross, *IT Governance: How Top Performers Manage IT Decision Rights for Superior Results* (Boston: Harvard Business School Press, 2004), 2.

18. Hunter and Westerman, *Real Business of IT*, Kindle locs. 344–345. Citing a 2004 study by Gartner and Forbes.com.

19. Heller, *CIO Paradox*, 100. Attributed to Heather Campbell, former CIO of Canadian Pacific who attributes it to her former boss.

20. McGowan, *IT Communication in Crisis*, 6.

21. Weill and Ross, *IT Savvy*, Kindle loc. 1867.

22. Variously 70%, 71%, 72% in the different sources. For example, 72% in Hunter and Westerman, *Real Business of IT*, Kindle loc. 284.

23. Douglas W. Hubbard, *How to Measure Anything: Finding the Value of Intangibles in Business* (Hoboken, NJ: Wiley & Sons, Inc., 2014).

24. Westerman, Bonnet, and McAfee, *Leading Digital*, 158.

25. Westerman, Bonnet, and McAfee, *Leading Digital*, 233.

26. Hunter and Westerman, *Real Business of IT*, Kindle loc. 427.

27. Westerman, Bonnet, and McAfee, *Leading Digital*, 157.

28. Mark Schwartz, *The Art of Business Value*, (Portland, OR: IT Revolution, 2016), ch 3.

29. Ken Schwaber and Jeff Sutherland, *The Scrum Guide: The Definitive Guide to Scrum: The Rules of the Game*, (Scrum.org and ScrumInc, 2016), 5, http://www.scrumguides.org/docs/scrumguide/v2016/2016-Scrum-Guide-US.pdf.

30. Schwaber and Sutherland, *Scrum Guide*, 5.

31. Schwaber and Sutherland, *Scrum Guide*, 5–6.

32. McGowan, *IT Communication in Crisis*, 6.

33. Mike Cohn, *Succeeding with Agile: Software Development Using Scrum* (Boston: Addison-Wesley, 2010), 221.

34. Jeff Patton, *User Story Mapping: Discover the Whole Story, Build the Right Product* (Sebastopol, CA: O'Reilly, 2014), 102. He is referencing Tom DeMarco, Peter Hruschka, Tim Lister, Steve McMenamin, James Robertson, and Suzanne Robertson, *Adrenaline Junkies and Template Zombies: Understanding Patterns of Project Behavior* (New York: Dorset House Publishing, 2008), Kindle locs. 3044–3067.

# Chapter 2

1. Carol V. Brown, "The Successful CIO: Integrating Organizational and Individual Perspectives," in *SIGCPR Proceedings of the 1993 Conference on Computer Personnel Research* (New York: ACM, 1993), 400–407.

2. Danny Maco, "Governance," in Dean Lane, ed., *CIO Wisdom: Best Practices from Silicon Valley's Leading IT Experts* (Upper Saddle River, NJ: Prentice Hall PTR, 2004), 126.

3. Tom DeMarco, *Why Does Software Cost So Much?: And Other Puzzles of the Information Age* (New York: Dorset House Publishing Company, 1995).

4. Heller, *CIO Paradox*, 73.

5. Arthur C. Clarke, 1973 revision of "Hazards of Prophecy: The Failure of Imagination," cited in Eric S. Raymond, *The Cathedral and the Bazaar: Musings on Linux and Open Source by an Accidental Revolutionary* (Sebastopol, CA, O'Reilly, 2008), 115.

6. DeMarco, *Why Does Software Cost So Much?*

7. Heller, *CIO Paradox*, 128. Attributed to Lyndon Tennison of the Union Pacific Corporation.

8. Hunter and Westerman, *Real Business of IT*, Kindle loc. 450.

9. Hunter and Westerman, *Real Business of IT*, Kindle locs. 154–156.

10. Hunter and Westerman, *Real Business of IT*, Kindle locs. 240–242.

11. Raymond, *The Cathedral & the Bazaar*, 115.

12. Raymond, *The Cathedral & the Bazaar*, 174.

13. Heller, *CIO Paradox*, 73.

14. Heller, *CIO Paradox*, 57. Attributed to Geir Ramleth of Bechtel.

15. Hunter and Westerman, *Real Business of IT*, Kindle loc. 650.

16. Weill and Ross, *IT Governance*, 235.

17. Jez Humble, Joanne Molesky, and Barry O'Reilly, *Lean Enterprise: How High Performance Organizations Innovate at Scale* (Sebastopol, CA: O'Reilly Media, 2015), 111.

18. Heller, *CIO Paradox*, 210.

# Chapter 3

1. "Manifesto for Agile Development," http://agilemanifesto.org.

2. "Manifesto for Agile Development," http://agilemanifesto.org.

3. Kent Beck with Cynthia Andres, *Extreme Programming Explained: Embrace Change*, 2nd ed. (Boston: Addison-Wesley, 2005).

4. Hirotaka Takeuchi and Ikujiro Nonaka. "The New New Product Development Game," *Harvard Business Review* (January 1986), https://hbr.org/1986/01/the-new-new-product-development-game.

5. Mary Poppendieck and Tom Poppendieck. *Lean Software Development: An Agile Toolkit* (Upper Saddle River, NJ: Addison-Wesley, 2003), xxv–xxviii.

6. Poppendieck and Poppendieck, *Lean Software Development*, 4.

7. Donald G. Reinertsen, *The Principles of Product Development Flow: Second Generation Lean Product Development* (Redondo Beach, CA: Celeritous Publishing, 2009). 73–75.

8. Reinertsen, *Product Development Flow*, 136.

9. Reinertsen, *Product Development Flow*, see discussions 112–199, principles B1–B9.

10. David Anderson, *Kanban: Successful Evolutionary Change for Your Technology Business* (Sequin, WA: Blue Hole Press, 2010).

# Chapter 4

1. Patton, *User Story Mapping*, 129.

2. Weill and Ross, *IT Savvy*, Kindle locs. 1822–1825.

3. Jerome Israel, "Why the FBI Can't Build a Case Management System," *Computer* 45, no. 6 (June 2012), 73–80.

4. Reinertsen, *Product Development Flow*, 44 (principle E5).

5. Jim Highsmith, *Adaptive Leadership: Accelerating Enterprise Agility* (Upper Saddle River, NJ: Addison-Wesley, 2014), 32.

6. Humble, Molesky, and O'Reilly, *Lean Enterprise*, 47.

7. Humble, Molesky, and O'Reilly, *Lean Enterprise*, 50.

8. Jeremy Hope and Robin Fraser, "Who Needs Budgets?" *Harvard Business Review* (February 2003), https://hbr.org/2003/02/who-needs-budgets.

9. Bjarte Bogsnes, *Implementing Beyond Budgeting: Unlocking the Performance Potential* (Hoboken, NJ: John Wiley & Sons, 2009), Kindle locs. 489–491.

10. Bogsnes, *Implementing Beyond Budgeting*, Kindle loc. 328.

11. Bogsnes, *Implementing Beyond Budgeting*, Kindle locs. 597–601.

12. Bogsnes, *Implementing Beyond Budgeting*, Kindle locs. 181–186.

# Chapter 5

1. Patton, *User Story Mapping*, 26.
2. Humble, Molesky, and O'Reilly, *Lean Enterprise*, 179.
3. Humble, Molesky, and O'Reilly, *Lean Enterprise*, 32. Citing R. Kohavi, "Online Experimentation at Microsoft," http://stanford.io/130uW6X.
4. I learned about hypothesis-driven development from *Lean Enterprise*, but Jez Humble says that he and his co-authors learned about it from *Lean UX* by Jeff Gotthelf. I have seen lots of references to HDD; at this point, I'm not sure what the original source was. See, for example, Humble, Molesky, and O'Reilly, *Lean Enterprise*, 177. Of course, the authors are thinking of products built for a market; we can amend this to <when we observe these changes in our metrics or these changes in user behavior>.
5. Humble, Molesky, and O'Reilly, *Lean Enterprise*, 96.
6. Ries, *Lean Startup*, 61.
7. Bill Wake, "INVEST in Good Stories, and SMART Tasks," XP123 blog, http://xp123.com/articles/invest-in-good-stories-and-smart-tasks/, proposed the INVEST criteria (independent, negotiable, valuable, estimable, small, and testable) for user stories. He defines Negotiable this way: "A good story is *negotiable*. It is not an explicit contract for features; rather, details will be co-created by the customer and programmer during development."
8. Gojko Adzic, *Impact Mapping: Making a Big Impact with Software Products and Projects* (Surrey, UK: Provoking Thoughts, 2012), Kindle loc. 525.
9. Ries, *Lean Startup*, Kindle loc. 1584.
10. Michael Porter, *Competitive Advantage: Creating and Sustaining Superior Performance* (New York: Free Press, 1985), 11–15.
11. Jim Highsmith, *Agile Project Management: Creating Innovative Projects* (Upper Saddle River, NJ: Addison-Wesley, 2009), ch. 2.
12. Humble, Molesky, and O'Reilly, *Lean Enterprise*, 172.

# Chapter 6

1. Michael Bloch, Sven Blumberg, and Jürgen Laartz, "Delivering large-scale IT projects on time, on budget, and on value," McKinsey & Company, Digital McKinsey (October 2012), http://www.mckinsey.com/business-functions/digital-mckinsey/our-insights/delivering-large-scale-it-projects-on-time-on-budget-and-on-value; Lars Mieritz, "Gartner Survey Shows Why Projects Fail," *GThisIsWhatGoodLooksLike* blog (June 1, 2012), https://thisiswhatgoodlookslike.com/2012/06/10/gartner-survey-shows-why-projects-fail/.
2. Weill and Ross, *IT Savvy*, Kindle locs. 860–863.

3.  Hunter and Westerman, *Real Business of IT*, Kindle locs. 284–286.

4.  Thomas Hobbes, De Corpore, in *The English Works of Thomas Hobbes of Malmesbury: Now First Collected and Edited*, vol. 1, by William Molesworth, (Charleston, SC: Nabu Press, 2012), 136–137.

5.  Martin Fowler, "Strangler Application," June 29, 2004, http://www.martinfowler.com/bliki/StranglerApplication.html.

6.  Michael Feathers, *Working Effectively with Legacy Code* (Upper Saddle River, NJ: Prentice Hall PTR, 2005).

7.  Paul Drnevitch and David Croson, "Information Technology and Business-Level Strategy: Toward an Integrated Theoretical Perspective," *MIS Quarterly* 37, no. 2 (June 2013): 487.

8.  Drnevitch and Croson, "Information Technology and Business-Level Strategy," 496.

9.  Drnevitch and Croson, "Information Technology and Business-Level Strategy," 496.

10. Drnevitch and Croson, "Information Technology and Business-Level Strategy," 496.

# Chapter 7

1.  Heller, *CIO Paradox*, 128. Attributed to Lynden Tennison, Union Pacific Corporation.

2.  Weill and Ross, *IT Savvy*, Kindle locs. 467–468.

3.  Weill and Ross, *IT Savvy*, Kindle locs. 1851–1853. Italics mine.

4.  Heller, *CIO Paradox*, 4. Attributed to Werner Boeing, Roche Diagnostics.

5.  Heller, *CIO Paradox*, 57.

6.  Drnevitch and Croson, "Information Technology and Business-Level Strategy," 485.

7.  Jean W. Ross, Peter Weill, and David C. Robertson, *Enterprise Architecture as Strategy: Creating a Foundation for Business Execution* (Boston: Harvard Business School Press, 2006), 4.

8.  Ross, Weill, and Robertson, *Enterprise Architecture as Strategy*, 47.

9.  Ross, Weill, and Robertson, *Enterprise Architecture as Strategy*, 206.

10. Ross, Weill, and Robertson, *Enterprise Architecture as Strategy*, 118.

11. Ross, Weill, and Robertson, *Enterprise Architecture as Strategy*, 50.

12. Weill and Ross, *IT Governance*, 233.

13. Hunter and Westerman, *Real Business of IT*, Kindle loc. 450.

14. Heller, *CIO Paradox*, 12. Attributed to Geir Ramleth, Bechtel.

15. Heller, *CIO Paradox*, 63. Attributed to Ralph Loura, Clorox.

# Chapter 8

1. Raymond, *The Cathedral & the Bazaar*, 117–118.
2. Heller, *CIO Paradox*, 65.
3. Raymond, *The Cathedral & the Bazaar*, 120.
4. Raymond, *The Cathedral & the Bazaar*, 117.
5. Raymond, *The Cathedral & the Bazaar*, 119.
6. Raymond, *The Cathedral & the Bazaar*, 118. Raymond says that use value is 95%, sale value is 5%.
7. Raymond, *The Cathedral & the Bazaar*, 120.
8. Plato, "Republic" in Edith Hamilton and Huntington Cairns, ed. *Plato: The Collected Dialogues* (Princeton: Princeton University Press, 1961). The Cave Allegory appears in Book VII of the Republic, 747–750.
9. Ray, C. Claiborne, "The Weight of Memory," *The New York Times*, October 24, 2011, http://www.nytimes.com/2011/10/25/science/25qna.html?_r=0. The analysis is credited to John D. Kubiatowicz, a computer science professor at the University of California, Berkeley.

# Chapter 9

1. Hunter and Westerman, *Real Business of IT*, Kindle locs. 1216–1231. Yes, I know I quoted the last part of this earlier in the book. I can't resist bringing it back again— it's awesome, isn't it?
2. Hunter and Westerman, *Real Business of IT*, Kindle loc. 1207.
3. Hunter and Westerman, *Real Business of IT*, Kindle locs. 866–867.
4. Hunter and Westerman, *Real Business of IT*, Kindle locs. 1492–1493.
5. Hunter and Westerman, *Real Business of IT*, Kindle locs. 1502–1503.
6. Patton, *User Story Mapping*, xii.

# Chapter 10

1. Leonard Mlodinow, *The Drunkard's Walk: How Randomness Rules Our Lives* (New York: Vintage Books, 2008), 5–6.
2. Mlodinow, *Drunkard's Walk*, 53–56.
3. John Allen Paulos, *A Mathematician Reads the Newspaper* (New York: Anchor, 1995), 136–137.
4. Highsmith, *Adaptive Leadership*, Kindle locs. 1782–1784.
5. Humble, Molesky, and O'Reilly, *Lean Enterprise*, 50.
6. Humble, Molesky, and O'Reilly, *Lean Enterprise*, 50.

7. Open Web Application Security Project (OWASP), "Welcome to OWASP," https://www.owasp.org/index.php/Main_Page, retrieved 7/30/2016.

8. Contrast Security, "The OWASP Top Ten and Beyond," https://www.contrastsecurity.com/blog/the-owasp-top-ten-and-beyond.

9. Rugged Software, "Rugged Software: Are You Rugged?" https://www.ruggedsoftware.org. Retrieved July 30, 2016.

10. *Rugged Handbook: Strawman Edition*, August 2012, 6, https://www.ruggedsoftware.org/wp-content/uploads/2013/11/Rugged-Handbook-v7.pdf.

# Chapter 11

1. Hunter and Westerman, *Real Business of IT*, Kindle loc. 360.

2. Aristotle, *Aristotle's Nicomachean Ethics*, trans. Robert C. Bartlett and Susan D. Collins (Chicago: UNiversity of Chicago Press, 1964), 31.

3. Karl E. Wiegers, "Seven Truths About Peer Reviews," *Cutter IT Journal* (July 2002), http://www.processimpact.com/articles/seven_truths.html, citing Dick Holland, "Document Inspection as an Agent of Change," *Software Quality Professional* 2, No. 1 (December 1999), 22–33.

4. "The Twelve-Factor App," http://12factor.net.

5. Atul Gawande, *The Checklist Manifesto: How to Get Things Right* (New York: Metropolitan Books, 2009).

# Chapter 12

1. GitHub, "About," https://github.com/about, as of July 23, 2016.

2. Raymond, *The Cathedral & the Bazaar*, 30.

3. Raymond, *The Cathedral & the Bazaar*, 80–81.

4. Raymond, *The Cathedral & the Bazaar*, 81.

5. Daniel Pink, *Drive: The Surprising Truth About What Motivates Us* (New York: Riverhead Books, 2011), Kindle loc. 631.

6. Pink, Drive, Kindle loc. 1062.

7. Raymond, *The Cathedral & the Bazaar*, Kindle loc. 3006.

8. Raymond, *The Cathedral & the Bazaar*, 60.

9. Raymond, *The Cathedral & the Bazaar*, 109.

10. Clippinger, *Biology of Business*, 5.

11. Clippinger, *Biology of Business*, 7.

12. Philip Anderson, "Seven Levers for Guiding the Evolving Enterprise," in Clippinger, *Biology of Business*, 133.

13. Clippinger, *Biology of Business*, 3.

14. Clippinger, *Biology of Business*, 23.

15. Clippinger, *Biology of Business*, 3.

16. Raymond, *The Cathedral & the Bazaar*, Kindle loc. 2930.

17. Raymond, *The Cathedral & the Bazaar*, Kindle loc. 2974.

18. Heller, *CIO Paradox*, 20.

19. Paul Kennedy, *Engineers of Victory: The Problem Solvers Who Turned the Tide in the Second World War* (New York: Random House, 2013).

# Chapter 13

1. Ries, *Lean Startup*.

2. Heller, *CIO Paradox*, 109.

3. Heller, *CIO Paradox*, 168.

4. Heller, *CIO Paradox*, 62.

5. Highsmith, *Adaptive Leadership*, Kindle locs. 899–900.

6. Heller, *CIO Paradox*, 200.

7. Daniel Pink, *To Sell Is Human: The Surprising Truth About Moving Others* (New York: Riverbed Books, 2012), 21.

8. Pink, *To Sell Is Human*, 36.

9. Bogsnes, *Implementing Beyond Budgeting*, Kindle locs. 159–163.

10. Bosgnes, *Implementing Beyond Budgeting*, Kindle locs. 181–183.

11. Heller, *CIO Paradox*, 62. Citing Ralph Loura, CIO of Clorox.

12. Hirotaka Takeuchi, and Ikujiro Nonaka, "The New New Product Development Game," *Harvard Business Review* (January, 1986), http://nbr.org./198610/the-new-new-product-development-game.

13. Craig Larman and Bas Vodde, *Scaling Lean and Agile Development: Thinking and Organizational Tools for Large-Scale Scrum* (Upper Saddle River, NJ: Addison-Wesley, 2009), 194.

14. Hunter and Westerman, *Real Business of IT*, Kindle locs. 117–118.

# Chapter 14

1. Heller, *CIO Paradox*.

2. Beck with Andres, *Extreme Programming Explained*, 78.

3. Highsmith, *Adaptive Leadership*, Kindle locs. 1932–1933.

# ACKNOWLEDGMENTS

This book grew largely from two sources: my experiences at USCIS and Intrax, and all that I have learned from the Agile and DevOps community. Many of the ideas in this book were hatched, tested, and refined through my work with the talented federal employees at USCIS and DHS. Josh Seckel has long been my co-conspirator in the plot to make federal IT agile. My deputies Keith Jones and Larry Denayer, CISO Andy Onello, jack-of-all-trades Yemi Oshinnaiye, and the rest of our IT leadership team—Regina Stokes, Norm Palmer, Rowena Furce, David Blair, Orest Fedak, and Greg Wittman—have all played key roles in bringing agility to USCIS. The amazingly resilient folks on our transformation program, who consistently bounce back from adversity and continue to do what they know is right, have taught me a lot about courage and about dealing with complexity. Chad Tetreault, Sarah Fahden, Rafaa Abdalla, Ken Moser, and Suzie Rizzo are among the USCIS IT employees whose ideas have contributed to those in this book. Thanks to all of you for making my time at USCIS so productive and enjoyable!

My collaborators "on the business side" have included Kath Stanley, who faced the ups and downs of the transformation program with me; Tammy Meckley, who has been working with me to reinvent program oversight; and Don Neufeld, Dan Renaud, Mariela Melero, and Joanna Ruppel at USCIS and Heidi Mispagel, Sherry Carpenter, and Paul Bydalek at Intrax. We could not have changed so much without leadership support, which came from Tracy Renaud, Kevin Kerns, Luke McCormack, Richard Spires, Margie Graves, and Chip Fulghum, who allowed me to "pilot" some of the governance ideas I present here. Eric Hysen and his team of US Digital Services folks taught us lots of neat new tricks and helped us work through challenges. But I could mention just about everyone at USCIS and across the DHS community. Thanks to all of you!

I have benefitted greatly from the ideas and support of Gojko Adzic, especially his ideas on company charters and red meat. Adzic has helped me make my ideas more precise and has kept my thinking honest. Adrian Cockcroft has been a great support and influence, as has Jez Humble, who still appears to be sane after a stint in the federal government. I have found myself sharing the stage at conferences with some of the brilliant minds of the DevOps and Agile communities, and have benefitted greatly from hearing their ideas. Gene Kim—always an inspiration and a guide—Josh Corman, Jason Cox, Topo Pal, Courtney Kissler, Heather Mickman, John Willis, Sam Guckenheimer, Damon Edwards, and many more. And of course thanks to Todd Sattersten and Anna Noak at IT Revolution.

I have borrowed heavily from *Lean Enterprise* by Jez Humble, Barry O'Reilly, and Joanne Molesky, and *Be the Business* and *The CIO Paradox* by Martha Heller. I thank all of you for putting ideas into my head that could then go through the strange blending and twisty logic that takes place there.

# ABOUT THE AUTHOR

Mark Schwartz is an iconoclastic CIO and a playful crafter of ideas, an inveterate purveyor of lucubratory prose. He has been an IT leader in organizations small and large, public, private, and non-profit. As the CIO of US Citizenship and Immigration Services, he provokes the federal government into adopting Agile and DevOps practices. He is pretty sure that when he was the CIO of Intrax Cultural Exchange he was the first person ever to use business intelligence and supply chain analytics to place au pairs with the right host families. Mark speaks frequently on the role of the CIO, innovation in IT, and Agile and DevOps approaches in challenging and low-trust environments. With a BS in computer science from Yale, a master's in philosophy from Yale, and an MBA from Wharton, Mark is either an expert on the business value of IT or just confused and much poorer.

Mark is the author of *The Art of Business Value*, which—he is proud to report—has been labeled by his detractors "The Ecclesiastes of Product Management" and "Apocryphal." The book takes readers on a journey through the meaning of bureaucracy, the nature of cultural change, and the return on investment of an MBA degree, on the way to solving the great mystery…what exactly do we mean by business value and how should that affect the way we practice IT? Mark promises that his new book, *Seat at the Table*, is more canonical and less apocryphal.

Mark is the winner of a *Computerworld* Premier 100 award, an *Information Week* Elite 100 award, a *Federal Computer Week* Fed 100 award, and a *CIO Magazine* CIO 100 award, which strongly suggests that there are less than 99 other people you could better spend time reading.

# More from Mark Schwartz

---

### Additional Material for *A Seat at the Table*

*A Reader's Guide to A Seat at the Table*

Continue your journey with *A Reader's Guide to A Seat at the Table*. This guide is intended to be used by readers as a way to further amplify the learnings from *A Seat at the Table*. For available formats, visit ITRevolution.com

### Previous Books by the Author

*The Art of Business Value*

Playful and thought-provoking, *The Art of Business Value* explores what business value means, why it matters, and how it should affect your software development and delivery practices. In *The Art of Business Value*, explore new ways to think about the cutting-edge of Agile practice and where it may lead.